Applications of Geographical Offender Profiling

Edited by

DAVID CANTER
and
DONNA YOUNGS
Centre for Investigative Psychology, University of Liverpool, UK

ASHGATE

Published by
Ashgate Publishing Limited
Gower House
Croft Road
Aldershot
Hampshire GU11 3HR
England

Ashgate Publishing Company
Suite 420
101 Cherry Street
Burlington, VT 05401-4405
USA

Ashgate website: http://www.ashgate.com

British Library Cataloguing in Publication Data
Applications of geographical offender profiling
  1. Criminal behavior, Prediction of 2. Crime – Regional disparities
  I. Canter, David II. Youngs, Donna
  364.3

Library of Congress Cataloging-in-Publication Data
Applications of geographical offender profiling / edited by David Canter and Donna Youngs.
    p. cm.
  Includes bibliographical references and index.
  ISBN-13: 978-0-7546-2720-3 (hardback)
  ISBN-13: 978-0-7546-2724-1 (paperback)
  1. Geographical offender profiling. 2. Criminal investigation--Psychological aspects. I. Canter, David V. II. Youngs, Donna.
  HV8073.5.A66 2007
  363.25--dc22

2007012590

ISBN: 978 0 7546 2720 3 (hardback)
ISBN: 978 0 7546 2724 1 (paperback)

Printed and bound in Great Britain by MPG Books Ltd, Bodmin, Cornwall.

Contents

Part 1   Empirical Bases

Part 2   Stylistic Variations

List of Figures

Acknowledgements

The editors and the Publisher wish to thank the following for permission to use copyrighted material.

Elsevier B. V. for Samantha Lundrigan and David Canter, 'A multivariate analysis of serial murderers' disposal site location choice', *Journal of Environmental Psychology*, 2001, 21, 423–32; David Canter and Paul Larkin, 'The environmental range of serial rapists', *Journal of Environmental Psychology*, 1993, 13, 63–69; Katarina Fritzon, 'An examination of the relationship between distance travelled and motivational aspects of firesetting behaviour', *Journal of Environmental Psychology*, 2001, 21, 45–60.

The Forensic Science Society for Craig Bennell and David Canter, 'Linking commercial burglaries by *modus operandi*: Tests using regression and ROC analysis', *Science and Justice*, 2002, 42(3), 153–64.

Institute of Forensic Research in Cracow for Masayuki Tamura and Mamoru Suzuki, 'Characteristics of serial arsonists and crime scene geography in Japan' in *Forensic Psychology and Law: Traditional Questions and New Ideas*, Czerederecka A. et al. (eds), 259–64.

International Association of Chiefs of Police for James L. LeBeau, 'The journey to rape: Geographic distance and the rapist's method of approaching the victim', *Journal of Police Science and Administration*, 1987, 15(2), 129–36.

John Wiley & Sons for Brent Snook et al., 'Predicting the home location of serial offenders: A preliminary comparison of the accuracy of human judges with a geographic profiling system', *Behavioral Sciences and the Law*, 2002, 20, 109–18; David Canter, 'Confusing operational predicaments and cognitive explorations: Comments on Rossmo and Snook et al.', *Applied Cognitive Psychology*, 2005, 19, 663–8; David Canter and Laura Hammond, 'A comparison of the efficacy of different decay functions in geographical profiling for a sample of US serial killers', *Journal of Investigative Psychology and Offender Profiling*, 2006, 3, 91–103.

Oxford University Press for Peter J. van Koppen and Robert W. J. Jansen, 'The road to the Robbery: Travel patterns in commercial robberies', *British Journal of Criminology*, Spring 1998, 38(2), 230–46.

Springer Netherlands for Janet Warren et al., 'Crime scene and distance correlates of serial rape', *Journal of Quantitative Criminology*, 1998, 14(1), 35–59; David Canter et al., 'Predicting serial killers' home base using a decision support system', *Journal of Quantitative Criminology*, 2000, 16(4), 457–78.

University of Toronto Press for Thomas Gabor and Ellen Gottheil 'Offender Characteristics and Spatial Mobility: An empirical study and some policy implications', *Journal of Criminology*, 26, 267–81.

Series Preface

Over recent years many aspects of law enforcement and related legal and judicial processes have been influenced by psychological theories and research. In turn concerns that derive from investigation, prosecution and defence of criminals are influencing the topics and methodologies of psychology and neighbouring social sciences. Everything, for example, from the detection of deception to the treatment of sex offenders, by way of offender profiling and prison management, has become part of the domain of a growing army of academic and other professional psychologists.

This is generating a growing discipline that crosses many boundaries and international frontiers. What was once the poor relation of applied psychology, populated by people whose pursuits were regarded as weak and arcane, is now becoming a major area of interest for many students and practitioners from high school through to postgraduate study and beyond.

The interest spreads far beyond the limits of conventional psychology to disciplines such as Criminology, Socio-Legal Studies and the Sociology of Crime as well as many aspects of the law itself including a growing number of courses for police officers, and those associated with the police such as crime analysts or forensic scientists.

There is therefore a need for wide-ranging publications that deal with all aspects of these interdisciplinary pursuits. Such publications must be cross-national and interdisciplinary if they are to reflect the many strands of this burgeoning field of teaching, research and professional practice. The *Psychology, Crime and Law* series has been established to meet this need for up to date accounts of the work within this area, presented in a way that will be accessible to the many different disciplines involved.

In editing this series I am alert to the fact that this is a lively new domain in which very little has been determined with any certainty. The books therefore capture the debates inherent in any intellectually animated pursuit. They reveal areas of agreement as well as approaches and topics on which experts currently differ. Throughout the series the many gaps in our knowledge and present-day understanding are revealed.

The series is thus of interest to anyone who wishes to gain an up-to-date understanding of the interplays between psychology, crime and the law.

Professor David Canter,
Series Editor

Preface

Over the past few years there has been a great increase in the number of studies of criminals' spatial patterns. Opportunities emerging from these studies are now being applied to more and more police investigations worldwide. Many different kinds of applications relating to where offenders live and carry out their crimes have found a place under the common umbrella heading of *Geographical Profiling*.

These studies and applications have origins in disciplines as varied as zoology, epidemiology, psychology, criminology and, of course, geography, leading to important publications appearing in many and diverse journals that are not always readily available to academics and practitioners across the different disciplines. Some of the seminal papers are also now quite old and difficult to come by. It is therefore appropriate to bring together a collection of the key papers so that researchers and investigators can consult the original source material in an easily available form.

The papers collected for the present volume are only a sample from the couple of hundred that could have been usefully drawn upon. They have been selected to give a flavour of the range of studies that have been conducted at different times and in different places as well as to provide an indication of the cumulative development of the methodologies and theories within this area of research and application. This has meant that there is a conscious emphasis on papers that have emerged from the Centre for Investigative Psychology in the UK and those who have been associated with that Centre. This gives more coherence to the topics studied than might otherwise be the case, as well as showing how the collaboration between a variety of researchers over 15 years has produced the basis for a set of theories, methods and applications that now are at the core of *Geographical Profiling*.

The present volume focuses on different kinds of study that underpin the applications of Geographical Offender Profiling. The first of these covers an important selection of empirical work on offender spatial behaviour. Within this, a subset of studies exploring the relationship between criminal spatial behaviour and stylistic variations in offending are included. The third section contains a range of studies that explore the potential investigative applications of the patterns in criminal geography. The field now covers such a range of issues and results that it was also deemed appropriate to produce an extensive introduction to the present volume that will help the reader to understand the context of the various papers included and the different ways in which they contribute to our growing appreciation of the complex issues incorporated in what started as a simple, some would say naïve, belief in the possibility of locating an offender's base from a study of where s/he offends.

The introduction ranges beyond the papers in the present volume to provide an overview of value to students and practitioners who wish to gain a full understanding of this rapidly developing area of study and application. A full bibliography of the many relevant publications is also given at the end of this volume to further support research and development.

This is an exciting area of research that has caught the imagination of Hollywood in recent times. The excitement this generates, though, should not mask the very serious research that is at the heart of these dramas and the implications this research has, not just for criminal investigations but for the broader understanding of all human activity.

David Canter and Donna Youngs

PART 1
Empirical Bases

Chapter 1

Geographical Offender Profiling: Applications and Opportunities

David Canter and Donna Youngs

Geographical Offender Profiling as an investigative application was born out of the contributions a number of individuals showed they could make to police investigations (Canter 1994, Canter 2004, Kind 1999, Rossmo 1995) by providing some systematic analysis of where the perpetrator of a given offence was likely to live. These early forays rapidly gave rise to the development of a number of different Geographical Offender Profiling tools, generating considerable interest among police and other law enforcement analysts. Yet, of course, the effectiveness of any such tools arises from the breadth and validity of the empirical work on which they draw. Beyond this, the actual utility of Geographical Offender Profiling tools to police investigations is also dependent upon the way in which the tools are implemented and integrated with the investigative process. Contemporary investigative applications of Geographical Offender Profiling should emerge then not from the expertise of individuals but from integrated scientific activity, consisting of three distinct components (Canter and Youngs 2008):

a) Studies of criminal spatial behaviour – basic research
b) Development of decision support tools that incorporate research findings
c) Explorations of how such tools may help police investigations and the effectiveness of these applications

Key Findings on Criminal Spatial Activity

The emerging studies of criminal spatial activity over the last decade have revealed a number of consistent findings that add to the possibilities for the operational and strategic applications of offender profiling. It is useful to draw together some of these findings so that their details are available for consideration.

Home to Crime Distances

Rhodes and Conly [1981][1] reported that offenders typically travelled less than three miles to carry out their crimes. Twenty years later with a new data set Costello and Wiles (2002) reported remarkably similar results. If we just consider burglary offences, as listed in Table 1.1, where the results from thirteen different studies, all in different locations are summarised, we can see a consistency in the average distance travelled from home to crime across many different places and time periods. The mean distances vary from 0.89 kilometres on the small island of Barbados to 3.87 kilometres in a small town in Southern England; all the other studies from many different places give mean distances between these extremes.

These distances are all calculated as the straightest line between the home and offence locations; 'crow flight' distances. There has been some discussion of whether the travel route would be a more appropriate way of calculating these distances, or even some route along a notional grid, as would be the case for many cities that have a network of roads either parallel or at right angles to each other, often known as a 'Manhattan' metric. However, as Phillips (1980) pointed out, the use of any sort of street distance is problematic because there is no guarantee that it reflects the actual route used by the offender and in any case there is a high correlation between street distances and straight line distances. Therefore, in general, researchers have used straight line distances such as those shown for burglary in Table 1.1.

For other types of crime there are different ranges of distances, but as Gabor and Gottheil [1984] report for Ottawa, quite different crimes such as sex offences, robbery or even auto theft are often carried out within the same overall range of distances that are found for burglary. The only crimes that typically appear to be carried out at much longer distances from home are serial murders and serial stranger rapes. Canter et al. [2000] report a mean of 46 kilometres for US serial killers, for example. Similarly, Warren et al. [1998] give a mean of 23 kilometres for US serial rapists.

There are still not enough detailed studies to unpack the processes that influence the distance offenders travel, or more particularly what special processes lead to the offenders travelling more than a few kilometres to carry out crimes. There are likely to be many factors involved. Targeting is one process (discussed in Canter and Youngs 2008); the degree of planning involved in the offence is like to be another [Fritzon 2001]. The density of opportunities for crime and the related density of guardianship will doubtless also prove to be influential on the distances offenders travel. Other social aspects of the crimes will need to be considered in addition. For example, if offenders carry out crimes together then it would be expected that their combined 'mental map' will be larger [Turner 1969].

The resources they have available beyond knowledge of places is another set of factors that will need to be considered. These relate to mode of transport [LeBeau 1987] and the amount of time a criminal can be away from a base without causing

---

1   Citations in [ ] are those included in these readings.

Table 1.1   Mean Distances (in kilometres) Burglars Travel to Offence Location

Study Author(s)	Location of Offences	When Offences Occurred	Type of Offence	Mean
White (1932)	Indianapolis, USA	1930	Burglary (N=121)	2.83
Rhodes & Conly (1981)	Columbia, USA	1974	Burglary (N=796)	2.61
Barker (2000)	Small towns in S. England	1981–1987	Burglary (N=30)	3.87
Snook (2004)	St. Johns (& surrounding areas), Canada	1989–1999	Burglary (N=41)	2.7
Wiles & Costello (2000)	Sheffield	1995	Domestic Burglary (N=1401)	3.02
	(Offender travel *within* Sheffield)	1995	Domestic Burglary (N=983)	2.94
	York	1995	Burglary	1.58
	Hambleton	1995	Burglary	2.70
	Sheffield	1995	Burglary	2.90
Dixon (2000)	Merseyside, UK	Unspecified	Residential Burglary (N=240)	2.84
Gittens (2004)	Parish of St. Michael, Barbados	1999–2005	Burglary (Residence) (N=43)	0.89
			Burglary (Business) (N=29)	1.48
Canter (2006)	Wandsworth, London	1998–2002	Burglary (Residential) (N= 825)	1.83

alarm or suspicion. Canter and Gregory [1994] propose that different resources will be available to different types of offenders. For example, younger offenders will travel shorter distances because they do not have access to vehicles and will be more likely to be missed if away from home for long periods of time. This hypothesis was supported by their findings that younger rapists did indeed travel shorter distances, reflecting the much earlier studies by Nichols (1980), Phillips (1980) and Baldwin and Bottoms (1976) that all show younger offenders do not travel as far as older ones. There may well be analogous processes that lead to criminals from ethnic minorities travelling shorter distances than others (Nichols 1980, Pettiway 1982), as Canter and Gregory [1994] show for rapists.

Variations across Types of Offence

The processes that give rise to differences in the distance travelled to offend may be regarded as having two sources of influence. One is aspects of the criminal and how s/he sets about committing the crimes. Impulsivity or planning are explored in Canter and Youngs (2008), as well as the resources of time, money and mode of transport. The other sources of influence are factors outside the individual's direct control, most notably the opportunities for crime and related land use patterns.

Both of these aspects combine in the nature of the crime. Different crime types require different amounts and forms of planning on the part of the offender and may require him/her to have access to different kinds or quantities of resources. But the opportunities for different crimes will also be spatial distributed in different ways. It is therefore not surprising that a number of researchers have explored differences in the distances offenders travel for different types of crime.

Broadly, published studies tend to indicate that offenders travel further to commit property crimes, which presumably take more planning and more direct targeting of particular opportunities that may be widely distributed, than to commit crimes against the person, as Rhodes and Conly [1981] indicate. Van Koppen and Jansen, [1998] showed that within property crimes in Holland there is some indication that the greater the value of the property stolen, the greater the distance travelled. A quarter of a century earlier, in the USA, Capone and Nichols (1975) showed that the distance robbers travelled is directly related to the value of the property they steal. Again it may be hypothesised that this is because more extended searches or specific targeting is involved in stealing higher value goods. But, such findings are certainly not uniform, which is unsurprising as the opportunities for property crime vary considerably from one area to another. Such variations draw attention to the relevance of the contextual backdrop for the spatial patterns.

Longer distances may also reflect a more general commitment to the course of action. Such a process is suggested by Capone and Nichols' (1975) report that armed robbers travel further than those who are not armed. Similar processes have been demonstrated within other types of offence. For example, Fritzon [2001] has shown that for arson, the more emotional offenses are committed at a shorter distance than those that have a very instrumental purpose. LeBeau's (1987) finding that rapists travelled furthest if they were using a vehicle, a mean of 11.7 miles, is also interesting here. Given that Wiles and Costello (2000) showed that, at the general level, increased mobility did not lead directly to longer home to crime distances, LeBeau's finding here may again be understandable in terms of levels of commitment.

The details of exactly how and why the crime is committed also need to be considered, not just its legal definition. For example, Warren et al. [1998] showed that different styles of stranger rape tended to be carried out by offenders who travelled different distances. Lebeau [1987] showed similar results considering the way the rapist approached the victim. He also showed that rapists' journeys to crime were shortest if the offence involved illegal entry, being less than a mile and thus similar to burglary distances.

No detailed models have been articulated to describe and explain all the differences that are found in criminals' travel patterns (Canter and Youngs 2007). Disentangling the influences from within the offender and relating those to the external aspects of land use and criminal opportunities requires very detailed and reliable data sets with information on both the criminals and on the localities in which they offend. There are likely to be complex interactions too. It may be, for instance, that different sorts of offenders, with different general travel tendencies, tend to be involved in the different sorts of crimes. Or it may be that it is the nature of the crimes, especially how impulsive they are, that leads to them having particular targets. The opportunities themselves may attract certain types of offenders, who have particular levels of resources, into a given area. Studies that try to disentangle the different aspects of the crimes, criminals and opportunities have yet to be conducted (Canter and Youngs 2007).

Decay Functions

Beyond the consideration of average distance has been the study of the distributions of the frequency of different distances. This distribution typically follows the shape shown in Figure 1.1 in which the rate of change in frequencies is not constant. As Turner [1969], describing the frequency of crimes against distance from home, puts it 'the proportion wanes with distance'. Such a shape to the distribution of journeys to crime has been repeatedly found in many subsequent studies [e.g. Rhodes and Conly

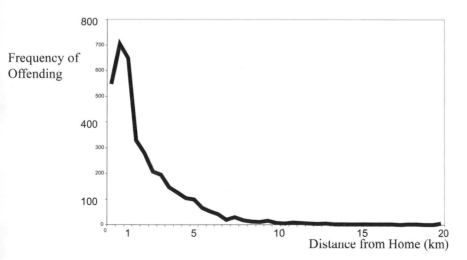

Figure 1.1   Illustration of a decay function (residential burglaries in London)

1981; van Koppen and Jansen 1998, Canter et al. 2000]. The further away a crime is from home the greater the distance has to be for a similar reduction in frequency. This rapid drop off in frequencies is usually referred to as 'decay' in the frequencies and the shape of any mathematical formula that describes this curve is known as a decay function. Such functions have been reported for many aspects of geographical activity, as varied as the distances leopards travel to make a kill [Mizutani and Jewell 1998] property values (Richardson, et al. 1990), migration (Kothari 2002) and even fishing (Beverton and Holt 1957).

The significance of the decay function for geographical profiling is that it implies that a simple averaging of the distances between offences, i.e. calculating their 'centre of gravity', or in other words the location that is the average minimum distance from all of the crime locations, will give too much emphasis to those offences committed at longer distances. The decay function leads to the hypothesis that the locations nearer a crime should be given more weight than those further away. Some researchers have consequently begun to explore exactly what mathematical function may best characterise the decay in frequencies of distances from home to crimes [Canter et al. 2000].

The decay function also draws attention to the weakness of using means as the way of capturing the central tendency of the distances travelled. Given this distribution, a median is possibly a better summary, although that has weaknesses too as it only describes one point in a somewhat complex system of values. All of this therefore shows how this field that started from such simple discoveries of the typical distances that offenders tended to travel has now evolved into a much more complex exploration of appropriate mathematical formulae for characterising the distribution of those distances.

One issue that has emerged from more intensive examination of decay functions is that they do not necessarily apply to individuals over their series of offences. As Van Koppen and Jansen [1998] show, individual offenders are more likely to exhibit a distribution around an optimum, or preferred distances, rather than the distance decay typical of aggregate data. However, Rengert et al. [1999] robustly challenged Van Koppen and Jansen's claim, opening further the debate as to whether decay functions are characteristic of individual offenders or more appropriately should be regarded as aggregates across cohorts of offenders. The resolution of this debate could have practical implications for how geographical profiling systems are developed.

The 'Buffer' Zone

In Figure 1.1 it can be seen that the peak of distance frequencies is around one kilometre. It is not at zero. This finding has been reported by a number of researchers, most notably Rossmo [1995], raising the possibility that the decay function is not uniformly negative, i.e. below about 1 km, offending becomes more, not less, likely as distance from home increases. So, in particular, it is proposed that there will be a zone around offenders' bases in which offences will be less frequent. This was put forward on a theoretical basis by Brantingham and Brantingham [1981]. They gave the label 'buffer zone' to the area around an offender's base, arguing that he would not commit crimes in that area for fear of being recognised or apprehended close to the crime scene. The evidence for a buffer zone though is mixed. Lundrigan and Canter [2001b] find no evidence for it. Rengert et al.'s [1999] results also provide no evidence of a buffer zone.

The reasons for the variations in results are not difficult to fathom. If a serial offender thinks he will be recognised near to home then he is likely to avoid offending in that area. This will depend on the nature of his crimes. Furthermore, if his criminal activity tends to take him to particular types of target, then there will be no evidence that he is specifically avoiding the area around his home. This takes us back to the issue of how likely it is that decay functions apply to individual serial offenders as opposed to aggregates of offenders. It is possible that some offenders avoid areas close to their home and others do not, but the overall decay function will hide these important distinctions. The scale over which offenders operate is also important to consider. Any buffer zone may be too small to identify if the overall range of distances travelled is great. So here, as in so many other aspects of geographical profiling, what started out as a simple assumption about criminal spatial behaviour has turned out to be a much more complex mix of offence and offender issues requiring detailed and precise data to examine further.

Criminal Range

The buffer zone draws attention to the possibility that the distance offenders travel may be characterised by a minimum as well as a maximum length. If these relate to each other in any systematic way, this implies that offenders will have characteristic criminal ranges over which they operate. There are a number of complexities within the notion of the criminal range that have not yet been fully specified (Canter and Youngs 2007). However, if offenders do have a criminal range that is typical for them, then it may be that, as Van Koppen and De Keijser (1997) indicate, the decay function is best thought of as a summary of the multiple optimum distributions of many different individuals. This draws on the idea that for any given offender there is likely to be a bell curve distribution around an optimum distance travelled to offend. Such discussions draw from the assumption that each offender does indeed tend to operate over a characteristic range of distances.

Evidence for this possibility is provided by a number of studies. Canter and Larkin [1993] show, for serial rapists, the high correlation between the distance an offender travels to a crime and the distance between offences, claiming that this supports the possibility that offenders make judgements about the appropriate spacing of their offences, whether from home or previous offences, that are somehow characteristic of them. Lundrigan and Canter [2001a] provide evidence from US serial killers that they can be assigned to distinct sub-groups on the basis of the distances they travel, with very little overlap between the journey to crime distances for different sub-groups of offenders. Lundrigan and Canter [2001b] develop this finding by demonstrating that there is a correlation between the length of the shortest distances offenders travel and the length of the longest distances. In other words, offenders who travel relatively short distances to the crimes nearest to home also tend to travel relatively short distances to their furthest crimes. This correlation, in effect, shows that the two extremes of the distances an individual travels are closely related in scale.

As indicated when looking at average distances travelled, these 'criminal ranges' for individuals may relate to the resources available to offenders of time and money, as well as the type of crimes in which they are involved. The implications of these findings have not been thoroughly incorporated into geographical profiling systems, but are taken into account by adjusting any formulae within the system calculations, so that they are independent of the actual size of area over which the offender operates. Usually this is done by calculating the average distance between all crimes in a series (known as the mean inter-point distance or MID). The MID is then taken as the unit against which other measures are adjusted [Canter et al. 2000]. However, other methods of calibrating the range have also been explored, notably the Q Range, sometimes producing better results than the MID [Canter et al. 2000].

Variations Across Types of Locations

As noted there are issues external to the offender that will also influence where and when s/he commits crimes. Clear differences have been found in relation to the types of locations in which the crimes are committed. In broad terms, offenders operating in rural areas will travel much further between their crimes than those in metropolitan areas. For example, Warren et al. [1998] give a mean distance travelled for serial rapists in rural areas of 3.3 miles, but the mean is 1.5 in urban areas. Once more there are a mixture of possible explanations for this that have not been thoroughly explored.

One possibility is that the density of opportunities is greater in urban areas. In other words, rural criminals just have to travel further to find the same number of targets. However another, not necessarily contradictory hypothesis, is that in rural areas there is more recognition of who is local and so offenders have to travel further to avoid detection. There is also the matter of guardianship and the likelihood that there will be different levels in different areas.

The density of the population in an area is thus certainly not the only likely predictor of offenders' journey to crime distances and patterns of offence activity. Many other socio-demographic issues are likely to come into play. These relate to patterns of land-use and transport routes. Further, the patterns of daily, weekly or seasonal use of the area are significant. Central business districts have very different patterns of routine use from dormitory suburbs. It is undoubtedly the case that the behaviour of any individual criminal is influenced by these temporal patterns. All of these considerations draw attention to a number of topics ripe for study.

Temporal Sequencing

As well as the geographical patterns of opportunities for crime and the particular predilections of the offender it has also been discovered that the actual experiences of committing crimes has an influence over subsequent spatial behaviour [Lundrigan and Canter, 2001]. In general offenders will tend to avoid an area close to where they have previously committed a crime. This is more likely to be the case if they may be recognised in that area or if there was subsequently heightened alertness or police presence.

Lundrigan and Canter [2001] also showed that the influence of a previous crime location was greater for crimes occurring over a smaller area. This makes sense because if the criminal's range is smaller then he is more likely to be vulnerable to detection in that area. However, their comparison of sequential and alternate crimes is only one aspect of a much more complex consideration of the temporal issues relating to crime series. As Canter (2005) illustrates, some offenders have long and involved criminal journeys that unfold over many locations over a long time period. The opportunities that offenders seek out may influence these journeys, but variations relating to different forms of crime may also be very important. The casual crime done locally to provide funds or instant access to drugs may be very differently located from subsequent crimes, by the same offender, that are planned more thoughtfully.

Figure 1.2　Showing the area within which the home/base is likely to be found around a designated crime, where the radius of the circle is drawn from the distribution of the frequency of crimes at various distances from the home/base

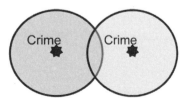

Figure 1.3　Showing overlap of two crime ranges, indicating the increased probability of the home being in the area of overlap

Development of Decision Support Systems

The findings that have emerged from various studies have been drawn upon to develop decision support systems, as discussed in Canter et al. [2000]. These can be distinguished from 'expert' systems because they do not aim to give the investigator a direct answer of where to find the offender. Rather, their objective is to systematise the information available to the police in a way that facilitates detectives' understanding of the crimes and the patterns within them. This support can then be drawn upon and combined with the investigators' specialist and local knowledge to reach a decision about how to proceed.

Locating Priority Areas

The stages in developing these decision support systems can be outlined as follows. The first is the indication that an offender is likely to live within an area related to any given crime, as shown in Figure 1.2.

If there is more than one crime then it is possible to combine the areas around the crimes and give more weight to those areas that overlap as shown in Figure 1.3.

Adding further crimes can increase the detail in the distribution of probabilities of where the home/base may be. This pattern of probabilities can be developed further by adjusting for the distance from the crime, taking account of the frequent finding that there are likely to be fewer crimes further from the offender's home. This adjustment can take the form of a decay function so that the probabilities decrease more rapidly as the distances get further away.

A third stage in the process is to assume that the offender's home is within the area circumscribed by the crimes linked to him as shown in Figure 1.4.

The actual shape of the probability surface is modified by the actual decay functions incorporated into the software as shown in Figure 1.5.

Area of highest probability is indicated by the arrow.

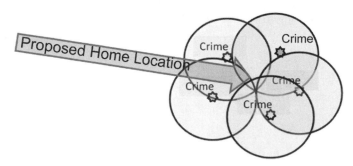

Figure 1.4   Indicating how a series of crimes help to define an area within which the offender's home/base is likely to be

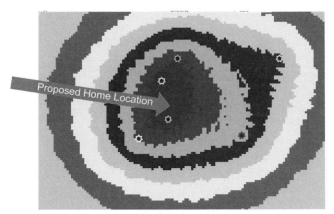

Figure 1.5   **Showing how the probabilities are added together from each of five crimes (indicated by stars) to give an overall probability surface of the likely base of the offender**

It should be noted that these analyses do not take any account of the patterns of land use, modes or routes of transport or other information relating to the details of where the crimes occur. They are operating on the geometry of the points rather than their significance as actual places.

Operational Strategies and Tactics Incorporating Geographical Profiling

It is useful to consider briefly the actions that law enforcement agencies can take as a result of geographical profiling analysis. The fictional idea that the computer gives a name and address so that all the police have to do is knock on a door, is of course very misleading, although there have been cases that get close to that as discussed by Canter (2005). It is also important to emphasise that geographical profiling systems offer a probability surface, i.e. they indicate an area with different degrees of probability that the offender has some association with that area, not just a point with distances from it.

The probability of different locations being of significance provides a set of priorities that can be acted on in a number of different ways. The particular action will depend on the nature of the crimes and the circumstances under which they occur. Five main tactics can be identified on which investigators can draw once they have the 'geographical profile'

- Surveillance – The high priority areas can become the focus of attention for overt or covert police observation, watching for offenders going to or returning from a crime.
- Arrest and questioning – If there is clear evidence of who is likely to be involved, derived from geographical and other analyses, then suspects can be arrested and interviewed.

- TICs – Geographical profiling principles can be used to identify other offences (that are 'Taken into Consideration' known as TICs) potentially committed by the same offender for consideration. These may be unsolved crimes identified on the basis of their relationship to the offender's home or linked by their proximity to the initial offence under investigation.
- Covert development – The area of focus can be used as a basis for seeking out further information, for example, from local informants or house to house enquiries.
- Prevention or disruption – Geographical profiling can also serve to highlight those areas most at risk and possibly the sorts of criminals they are at risk from. This can therefore be drawn on for crime reduction and other forms of disruption of criminal activity.

Finally, it is worth mentioning that an analysis that shows the geographical distribution of crimes and links that to the base of a known offender can strengthen the case presented in court. It is possible even that this information could be used by the defence if the defendant can demonstrate a lack of association or access to that area. But to date it has not been possible to identify any actual cases in which this strategy has been used.

The Lack of Need for Precision

One further point that derives from the various law enforcement tactics outlined above is that they do not require a very high degree of precision for the geographical profile to be of value. The one exception may be the identification of the most likely culprit to arrest, where some degree of precision is necessary. But even in this case the degree of geographical precision necessary depends on the density of possible suspects in that area. For example, in the often quoted identification of John Duffy as the Railway Rapist [Canter 2004] there was only one of the main suspects who lived in the area of London indicated from the geographical analysis. This was quite a large area of London, but the specificity of the criteria for selecting suspects meant that only one person in that area fitted those criteria.

The lack of a need for great precision, in most cases, also shows that the studies by Snook et al. [2002] although of some theoretical interest are, as Canter [2005] has argued in some detail, of little practical import. Snook et al.'s [2002] studies and subsequent similar studies (Snook et al. 2004) consider the ability of people to estimate the centre of gravity of a set of points. These points are then regarded as if they had been crimes on a map so that the centre of gravity may be treated as a guess of where an offender might live. The distance from the centre of gravity estimate to the known base of an offender is then used as some indicator of the 'success' in estimating where an offender's base might be. The length of this distance is then compared with the lengths from various points established through geographical profiling systems.

Given that geographical profiling systems indicate an area rather than a point and that they do so following consistent rules, it matters little that on average people can make an estimate of a point that is more or less as close to the actual home as the computer system's highest priority location. Some people will be less accurate, some may be more. Any given person may be influenced by irrelevant factors, and will certainly not be as consistent as a computer system. But most importantly, effective systems indicate a priority order of areas to be considered, not just points. So, if the point of highest probability is in the middle of a park, the next search location is considered.

One further development that has been introduced into the latest system, iOPS (Canter et al. 2006) is that suspects can be drawn from police records and placed in order of priority by the computer system. Other details of possible suspects can then be examined, such as whether they were imprisoned at the time of the offences, to allow a filtering of priorities. This computer system allows very rapid explorations through various archives and records before there is a need to knock on any doors or institute any other tactical responses.

Evaluation of 'Systems'

These developments also show how complex are the questions about the effectiveness of geographical profiling systems. Attention has already been drawn to the naivety of regarding the approach by Snook and his colleagues as having any practical significance [Canter 2005]. Canter et al. [2000] have already shown that rather than considering single distances between a highest probability point and the offender's base, it is more appropriate to examine some function that relates the proportion of the area searched to the proportion of offenders located. This 'search cost function' [Canter et al. 2000] can be used to compare different algorithms and different types of crime, but it only deals with one aspect of the utility of any system.

A US National Institute of Justice working party (Wilson et al. 2004) has outlined a number of other factors that need to be taken into consideration when evaluating any investigative decision support system. These include such mundane, but crucial, matters as how easy the system is to use and over what range of computer platforms it will operate. However, so far there has been little consideration of the research base on which any system is built and how well articulated are the underlying theories that the system implies. As the underlying theories become more developed we can expect that the systems on which they are built will become more sophisticated and the procedures used for evaluating them will also become more advanced.

Limitations in Studies of Criminals' Spatial Activity

Focus on Location

Although some real progress has been made in the understanding of offenders' geographical activity and the application of this understanding to police operations, there is still a great deal to be studied further and many improvements necessary in existing geographical profiling systems. Indeed, the interplay between theory and application is still one of the least developed aspects of this whole approach. The excitement over being able to develop commercially viable geographical profiling systems and the dramatic visualisation of crimes on a map has tended to draw more attention to the technologies involved than to the underlying questions about criminal spatial behaviour. The great increase in the availability and sophistication of geographical information systems (GIS) has also encouraged people to explore the geometries of criminals' maps at the expense of any consideration of what those geometries may signify or the psychological and social processes that may be generating them. Yet variations in these processes could produce entirely different geometrical distributions. The emphasis on the nuances of the mathematics that can be applied to the dots on a map also masks the much more fundamental need to establish reliable and valid data on which to carry out the calculations.

This emphasis on the dots on the map has drawn attention away from understanding the nature of the places where the dots are located. The opportunities those places provide, the readiness of access to them, guardianship and other land-use and geo-demographic issues also need to be considered to assist in understanding why any particular location was chosen to commit a crime. These matters can then be related to what is known about offenders to build much more subtle models of offence location choice.

One particularly interesting direction is the consideration of the opportunity distribution of crimes. This could take research into the examination of possible targets for crime that are not acted on. It is very likely that many offenders deliberately avoid certain venues, rather than consciously choosing others. It may therefore be more feasible to model offence location choice by taking account of where the offender does not go in any particular locality rather than where she or he does go.

Clustering

Currently research on the geography of criminals' actions tends to deal with each crime location as a distinct point. However, there are many reasons to think that offenders may carry out multiple crimes in sub-sections of areas, rather than their crimes being randomly distributed across a domain. The opportunities, access or particular types of targets as well as many other processes would be expected to give rise to an uneven spatial distribution of crimes. Currently, though, geographical profiling systems do not take account of this 'clumping' and research has not been published to indicate what the implications may be.

In practice, experts using geographical profiling systems may treat a group of crimes committed in one area over a short period of time as just one input point, so that they do not receive undue weight in the calculations of probability surfaces. But because the reasons for clustering have been little studied the decision as to whether to deal with two or more crimes as if they were one location is currently subjective and arbitrary. Much more needs to be known about how and why serial offenders group their offences in time and space.

Temporal Sequences

Geographical profiling, as the words indicate, has centred on where things happen rather than when. Yet, just as a person cannot be in two places at one time, hence laying the basis for mapping offences, so a person can only commit a crime at one point in time. This means there will always be a temporal as well as a spatial structure to criminal activities. This structure can be observed at the level of the time and day of crimes in a series, or at the level of the development of the offender over his criminal career.

There is doubtless a pattern to criminal temporal occurrences, as with all human activity. This pattern may be driven by processes within the offender as direct as the need for drugs, or shaped by external matters such as the changes in guardianship over the working day and the working week. Other seasonal processes, relating for example to the hours of darkness, are also likely to have an influence. There is also some general indication that matters such as temperature and climate provide a framework that correlates to criminal incidents (cf. Ceccato 2005).

Time does, of course, interact with place. The distance between crimes reflects the time it takes to travel from one to another, as does the distance from crime to home base. Therefore in modelling crimes there is a need for a lot more research that considers both when and where they occur. This research will benefit from considering the likely criminal journeys directly, and the actual movements that make these up rather than the notional 'journey to crime' models that are currently proposed. Issues to consider here would include the preferred mode of travel for offenders. This may not always be obvious without careful consideration of the risks and objectives of criminal travel. For example the delivery of drugs by bicycle may make contact with buyers easier because they do not have to lean into cars, and readiness of escape away from main road routes that may have CCTV, say through parks, may be seen as safer, despite the advantages of speed offered by motor vehicles.

One interesting prospect here is that conventional journey patterns, widely studied and explored by traffic engineers and planners, may be fruitful models for criminal journeys. The potential complexities of such studies are very great. Ad hoc explorations are thus likely to prove unproductive. Instead, what is needed is a more developed set of models/theories of criminal activity from which clear hypotheses can be derived and tested on the growing data becoming available.

The Social Psychology of Criminal Spatial Behaviour

All current publications on the spatial activity of offenders deal with them as if they were lone individuals. Even the spatial implications of offenders working in pairs or teams are rarely considered, much less studied closely. It is not yet clear how the relationship between offence location and one offender's home base is influenced by the locations of the homes of his/her co-offenders. Yet as the review by Canter and Alison (2000) illustrates, the great majority of crime is best considered as a social process. Criminals co-offend with others. They learn of criminal opportunities from other offenders. They are also often part of a distribution network; selling on stolen goods, buying and selling illegal drugs, and obtaining illegal weapons.

The range of contacts implied in all these processes each has a geographical location and each location is likely to influence other locations. How far apart from each other co-offenders live may, for instance, have an impact on how widespread their crimes are. Where they obtain illicit drugs or other products may have an impact on where they go to obtain funds to purchase those products, and so on. In order to examine the geographical implications of these processes the social networks of which criminals are a part will need to be mapped and those maps carefully analysed.

Geo-Behavioural Profiling

As richer and more subtle theories emerge that incorporate the location of crimes, when they happen and the journeys between them, it will become increasingly important to distinguish between different types of criminal activity. For instance, it seems very likely that models derived from some notion of the daily non-criminal activities of offenders may be more relevant to, say, property crimes that have a strong instrumental component than to crimes against the person that may be highly emotional. To take a different perspective, offenders' familiarity with an area, that may emphasise their domocentricity, might be of more significance for young offenders, or those early in their criminal 'career' than for experienced offenders, but this may only apply to those offences that have careful planning involved.

To date, studies tend to have been rather univariate in their focus. For although there is a growing literature on the multivariate structure of crimes (reviewed by Canter and Youngs 2003) there are still very few studies that relate these structures to the distances offenders travel, in the way that Fritzon [2001] has attempted for arson. Such developments would integrate geographical profiling with the behavioural profiling that has so far had an independent existence, giving rise to a much more sophisticated area of geo-behavioural profiling.

This combination of behavioural and geographical analyses would allow a careful consideration of the variations between offenders. They could be distinguished on the basis of indications, for example, of what they reveal of their criminal background through the way they commit their crimes. It will also be productive to take into account the resources, of money, time and skills, available to criminals. All these considerations can be informed by a better understanding of offenders' search strategies and their crime related decision making processes.

With such considerations the criminal life of the offender needs to be examined as a dynamic changing process. This may be day to day changes or major life changes, which might, for instance, be a product of a time in prison. To model such complex systems sophisticated computer support will be essential, but such support will be of little value without a clear framework for determining what the computer should be called upon to help do.

Conclusions and the Future of Geo-behavioural Profiling

Implications for Studies of Criminal Spatial Behaviour

Most crime has a distinct geographical location, as well as a number of behavioural and related psychological characteristics. Therefore the process of studying the interplay of offence actions and locations is an interesting route into understanding the psychology of crime. It helps to elucidate the degree of structure to criminal actions as well as the forms of implicit or explicit planning involved. Taken together with opportunities for crime, the study of individuals can help to determine how much crime is likely to occur because it is possible and how much will be generated by the demands of individual criminals.

Some of the more fundamental questions of how people create internal representations of their surroundings and how those representations may influence their place-related activities can also be illuminated by criminal geography. Offending may turn out to be an especially productive arena in which to explore these more fundamental environmental psychology problems because offenders often need to explore and make use of urban or rural environments rather more thoroughly than people not offending typically do. The ways in which access routes and transport networks interact with criminal opportunities, to create a framework that offenders need to make sense of, could provide a paradigm for many different ways of interacting with the physical surroundings. Paradoxically, study of these illegal activities may be more open to study than legal use of the surroundings, because of the records kept by law enforcement agencies.

A central challenge, though, is to move from the individual criminal to the aggregate and back again. The geographical profiling theories and systems currently available all assume that the aggregate distributions of crime journeys can be applied to any single offender. As mentioned above there is growing evidence that decay functions in particular do not characterise the journey to crime distances for individual offenders over a series, even though they have been consistently found to characterise the frequency distributions of samples of offenders. The proposal of criminal ranges implies that there are a range of optimal travel distances each typical for any given offender.

Such offender idiosyncrasies are likely to exist for all the other aspects of offender geography. This is a parallel challenge to that in psychological personality theory, where broad traits can be used to describe sub-populations but may be of little value at the individual level. This means that an important direction for future research and development is to find ways of classifying offenders so that their geo-behavioural patterns can be distinguished from one another. It is unlikely that such a classification can effectively be based solely on the spatial geometry of their crimes. It seems inevitable that use will need to be made of all aspects of their criminal actions.

Further there is a need to move towards a broader notion of geographical profiling that goes beyond the focus on the home or base. By taking on board the social psychology of crime as well the dynamic, changing nature of criminal spatial behaviour a much richer set of theories and, in turn, investigative tools will emerge. These will move away from the idea that what is being studied is some notional 'journey to crime'. It seems unlikely even at our present level of understanding that criminals set out from home on a simple trip to their intended offence target. It is much more likely that crime evolves out of offenders' criminal lifestyle, shaped by many of the processes that shape the activities and locations of non-criminal behaviour. Understanding, modelling and eventually incorporating such models into geo-behavioural profiling systems will demand much more than geometrical analyses of dots in an abstract geographical space.

It should also not be forgotten that offender spatial activities are only one subset of human activities. If routine activity holds sway then it can be assumed that criminal journeys will not be that different from other forms of legal journey. Certainly some of the patterns mentioned above, such as decay functions, are similar between legal and illegal activity. There is therefore a great deal to be learnt from studies of the spatial patterns of legal activities. This will enrich our models and theories of criminal behaviours in many ways.

One particularly powerful illustration of how studies of legal human spatial activities can enrich our conceptualisations of criminal geography are the very detailed studies of street traders reviewed by Bromley (1980). He explores the distinction between mobile and fixed traders and shows that quite different logical cycles can be modelled on the basis of different assumptions. His cycle 2b in Figure 4.4. is remarkably similar to the 'marauding' pattern found for serial killers by Lundrigan and Canter [2001a] and other types of criminals. So, the existence of other market cycles raises the possibility that we should be looking for them within criminal geographies. Many other issues raised by Bromley open up possible parallels with criminal activities. To take just one example, he draws attention to differences in part-time traders and those for whom it is a full time job. There are clear analogies here with casual offenders, who are often younger, and 'career' criminals whose life is devoted to crime. Are there important differences in how these different types of offender make use of their surroundings?

Some of the patterns of traders' spatial mobility can be seen as a natural result of the economy of opportunities. They wish to maximise their access to markets whilst minimising the effort involved. When the process has such a strong relationship between effort expenditure and benefits it is to be expected that there will be parallels in the animal kingdom. Mitzutani and Jewell (1998) show such parallels in the movement of leopards and their ranges of activities, as well as the location of their kills [Mitzutani 1995]. These studies are conducted by monitoring electronic tags on the animals. Developments in criminal justice may make closely similar studies possible with criminals in the future.

These animal studies do show that some, at least, of the processes we have been summarising have a fundamental logic to them and are thus a consequence of natural activities. We should therefore not be surprised that more than a century and a half ago models of human spatial activity were proposed to help explain non-criminal phenomena. In particular the cause of an outbreak of cholera in London was explained by locating the patients on a map and relating that to the available water sources on well pumps [Snow 1855]. The clear correlation between the density of cholera cases and the location of particular wells was used to support the view that cholera was water borne. The assumption here was that people would use their nearest well, just as we assume offenders will not travel far to commit their crimes. The well plays a role analogous to the criminal's base and the cholera cases are distributed like crimes around that location. Snow's study is often heralded as the origin of modern epidemiology. It serves to show us that the patterns of criminal behaviour we are finding are not unique to criminals and, equally, that there is much that can be learnt about criminals' spatial activity from considering similarities in other domains of activity.

All of these developments will serve to move the scope and aims of geographical profiling beyond those that were similar to early 'offender profiling' in which the purported objective was to identify and locate the offender. They move the whole conceptualisation of what is being explored in geographical offender profiling away from the notion of simply identifying an address to which to dispatch a police officer. Providing direct input into the process of arresting a culprit will increasingly become only a small component of geographical profiling as it evolves into a wide-ranging set of studies that enrich our understanding of criminals and non-criminals alike.

References

Baldwin, J. and Bottoms, A.E. (1976). *The Urban Criminal. A Study in Sheffield.* London: Tavistock Publications.

Barker, M. (2000). The criminal range of small-town burglars. In D. Canter and L. Alison. (eds), *Profiling Property Crimes* (pp. 57–73). Aldershot, UK: Dartmouth.

Beverton, R.J.H. and Holt, S.J. (1957). 'On the dynamics of exploited fish populations'. *Fish.Invest.Lond.* Ser II, Vol. XIX.

Brantingham, P.L. and Brantingham P.J. (1981). Notes on the geometry of crime. In P.J. Brantingham and P.L. Brantingham (eds), *Environmental Criminology* (pp. 27–54). Beverly Hills: Sage Publications.

Bromley, R.J. (1980). Trader mobility in systems of periodic and daily markets. In D.T. Herbert and R.J. Johnston (eds), *Geography and the Urban Environment* (pp. 133–174). New York: John Wiley & Sons Ltd.

Canter, D. (2004). Geographic profiling of criminals. *Medico-legal Journal*, 72, 53–66.

Canter, D. (2005). Confusing operational predicaments and cognitive explorations: Comments on Rossmo and Snook et al. *Applied Cognitive Psychology*, 19(5), 663–668.

Canter, D. and Alison, L.J. (2003). Converting evidence into data: The use of law enforcement archives as unobtrusive measurement, *The Qualitative Report, June*, 8(2).

Canter, D.V. and Gregory, A. (1994). Identifying the residential location of rapists. *Journal of the Forensic Science Society*, 34, 169–175.

Canter, D. and Hammond, L. (2006). A comparison of the efficacy of different decay functions in geographical profiling for a sample of US serial killers, *Journal of Investigative Psychology and Offender Profiling*, 3(2), 91–104

Canter, D. and Larkin, P. (1993). The environmental range of serial rapists. *Journal of Environmental Psychology*, 13, 63–69.

Canter, D. and Youngs, D. (2003). Beyond offender profiling: The need for an investigative psychology. In R. Bull and D. Carson (eds), *Handbook of Psychology and Legal Contexts,* (pp. 171–205).

Canter, D. and Youngs, D. (2007). Beyond geographical offender profiling: The investigative psychology of criminal spatial activity – an emerging research agenda *(Submitted).*

Canter, D. and Youngs, D. (2008). *Principles of Geographical Offender Profiling.* Aldershot, UK : Ashgate.

Canter, D., Youngs, D. and Newman, F. (2006). iOPS: An Interactive Offender Profiling System. *In Press.*

Canter, D., Coffey, T., Huntley, M. and Missen, C. (2000). Predicting serial killers' home base using a decision support system. *Journal of Quantitative Criminology*, 16, 457–478.

Capone, D.L. and Nichols, W.W. (1975). Crime and distance: An analysis of offender behaviour in space. *Proceedings of the Association of American Geographers, 7*, 45–49.

Ceccato, V. (2005) Homicide in Sao Paulo, Brazil: Assessing spatial-temporal and weather variations. *Journal of Environmental Psychology, 25, 3, 307–321.*

Costello, A. and Wiles, P. (2001). GIS and the journey to crime: An analysis of patterns in South Yorkshire. In A. Hirschfield and K. Bowers (eds), *Mapping and Analysing Crime Data: Lessons from Research and Practice* (pp. 27–60). London: Taylor and Francis.

Dixon, L. (2000). Merseyside uncovered: Examining the relationship between thematic behavioural actions, spatial mobility and demographic characteristics in residential burglary. Unpublished Master's Dissertation, The University of Liverpool, England.

Fritzon, K. (2001). An examination of the relationship between distance travelled and motivational aspects of arson. *Journal of Environmental Psychology, 21, 45–60.*

Gabor, T. and Gottheil, E. (1984). Offender characteristics and spatial mobility: An empirical study and some policy implications. *Journal of Criminology*, 26, 267–281.

Gittens, E. (2004). *A Geographical and Thematic Exploration of Burglary in Barbados*. Unpublished Master's Dissertation, The University of Liverpool, England.

Kind, S. (1999). *The Sceptical Witness: Concerning the Scientific Investigation of Crime Against a Human Background*. Harrogate: The Forensic Science Society.

Kothari, U. (2002). *Migration and Chronic Poverty*. Institute for Development, Policy and Management, University of Manchester. Working Paper No. 16.

LeBeau, J.L. (1987). The journey to rape: Geographic distance and the rapist's method of approaching the victim. *Journal of Police Science and Administration*, 15, 129–136.

Lundrigan, S. and Canter, D. (2001a). A multivariate analysis of serial murderers' disposal site location choice. *Journal of Environmental Psychology*, 21, 423–432.

Lundrigan, S. and Canter, D. (2001b). Spatial patterns of serial murder: An analysis of disposal site location choice. *Behavioural Sciences and the Law*, 19, 595–610.

Mizutani, F. (1993). Home range of leopards and their impact on livestock on Kenyan ranches. *Symposium Zoological Society London*, 65, 425–439.

Mizutani, F. and Jewell, P.A. (1998). Home-range and movements of leopards (*Panther pardus*) on a livestock ranch in Kenya. *Journal of Zoology*, 244, 269–286.

Nichols, W.W. Jr. (1980). Mental maps, social characteristics and criminal mobility. In D.E. Georges-Abeyie and K.D. Harries, (eds), *Crime: A Spatial Perspective* (pp. 156–166). Columbia University Press.

Pettiway, L.E. (1982). Mobility of burglars and robbery offenders. *Urban Affairs Quarterly*, 18(2), 255–270.

Phillips, P.D. (1980). Characteristics and typology of the journey to crime. In D.E. Georges-Abeyie and K.D. Harries (eds) *Crime: A Spatial Perspective*. New York: Colombia University Press.

Rengert, G.F., Piquero, A.R. and Jones, P.R. (1999). Distance decay re-examined. *Criminology*, 37(2), 427–425.

Rhodes, W.M. and Conly, C. (1981). 'Crime and mobility: An empirical study'. In P.J. Brantingham and P. Brantingham (1981). *Environmental Criminology*. Waveland Press Inc: Prospect Heights, Illinois.

Richardson, H.W., Gordon, P., Jun, M.J., Heikkila, E., Peiser, R. and Dale-Johnson, D. (1990). 'Residential property values, the CBD, and multiple nodes: Further analysis'. *Environment and Planning*, 22(A), 829–833.

Rossmo, D.K. (1995). Place, space, and police investigations: Hunting serial violent criminals. In J.E. Eck and D.L. Weisburd (eds), *Crime and Place: Crime Prevention Studies, Vol. 4* (pp. 217–235). Monsey, NY: Criminal Justice Press.

Snook, B., Taylor, P.J. and Bennell, C. (2004). Geographic profiling: The fast, fast, frugal, and accurate way. *Applied Cognitive Psychology*, 18, 105–121.

Snook, B., Canter, D. and Bennell, C. (2002). Predicting home location of serial offenders: A preliminary comparison of the accuracy of human judges and a geographic profiling system. *Behavioral Sciences and Law*, 20, 109–118.

Snow, J. (1855). *On the Mode of Communication of Cholera*. Explanation of the Map showing the situation of the deaths in and around Broad Street, Golden Square. Retrieved February 25th, 2006, from http://www.ph.ucla.edu/epi/snow/snowbook2.html.

Turner, S. (1969). Delinquency and Distance. In Sellin, T. and Wolfgang, M. E. (eds). *Delinquency: Selected Studies* (pp. 11–26). New York: John Wiley & Sons.

Van Koppen, P.J. and De Keiser, J.W. (1997). 'Desisting distance decay: On the aggregation of individual crime trips'. *Criminology*, 35(2), 505–513.

Van Koppen, P. J. and Jansen, R.W. (1998). The road to robbery: Travel patterns in commercial robberies. *British Journal of Criminology*, 38(2), 230–246.

Warren, J., Reboussin, R., Hazelwood, R.R., Cummings, A., Gibbs, N. and Trumbetta, S. (1998). Crime scene and distance correlates of serial rape. *Journal of Quantitative Criminology*, 14(1), 35–59.

White, R.C. (1932). The relation of felonies to environmental factors in Indianapolis. *Social Forces*, 10(4), 498–509.

Wiles, P. and Costello, A. (2000). *The 'Road to Nowhere': The Evidence for Travelling Criminals*. Home Office research study 207. Section 5, (pp. 29–42).

Wilson, R., Rich, T. and Shively, M. (2004). *A Methodology Evaluating Geographic Profiling Software*. Cambridge, MA.: Abt Associates Inc.

Chapter 2

A Multivariate Analysis of Serial Murderers' Disposal Site Location Choice

Samantha Lundrigan and David Canter

Introduction

In recent years, the spatial behaviour of criminals has been related to other studies of human experiences and use of places. This has generated a framework for considering the rationale behind the locations at which criminals commit their crimes (Brantingham and Brantingham 1981; Rengert and Wasilchick 1985; Canter and Larkin 1993). This has indicated that these locations are not arbitrary, but as with non-criminal aspects of location choice, relate to the specific experiences of the individuals themselves. This implies some form of selection on the part of the criminal, even if the basis of the selection is not always clear to the criminals themselves. The present study examines U.S. serial murderers as a way of developing the understanding of these geographical patterns of offence behaviour.

Although very rare, and certainly not a conventional topic for environmental psychology, serial murderers are interesting to consider because they are typically thought of as bizarre, genetically disordered individuals who randomly prey on victims (Revitch and Schlesinger 1981). Logical or rational action is not usually assumed to be the hallmark of such offenders. It may therefore be considered very difficult to model their actions in any way. However, although the motivations and causes of these offences may be difficult to determine, it is possible that the offenders' selection of the locations in which to act may have an inherent logic that bears commonalties with other offending and nonoffending behaviour. For although individual motivations for murder are often thought to be the result of a unique combination of biogenetic, sociological and psychological factors, it is hypothesized that the manner in which any individual interacts with the environment will be influenced by a number of spatial processes that are generic to both criminals and noncriminals alike.

For instance, a serial murderer whose motivation is a bizarre desire for sadistic sexual excitement is unlikely, in terms of motivation and murder actions, to share any similarities with other types of offender. However, the extreme nature of his motivation and murder actions will not necessarily be reflected in his spatial behaviour. For although driven by a unique motive intrinsic to himself, in order to maintain some control over his actions and perpetuate his criminal activities, he will need to take account of locational possibilities, as shaped by his own cognitions of the larger environment. Therefore, it is proposed that generic spatial processes will influence the spatial decision making of serial murderers. Such spatial processes include the psychological importance of the home (Canter and Larkin 1993), familiarity with surroundings (Brantingham and Brantingham 1981), individual representations of the environment (Downs and Stea 1973), rational choice considerations (Cornish and Clarke 1986) and the evident need to reduce the risk of detection.

Human spatial activity is a reflection of each individual's cognitive map of the spatial environment. From its earliest, cognitive mapping research has shown the importance of residential location in giving focus to a person's internal representations and subsequent location selections (Trowbridge 1913). The power of an individual's residential location is also reflected in their 'home range; the geographical area around a home which is traversed and used more regularly than areas a greater distance from the home. This area would typically contain the shops, the homes of friends and relatives and the social activities a person frequents. Rengert and Wasilchick's (1985) investigations reflect this concept in their suggestion of the importance of the journeys criminals habitually take around the areas close to their homes. They propose that such journeys provide criminals with information around which they plan their next crime. They emphasize that it is not only the physical dynamics of the area which are important in structuring criminals' behaviour, but that the information which they gather on their 'way home' is also important. Places frequented by the criminal while travelling home, such as, bars, shops and restaurants are therefore proposed as defining their criminal range, tuning perceptions as to which areas are 'safe; both geographically and psychologically.

Centrality of Offenders' Residential Location

Brantingham and Brantingham (1981) suggest that the concentration of activity around the home is influenced by biased information flows. In other words, more information will be available about locations close to the home base and therefore offenders are more likely to be aware of criminal opportunities in such areas. For serial murder this leads to the proposition that such killers may become aware of potential victim opportunities whilst engaged in noncriminal activity They similarly may also become aware of suitable locations to dispose of their victims' bodies.

The usual procedures for exploring mental representations of the surroundings and the way these influence location choices are through interviewing and sketch mapping. Whilst these procedures have proven their value since the earliest work of Lynch (1960), and have recently been shown to be fruitful when used with some offenders (Canter and Hodge 2000) they have both practical and theoretical limitations in relation to serial killers.

At the practical level such material is hard to come by, but even if interviews with these criminals were possible there would be an important question about the extent to which they could be trusted to give valid accounts that were not self-serving. At the theoretical level there is the question as to whether, whatever an offender might say or think about his choice of crime locations, these choices can modelled using *a priori* logical principles. The establishment of such principles may then offer a fruitful basis for later interviews that would therefore be less prone to bias from the interviewee as the sole source of any explanatory framework.

Rational Choice theory (Cornish and Clark 1986) provides a productive starting point for considering the logic that may be implicit in offenders' site selection. Rational choice proposes that offenders seek to benefit themselves by their criminal behaviour and this involves the making of decisions and choices which exhibit a trade-off between increased opportunity and greater reward, the further an offender travels from home, and the costs of time, effort and risk. The benefits of a criminal action are the net rewards of crime and include not only material gains but also intangible benefits such as emotional satisfaction. The risks or costs of crime are those associated with formal punishment should the offender be apprehended.

However, models of Rational Choice have been concerned with overtly instrumental crimes such as burglary and robbery. Violent crimes that have a strongly expressive component, such as murder and rape, have rarely been subject to analysis from this perspective. The few relevant studies in this area (notably, Athens 1980 study of rape and homicide) suggest that many such offences do exhibit a substantial degree of rationality.

Criminal Range

For serial murder the Rational Choice framework offers some processes from which important hypotheses can be derived. One is that the offender needs to balance the effort required to travel from his residential base, including the risks associated with being in possession of the body while travelling, with the benefits of leaving his victims' bodies as far from his home as possible. The simplest assumption is that, in general, the balance of risks and rewards would remain similar for each offender from one offence to another. Therefore, if his cognitive map of disposal locations is shaped by the location of his home base it would be hypothesized that, no matter what scale of distances he travelled on average, his location choices would tend to be within the same range. In other words there would be the possibility of distinguishing offenders in terms of the general size of the area over which they operate. If they tend to travel far from home for some crimes they will for others and vice versa. Canter and Larkin (1993) offer support for this assumption for serial rapists in the South of England by showing that there is a very high correlation between the smallest distances they travel from home and the largest. In other words those offenders tended to have a consistent 'criminal range' over which they operated.

It might be expected that once an offender located an area that he found suitable for his criminal activity that he would then use it consistently. Yet, whilst there are examples of such offence behaviour, the risks involved in such a course of action are self-evident. It might therefore be expected that the offender will maintain the criminal range from his home in committing his crimes, (referred to by Brantingham and Brantingham [1981] as a 'buffer zone') but that his criminal activity will be distributed around his home. This is a directly testable hypothesis.

Crime Locations

Although there are a number of geographical locations associated with any one murder in a series (e.g. point of encounter, murder scene, containment location), the present study focuses on the locations and meaning of the body disposal sites that the offender selects. It is assumed that a murderer will choose to dispose of a victim's body in a location that minimizes the likelihood of apprehension. Although each and every location used by an offender in the commission of a murder is of psychological and investigative importance, the location at which the victims' bodies were left was used because it is the least contentious, most objective information available about the location of a murder. Interestingly, in an analysis of the Hillside Strangler case, Newton and Swoope (1987) discriminated between point of fatal encounter, site were the body was left, and victim residence. They found that the geographic centre of the location where the body had been placed most accurately predicted the location of the residence of murderer Angelo Buono.

The body disposal site will often be the only location known to investigators simply because it is the discovery of a body that alerts the authorities to a murder (of course, the location at which the body is found may also be where the murder was carried out or they may be two separate locations). The body disposal location will usually be the 'final resting place' for the victim. It signifies the culmination of the act and therefore may have particular significance to the offender and therefore be particularly relevant to an understanding of his spatial behaviour. Furthermore, the body disposal site may be of particular importance as it is perhaps where the offender has the most locational choice. For example, the choice of an encounter site will be influenced by the distribution of suitable victims while the murder site will be influenced by the difficulty of constraining/transporting a 'live' victim. Once the victim has been murdered, these constraints are no longer factors. Of course, other constraints arise after the victim has been murdered. For example, it can be argued that the offender is at his most vulnerable at this stage of the murder and the risk of being apprehended with such incriminating evidence may influence the mobility of the offender. Therefore, it is proposed here that body disposal locations will reflect the spatio-cognitive frameworks within which serial murderers operate. Furthermore, whilst the murder itself may be assumed often to take place in the heat of emotion it is more likely that the disposal site is selected after some consideration before or after the murder.

Serial Murder and Spatial Behaviour

Serial murder has been the subject of extensive research (Egger 1990; Holmes and Holmes 1989). In particular, many researchers have attempted to provide typologies of serial murder. Such typologies have typically been based on motivation (Holmes and De Burger 1988) or crime scene behaviour (Ressler et al. 1986). Inherent within these typologies has been discussion of the spatial behaviour associated with the different 'types'. In their organized/disorganized dichotomy, Ressler et al. suggest that one of the behaviours that distinguish the two types is the distances they typically travel to carry out a murder. They suggest that the disorganized murderer is likely to remain close to home while the organized killer will travel further afield.

Although most researchers recognize the vital part that an understanding of spatial behaviour plays in any definition or exploration of serial murder, there is surprisingly little empirical research that examines this aspect of the crime. The few attempts to address the spatial mobility of serial killers have typically focused on describing the distances such offenders travel from home to offend.

Based on interviews and analysis of over 400 cases of serial murder, Holmes and De Burger (1988) proposed a distinction between geographically stable and geographically transient serial killers. According to the authors, geographically stable killers live in the same area for some time, kill in the same or nearby area and disposes of bodies in the same or nearby area. In contrast, the geographically transient killer travels continuously from one area to the next and disposes of bodies in far-flung places. They go on to suggest that, contrary to the popular belief that nomadic serial murderers drive thousands of miles in their hunt for victims, most 'never lacked for readily available victims within their own neighbourhood; [and] their rational explanation for their travel is that it was used to confuse police: This suggests that the decision to travel a great distance to offend is greatly influenced by the desire to avoid apprehension, in itself, a rational consideration. Were this risk not present then these offenders would remain within a familiar environment. In other words, it may be an external influence that prompts serial murderers to travel large distances. Although a useful distinction, there is a lack of precision in that there is no attempt to define the distances travelled or the size of area for each group.

Hickey (1991) draws attention to a threefold classification of serial killers that he calls a) 'travellers' crossing state boundaries, covering thousands of miles; b) 'locals' who remain in their home state and c) place specific killers who do not leave home to kill. Hickey found that 50% of the male offenders were categorized as local killers and the majority (71%) operated in a specific place or general urbanized area but did not travel into other states.

Although clearly of value this classification takes no account of the possible role of a base even in the offenders who cover great distances or of the other processes that have been put forward here that may account for the patterns. It is intended more as a general classification that draws together many different descriptive features of the men Hickey studied. As with the classification proposed by Holmes and De Burger,

Hickey's definition of these three groups also lacks some precision in that no actual distance ranges are suggested to differentiate between the groups. Furthermore, it is not clear what the distances they report are describing. In other words there is no indication of whether they are describing distance travelled to encounter, murder or disposal site or a combination of them.

The studies above are all descriptive of the distances that serial murderers travel. From a different perspective, Rossmo (1997) proposed a hunting typology to describe the processes that underlie their patterns of mobility. He breaks the serial killer hunting process into two components, the search for a suitable victim and the method of attack. He suggests that the first influences the selection of victim encounter sites and the latter, disposal sites.

As can be seen, the few studies that have explored serial murder from a spatial perspective typically separate such behaviour into broad categories according to the scale of the offender's mobility There has been no attempt to quantify the categories within specific distance ranges. Instead, more general geographical units such as 'neighbourhoods' and 'states' are used to suggest the scale of movement in each category. Such typologies also suggest that the spatial behaviour of serial murderers can be easily divided into groups. This is in contrast to spatial research for other types of offender. Typically, other types of offender are differentiated by offence or offender characteristics. Rarely, are typologies based solely on distance differences. This is interesting as it suggests that there may be a greater need to do this for serial murder because the distances involved cover a wider range of distances than other types of crime, which may remain more local in nature. In other words, serial murderers, although not only being at the extreme of a criminal continuum in terms of violence and brutality are also at the extreme of a mobility continuum, travelling far greater distances than other types of offender. The question is that, if this is the case, are the same processes used to explain other types of criminal movement applicable to the extreme behaviour of serial murderers?

Data Collection

Within the literature, there are many definitions of serial killers usually differing in terms of the number of victims any given offender must kill in order to be termed a serial killer. The most common number is a minimum of three victims (Holmes and Holmes 1996). However, some researchers such as Jenkins (1988) use four or more victims as the cut off point. Our definition recognizes serial killers as those individuals who have killed 'two or more victims over a period of time with a cooling off period between each murder'. The inclusion of a cooling off period' ensures that mass murderers are excluded from the definition. The use of 'two or more victims' as the defining number allows for those serial killers who, although being responsible for only two known murders, may still exhibit the traits of serial killers who are known to have killed more than twice.

In order to examine the spatial behaviour of serial murderers, information on serial killers from the U.S.A. (*n* = 120) were obtained from published sources and police records. The data for each murderer was drawn from the qualitative measurement process of content analysis. Sources included newspapers and magazine articles, true crime books and academic texts. It should be noted that many of these sources are published reports from individuals who were involved in the original investigations, such as Keppel's accounts (Keppel 1997). Furthermore, in many cases, the opportunity was taken to verify details with police sources close to the investigations. The use of such data sources was detailed by Webb et al. (1966) and has been used in previous research on serial murder (Leyton 1986; Hickey 1991).

For the purposes of the present research, locational information concerning all the 120 American serial murderers was collected. This information consisted of the home addresses of the offenders and the locations where the bodies of their victims were found. The sample was limited to those cases for which clear and corroborated locational information was available.

Procedure

Collectively, the U.S. killers were known to have murdered 898 victims. They had been convicted of killing between 2 (1) and 24 (1) people each. Once the relevant geographical information had been collated, the offenders' home base and the sites at which they left the bodies of their victims were recorded onto local street maps. Where more than one base was known the one that was used during any particular series of killings was recorded. Thus the base recorded was always linked directly to the offences known to have been committed from that base. The base and body disposal site locations were mapped onto a specially developed Geographical Information System 'Mplot; that recorded the points as relative coordinates in a 2-dimensional Euclidean space, together with a specific scale for each offender. The software calculates a variety of distances from the coordinates as well as statistical derivations of these distances.

For the purposes of the present research, it is necessary to consider the relationship that every location has to every other and to examine those locations in sequential order. It can be argued that the locations of an offender's disposal sites around his home area may be illustrating a sort of criminal cognitive map. Mapping the sites of criminal activity over time could be seen as an illustration of how an offender discovers and uses his environment, learning about it in terms of the opportunities for criminal activity it can offer him.

An appropriate statistical procedure for testing this is smallest space analysis (SSA) which is a multi dimensional scaling technique that finds the best fit within a specified dimensionality between a matrix of associations, in this case, the mean distances between all locations and a geometric representation of these associations as distances in a Cartesian space. In effect, a geometric representation of the distances between all the locations allows for the testing of a multivariate model of offender mobility. Therefore, SSA can be used to explore both the relationships between home and the disposal locations and between the disposal locations themselves. Two hypotheses can therefore be made that relate to these two facets of spatial patterning:

1. There will be some order to the distances between the disposal sites and home with the home being central to that order.
2. There will be ordered differences in the temporal sequencing of disposal sites in terms of both distance and direction.

In order to investigate these proposed relationships, the sample was divided into three subgroups according to mean interpoint distance (MID). For each offender, the MID was calculated by adding the distances between every offence and dividing by the number of distances measured. The first group included all those offenders who operated within mean interpoint distances of 10 km. The second group consisted of those offenders whose mean interpoint distance was between 10 and 30 km. The final group consisted of those offenders whose mean interpoint distance was greater than 30 km. Table 2.1 summarizes the three groups.

In order to investigate whether these groups are distinct from each other, an Anova was carried out. The results were significant ($F = 43.47$ $p < 0.0001$ df 2). In order to establish which of the groups were significantly different from each other, a post hoc Scheffe test was carried out. This indicated that group 3 was significantly different from the other two. A Kruskall Wallis test was also carried out as the data is not normally distributed. This was also significant (Chi Sq 105.5 $p < 0.0001$).

If serial killers are reasonably consistent in their disposal site choices, there should be a correlation between the minimum distance they travel from home and the maximum. Therefore, the minimum and maximum distances travelled from home were correlated for each group. The correlations between the nearest and the farthest distances from home to a disposal site are:

- Group 1– $r = 0.41$ ($p < 0.05$)*
- Group 2 – $r = 0.59$ ($p = 0.08$)
- Group 3 – $r = 0.67$ ($p < 0.001$)*

For groups 1 and 3, it was found that an increase in the maximum distance travelled from home was accompanied by a parallel increase in the minimum. The relationship between minimum and maximum distance was not quite significant for group 2.

Smallest Space Analysis

Smallest space analysis was developed by Guttman (1968). The procedure deals with the off-diagonal elements of a square, symmetric matrix of association coefficients

(Lingoes 1973). The advantage of SSA over other algorithms lies in its robustness and rational step-size (Lingoes 1973). This is mainly because the algorithm only attempts to find the best fit between the ranks of the association coefficients and the ranks of the distances in the geometric space. Such a matching of ranks can be shown to give a mathematically more efficient solution as well as being less sensitive to extreme values. It also leads to the procedure being recognized as nonmetric. In the present analysis the hypotheses are about the relative associations between locations rather than their absolute differences. The hypotheses here are not precise enough to say how much bigger or smaller the relative distances are in comparison with each other, rather that there are consistent differences in rank. The resulting geometric representation is thus more open to direct interpretation than would procedures using metric algorithms.

A triangular association matrix was generated for the SSA analysis using the mean interpoint distances that serial murderers travelled between their home base and all their disposal sites. The distance metric used to generate the SSA is based on Euclidean distances.

Results

SSA for Offenders with MIDs of Less than 10 km

Figure 2.1 shows the three-dimensional solution for those offenders who travelled mean distances of less than 10 km. The coefficient of alienation indicates the 'goodness of fit' between the correlations and their graphic representation. The score ranges from zero, denoting a perfect fit, to one, a poor fit. The smaller the coefficient, the better the fit. An acceptable score is between 0·15 and 0·24 (Donald and Canter 1990). The coefficient here is 0·15 indicating a good fit. Each point in the SSA plot represents an average location so the relative distances across the plot represent the relative distances the murderers travelled on average from their home bases to dispose of their victim's bodies as well as the average distances between each and every disposal site. A star represents the serial murderers' home base. So, for example, Figure 2.1 shows that the average distance from home to the first disposal site was considerably less than the average distance between the seventh and tenth disposal sites.

In Figure 2.1, the home is clearly located within a region surrounded by the disposal sites. This clearly demonstrates the important influence of the home base as a spatial focus for this group of serial murderers. The best solution that the SSA algorithm can find positions the home in a location so that all the disposal sites surround it, therefore supporting the hypothesis that the home exerts a central significance on the offender. The three-dimensional solution clearly illustrates the strong conceptual influence of the home on this group's disposal site location choices.

Turning to the relative positioning of the disposal sites around the home base, it can be seen that they are reasonably clustered around the base. Interestingly, the

Table 2.1   Breakdown of sample

MID of group	Number	Mean number of offences per offender	Overall mean distance for group	Range
less than 10 km	36	5·7	4 km	0·69–9·63
10–30 km	44	7·4	19 km	10·13–28·40
greater than 30 km	40	6·6	40 km	34·55–643·45

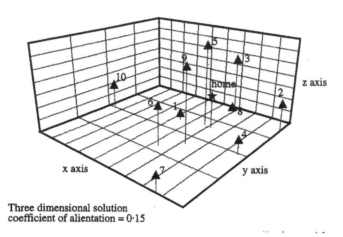

Three dimensional solution
coefficient of alientation = 0·15

Figure 2.1   Three-dimensional solution for those offenders with MIDs of less than 10 km

SSA positions the first four disposal sites closest to the home base but at different locations around it. Sites one and two and sites three and four are located opposite each other on either side of the home. This suggests that this group of offenders use the first four disposal sites to explore the area directly around the home base.

The SSA further illustrates that there are other processes at work that influence the disposal site choices of the offenders. In the third dimension, the influence of previous disposal location choices on subsequent choices can be clearly seen. In other words, the SSA shows a distancing between chronologically related sites. No two chronologically related sites maintain the same position on the z-axis. For example, disposal site one occupies a location on the z-axis distinct from site two and site three is distinct from site two and so on. One of the clearest examples of this is the positioning of sites eight and nine at opposite points on the third dimension. This further illustrates the important finding that the location of previous disposal activity exerts an influence on subsequent location choice. In other words, the offenders appear to be moving to different locations around the base for each subsequent site so that no two sites are in the same general area. The small area over which these offenders are operating can explain the deliberate separation between subsequent sites. It may be that, in order to maintain a perceived safe distance between disposal sites, the offender has to move to separate areas on each occasion.

SSA for Offenders with MIDs between 10 and 30 km

Figure 2.2 shows the three-dimensional solution for those offenders whose mean interpoint distances were between 10 and 30 km. The coefficient of alienation is 0.4 indicating a good fit. As before, the SSA positions the home base at a location where it is surrounded by the disposal locations, again lending support to the home acting as a focus for the offender's spatial behaviour. Interestingly, the overall pattern displayed here is more dispersed than that for the offenders operating over the smaller area. In other words, the SSA accounts for the larger relative distances by spreading the locations further around the plot.

A more complex process to the previous SSA is revealed in terms of the positioning of the disposal sites relative to each other. The first site is located directly adjacent to the home base as before. However, the three subsequent sites are further away towards the periphery of the plot. The last three sites (8, 9 and 10) are a little separate from the previous sites suggesting that the offenders may have a tendency to move to a slightly different area away from the earlier locations.

It appears that, for these offenders operating over larger ranges, the home, although still playing a pivotal role in influencing disposal site choice, is not as strong an influence as was found for the sample operating over ranges of less than 10 km.

SSA for Offenders with MIDs over 30 km

Figure 2.3 represents the three-dimensional projection for those offenders with mean interpoint distances greater than 30 km. The coefficient of alienation is 0-12 indicating a very good fit.

As with the previous plots, the SSA positions the home in a relatively central location and the disposal sites are widely dispersed around this central location. Interestingly, the first four sites are all positioned to the left side of the plot in a distinct region. This suggests that the offender uses the first four sites in a very different way to the other two groups. Here, the first offence is located some distance from the home base while the second site is the closest to home. The offender may deliberately place a greater distance between his home and first disposal site because of extra vigilance on embarking on his series of murders. He then appears to move towards home again and then spread to the opposite side of the home for the third and fourth disposal sites. Disposal sites 7, 8 and 9 are located at the same level on the z axis, again suggesting a move on the part of the offender to a separate area at the late stage of his series. It may be that for this group of offenders, the locations of

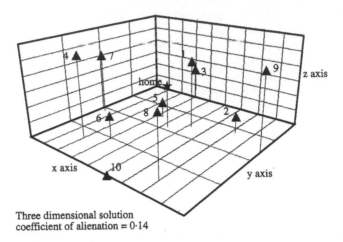

Three dimensional solution
coefficient of alienation = 0·14

Figure 2.2   Three-dimensional SSA for those offenders with MIDs between 10–30 km

previous disposal sites have less of an influence on the location of subsequent sites. This seems reasonable because of the far greater distances that the offenders are travelling and, as a result, leaving between their sites. The need to place a perceived safe distance between chronological offences is no longer a consideration because of the great size of the area they typically utilise as their disposal zone.

Temporal Proximity

Table 2.2 shows the mean distances travelled for each group in relation to temporal proximity. These findings further support the spatial patterns uncovered by the Smallest Space Analysis. For group 1, those offenders with MID's of less than 10 km, there is significant difference between the mean distances they put between chronologically adjacent sites and between odd and even sites. These offenders appear to place a greater distance between chronologically subsequent sites than the sites that are not chronologically adjacent.

For group 2, those offenders operating with MIDs between 10–30 km again appear to place greater distances between their chronologically adjacent sites than their odd and even sites, although the differences are not significant.

For group 3, those offenders with MIDs over 30 km, a different pattern emerges, already uncovered in the SSA. Here, there is no increase in distances between chronologically adjacent sites compared to the odd and even sites. In fact, there is a significant difference between the groups but it is in the opposite direction. The chronologically adjacent sites are closer together than the non-chronological sites. This further suggests that the influence of home and the location of subsequent sites may not be as important to those offenders travelling greater distances.

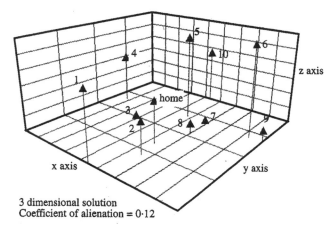

Figure 2.3   **Three-dimensional SSA for serial murderers with MIDs over 30 km**

Table 2.2   **Temporal proximity and distance travelled**

Group 1	N	Min	Mean	Max
Chronologically adjacent	36	0·63	5·57	13·00
Odd	36	0·51	3·47	8·31
Even	36	0·00	3·22	9·31
Friedman Nonparametric Anova $p < 0·05$ Chi sq=6-16 (df. 2)				

Group 2	N	Min	Mean	Max
Chronologically adjacent	44	8·33	23·66	94·85
Odd	44	0·87	19·84	38·65
Even	44	0·00	22·17	54·62
Friedman Nonparametric Anova $p < 0·66$ Chi sq = 0·82 (df. 2)				

Group 3	N	Min	Mean	Max
Chronologically adjacent	40	11·30	101·02	300·83
Odd	40	24·51	138·98	412·16
Even	40	0·00	138·22	718·37
Friedman Nonparametric Anova $p < 0·001$ Chi sq = 9·56 (df. 2)				

Conclusions

The present study examined the disposal site locations of a sample of serial murderers in order to identify whether more traditional explanations for spatial behaviour could also explain the behaviour of serial murderers. It was found that the home location of serial murderers had a strong centralizing influence on the spatial patterns of disposal locations. This finding supports the hypothesis that the more generic explanations of familiarity, mental mapping and the psychological role of the home can go some way to explain the spatial behaviour of this unique type of offender.

Furthermore, it was found that the locations of previous disposal locations also exerted an influence on the locations of subsequent disposal sites. It appeared that there was more of a conceptual continuum where the distances the offenders typically put between their disposal sites was determined by their perception of a 'safe' distance. The evidence for the influence of such safe distances was greater for those offenders operating over smaller areas. As the distances the offenders typically travelled increased, it appeared that the influence of previous sites decreased. It can be argued that an offender who operates over a small range may be more likely to consider the locations of his previous disposal sites and the risks associated with disposing of further bodies in a similar area. On the other hand, an offender operating over a range covering hundreds of miles may not be influenced by such constraints simply because of the larger distances involved.

The 'safety space' was also found to exist for the distances the offenders typically put between their home and their disposal sites. Conceptually, this suggests that although the home acts as an important focus to the offenders, their patterns of behaviour are equally influenced by the locations of their previous sites. Therefore, the concept of familiarity is far more complex than first suggested by the Brantinghams (1981). Although serial murderers may commit their offences within an environment familiar to them, the specific locations of their disposal sites will also depend on the locations already utilized for criminal activity. The distance they feel comfortable travelling from home may also apply to the distance they feel comfortable putting between their offences. These characteristic distances will be a reflection of the spatial constraints the offender is operating within.

References

Athens, L.H. (1980). *Violent Criminal Acts and Actors*. Cambridge, Mass: Routledge and Kegan Paul.

Brantingham, P.J. and Brantingham, P.L. (1981). *Environmental Criminology. Beverley Hills:* Sage Publications.

Canter, D. and Hodge, S. (2000). Criminals' mental maps. In L.S. Turnball, E. Hallisey-Hendrix and B.D. Dent (eds) *Atlas of Crime*. Oryx Press, pp. 187–191.

Canter, D. and Larkin, P (1993). The environmental range of serial rapists. *Journal of Environmental Psychology*, 13, 63–69.

Canter, D. (1977). *The Psychology of Place*. London: Architectural Press.

Cornish, D.B and Clarke, R.V. (1986). *The Reasoning Criminal: Rational Choice Perspectives on Offending*. New York: Springer-Verlag.

Donald, I. and Canter, D. (1990). Temporal and trait facets of personal Assessment. In L.S. Dancer and S.L. Hans (eds) *Applied Psychology: An International Review*, 39, 413–129.

Downs, R.M. and Stea, D. (1973). *Image and Environment*. Chicago: Aldine Publishing.

Egger, S.A. (1990). *Serial Murder: An Elusive Phenomenon*. New York: Praeger

Guttman, L.A. (1968). A general non-metric technique for finding the smallest coordinate space for a configuration of points. *Psychometrika*, 33, 495–506.

Hickey, E.W. (1991). *Serial Murderers and their Victims*. Pacific Grove, CA: Brooks/ Cole Publishing.

Holmes, R.M. and De Burger, J. (1988). *Serial Murder*. Beverly Hills: Sage.

Holmes, R.M. and Holmes, S.T. (1996). *Murder in America*. Beverly Hills: Sage.

Jenkins, P. (1988). Serial murder in England 1940–1985. *Journal of Criminal Justice*, 16, 1–15.

Keppel, R.D. (1997). *Signature Killers*. New York: Pocket Books.

Leyton, E. (1986). *Hunting Humans: The Rise of the Modern Multiple Murderer*. Toronto: McClelland and Stewart.

Lingoes, J.C. (1973). The multivariate analysis of qualitative data. *Multivariate Behavioural Research*, 3, 61–94.

Lynch, K. (1960) *The Image of the City*. Cambridge, Mass.: MIT Press.

Newton, Jr. M.B. and Swoope, E.A. (1987). *Geo-forensic Analysis of Localised Serial Murder: The Hillside Stranglers Located*. Unpublished manuscript.

Rengert, G.F. and Wasilchick, J. (1985). *Suburban Burglary: A Time and a Place for Everything*. Springfield, ILL: Charles C Thomas.

Revitch, E. and Schlesinger, L.B. (1981). *Psychopathology of Homocide*. Springfield, Charles C. Thomas.

Rhodes, W.M. and Conly, C. (1981). Crime and mobility: An empirical study. In P.J. Brantingham and P.L. Brantingham (eds), *Environmental Criminology*. Beverly Hills: Sage.

Rossmo, D.K. (1997). Geographic profiling. In J.L. Jackson and D.A. Bekerian (eds) *Offender Profiling: Theory, Research and Practice*. Wiley and Sons.

Trowbridge, C. (1913). On fundamental methods of orientation and imaginary maps. *Science*, 38, 990.

Webb, E.J., Campbell, D.T, Schwatz, R.L. and Sechrest, L. (1966). *Unobtrusive Measures: Nonreactiue Research in the Social Sciences*. Chicago: Rand McNally.

Chapter 3

Offender Characteristics and Spatial Mobility: An Empirical Study and Some Policy Implications

Thomas Gabor and Ellen Gottheil

Many criminological studies and prevention programs are predicated on the assumption that offenders are confined to fixed geographic areas when they engage in criminal activity. Correlations in ecological research between urban characteristics and crime rates assume that these rates are produced exclusively by persons residing within the relevant zones.[8,42] Similarly, the location of preventive services in urban communities is often dictated by levels of crime, with the most crime-ridden areas frequently attracting the bulk of these services.[46] Little consideration is given to the possibility that sites attracting the greatest criminal activity may not be inhabited by the highest concentration of offenders.

The spatial nobility patterns of offenders, in all likelihood, are not radically different from those of non-offenders of similar socioeconomic status.[35] The development of satellite communities in most urban areas and their dependence on the automobile, as well as improvements in mass transportation systems, have greatly increased public mobility.

Since a great deal of critic is opportunistic in nature,[30] some offences will be committed in the course of transit. Thus, even where an offender is disposed to committing criminal acts in his own neighbourhood, situations and opportunities may lead to an occasional departure from this tendency. It is therefore imperative that a truly dynamic criminology gauge offender movements in urban areas. The present study sought to do this by using criminal justice data to determine the distances various types of offenders travel to commit their offences. Before we describe this study, the potential of mobility studies and the previous research is discussed.

The Value of Mobility Studies

One obvious by-product of mobility studies is knowledge regarding the source of a community's crime problem. Such studies can indicate the extent to which this problem derives from sources outside of that community and can identify the areas containing the highest concentrations of offenders. These studies can also examine the differential mobility patterns of varying types of offenders.

The finding that a significant proportion of crime is committed by persons residing outside of a community will have clear implications for crime prevention. Primary preventive strategies are of little relevance to areas producing only small numbers of offenders. A logical approach would be an exploration of those factors within the community that serve to attract offenders living elsewhere. A resulting measure may be victim-oriented – reducing criminal opportunities that serve as an attraction. It may also involve redesigning the physical environment through such steps as sealing off an exit from an adjacent freeway to reduce the accessibility of the community to outsiders in transit and transients. Or, it might involve stepping up police activity in the community, as well as increasing co-operation with police departments operating in areas that spawn many of these offenders. A great deal of interjurisdictional crime in an area may warrant the consolidation of local law enforcement agencies into a regional police force.[31]

The political-legal implications of crime spillovers from one jurisdiction to another may be profound. Non-reciprocal spillovers from one jurisdiction to another may produce antagonistic relations between the two areas, possibly exacerbating inter-racial or inter-class tensions. The recipient community may retaliate by curtailing the movement of desired goods to the source of these spillovers or reciprocating with a negative externality of their own. This problem is often encountered in international relations when one nation produces consumer goods (e.g., television programs) that may be "consumed" free of charge by a neighbouring country. This free consumption may have an adverse effect on the country of origin's economy. This can be rectified through the pursuit of an optimal exchange of goods whereby there is an essentially equal benefit on both sides in the sum total of exchanges.[16] To promote inter-regional harmony, a serious imbalance in crime spillovers between two areas may necessitate that the community of origin provide some compensation to its neighbour, if such spillovers are serious and/or frequent enough to produce a sub-optimal situation.

By identifying those areas most prone to attract (import) and those most prone to expel (export) crime, we can also determine the factors associated with offender movements. The identification of these "push" and "pull" factors can illuminate offender motivation and, consequently, aid in theory development. Specifically, the relative appropriateness of situational versus more traditional etiological approaches can be weighed. Evidence that offenders are travelling from socioeconomically diverse neighbourhoods to a limited number of crime-ridden areas may indicate the prominence of factors providing temptations to offenders ("pull factors") over etiological factors operating in the home areas of offenders. On the other hand, the apparently arbitrary selection of crime targets in an area – i.e., no pattern can be discerned in target selection – may indicate less selectivity and a greater impulsivity (expressiveness) of offenders. A knowledge of offender motivation, in turn, can enlighten us as to whether the most appropriate preventive policies are those based on deterrence or those focusing on individual or social deficits.

One particular theoretical perspective that can be examined through mobility studies is social reaction theory. It might be assumed that the extent of the adverse social reaction to a person's criminal record, such as police harassment or the reticence of prospective employers to hire him, is inversely related to the distance of his current residence from the site(s) of his former misconduct. If the offender is particularly notorious, the location of his residence is probably irrelevant, as police departments nationwide will be alerted about his movements. Also, the community where such an offender resides may become informed of his presence there. However, a less serious offender may be able to keep a lower profile. If the history of this second type of offender reveals offences in different neighbourhoods or, more importantly still, different regions, the attribution of these offences to increased police vigilance or social stigma becomes less tenable.

Finally, observations of the differential spatial mobility of offenders can aid in the development of criminal typologies. Variables such as age, sex and experience in crime might distinguish the personality of offenders if the level of mobility reflects offender motivation. It might be reasonable to suggest that high mobility reflects selectivity and rationality and low mobility reflects greater impulsivity, all else being equal. The present study is concerned with this last dimension, relating offender characteristics with their levels of mobility.

The Literature on Offender Mobility

Studies of offender mobility have almost exclusively been conducted in the United States. Given cross-national differences in transportation systems, in the geographic configuration of cities, in the extent of urbanization, and in the nature of crime itself, one must be circumspect in assessing findings conducted primarily in one country. These studies have utilized two principal methodologies. The first involves measuring the distance from the residence of arrested offenders to the site of the offence. The means of measurement range from simple estimation procedures[51] to more sophisticated cartographic techniques.[38,41] The second method uses interviews with offenders to obtain information regarding their movements[11,39] or with victims to get their impressions of where the offenders reside.[50]

Certain generalizations can be drawn from the literature on mobility. The majority of offenders tend to operate within their own neighbourhoods, although there is a small proportion willing to travel long distances to commit crimes. Distances travelled for property offences tend to exceed those for personal violent offences. There is contradictory evidence about the direction of offender movements. While some studies indicate that the predominant travel patterns involve movements of offenders from poor to more affluent areas to commit their offences, the opposite has been found in an approximately equal number of studies.

One fact is clear. All cities have areas that contain a disproportionate amount of crime due to the opportunities they present. Offenders travel to these areas from throughout a city, although some areas may contribute more than others. Not only do many offenders exhibit selectivity in the general area they choose for their criminal activities, but they are often very precise in their selection of a specific target – be this a person, residence or organization. Such selections are often based on perceptions of target vulnerability and of risk to the offender.

Finally, the variables of age, experience in crime and race have been shown to be relevant to mobility in a limited number of studies. The young, inexperienced and those belonging to visible minority groups have tended to be least mobile.

More specifically, with respect to distances travelled to commit offences, Boggs, almost twenty years ago, made the observation that areas where offences are committed often differ from those where offenders live.[5] She found a low association between the areas in St. Louis where commercial robbery and burglary, rape and grand larceny tend to occur and the residences of those offenders; whereas, she found that offence and offender areas did tend to coincide for the crimes of homicide, assault and residential burglary.

In support of the general pattern of greater mobility for property as opposed to purely violent crimes, Pyle, in Cleveland, found that 61% of all those arrested for crimes against the person over a two-year period resided in the same census tract as where the crime occurred, while this was the case in only 48% of the property crimes.[38] White, in Indianapolis, found that the mean distances to the offender's residence for homicide, assault and rape were .11, .91 and 1.52 miles, respectively; whereas for auto theft, embezzlement, robbery, burglary, grand and petty larceny, these distances were 3.43, 2.79, 2.14, 1.76, 1.53 and 1.42 miles, respectively.[51] Rhodes and Conly, in Washington, D.C., found the mean distance travelled for rape, burglary and robbery to be 1.15, 1.62 and 2.10 miles, respectively.[41]

Bullock, in a Houston study of homicide, found that 57% occurred within .4 miles of the perpetrator's residence.[9] Wolfgang found that over one-half of Philadelphia homicides occurred in the home of the offender or victim.[52] Since the offender and victim often cohabited, were related or at least acquaintances, it can be inferred that the offence very frequently occurred close to the offender's residence. Amir, in a Philadephia study of rape, found that 72% occurred within five city blocks of the offender's home. Turner's Philadelphia study of assault and vandalism committed by juveniles found the mean distance from the perpetrator's residence to be .4 miles.[47]

Research involving profit-oriented crimes, such as robbery, suggests greater offender mobility, as well as greater variation between studies. Reppetto, in Boston, found the mean distance travelled by robbers to be .6 miles.[39] Normandeau, in Philadelphia, found this distance to be 1.57 miles.[34] Capone and Nichols, in Miami, distinguished between armed and unarmed robbery in their study. They found that 77% of the armed cases and 64% of the unarmed cases occurred beyond one mile of the offender's residence.[47]

Residential burglary may be one of the few exceptions to the idea that offender mobility for violent offences exceeds that for property crimes. Reppetto found, in his interviews with adjudicated burglars, that the mean distance travelled was .5 miles.[39] Waller and Okihiro, in their survey of burglary victims in Toronto, found that one-half of the respondents who had confrontations with offenders thought that the principal offender lived within one-half mile of the victim's residence. Indeed, in over half the cases, the victim had some prior knowledge of the offender.[50]

Addressing the direction of criminal movements in a city, Fletcher, over a century ago, suggested that higher socioeconomic areas tend to be the collecting grounds for offenders and lower income areas the breeding grounds.[21] Carter and Hill contend that, with the exception of white collar crime, this statement still remains unchallenged.[11] The Chicago School of Sociology, however, showed that the crime rates of urban zones were inversely related to their distance from a city's central core and that many of the poorest areas were located near a city's center.[44] Thus, poor areas were receptacles for crime, as well as breeding grounds. Recent studies by Pyle in Akron and Cleveland, Ohio support this notion.[38] In an analysis of offender movements between census tracts, he found that the "import" areas for both personal and property crimes tended to be lower income areas and that "export" areas also often tended to be low income. Thus, a circulation of offenders among primarily lower class tracts was observed.

There is a great deal of evidence from ecological research supporting a negative association between income and crime – i.e., low income areas are likely to have higher crime rates than high income areas.[4,5,6,13,25,27,39,43,45,51] Most of those studies do not tell us the extent to which crime rates in a given area are attributable to mobile as opposed to local offenders.[24] What ecological studies (some using city blocks and even houses as units of analysis) do show is that target selection is far from random, indicating that many offenders are quite selective, if not highly mobile. Offenders tend to be sensitive to such features of the socio-physical environment of a potential target as its accessibility to major thoroughfares,[7,20,27] surveillance levels,[26,30,32,33] street lighting,[29,48] specific location, design and occupancy levels,[15,17,18,29,32,33,39] and the perceived risk of capture on the part of the offenders.[11,14,39]

Spatial crime displacements, of offender attempts to circumvent impediments to potential targets by relocating their activity, also reflect selectivity and mobility.[22,40] Evidence of these displacements has been provided by a number of authors.[12,23,28, 37,48,49]

The relationship between mobility and offender characteristics has barely been explored. The scant evidence that does exist indicates that age, race or ethnicity and criminal experience may affect levels of mobility. The young are said to not only be less mobile,[3,36,39,41] but to engage in less preparation for their offences than older, more seasoned offenders.[36] In an Oklahoma study, Carter and Hill found that black offenders were less diversified in their mobility patterns than were whites, preferring to operate in familiar surroundings more so than the latter.[11] Reppetto found that both races were reluctant to operate in neighbourhoods populated by the other.[39]

The Study

The present Ottawa study had several objectives. First, we wished to determine the proportion of offences in the area committed by persons residing elsewhere and typical distances travelled by Ottawa offenders for the respective offences examined. Next, we were interested in the extent of transiency in the offender population – i.e., those offenders without a fixed residence. Finally, we wished to determine the impact on mobility of a number of primarily personal attributes.

The data for this study was obtained from the files of the Ottawa Police Department. We set out to select a sample containing 20 persons arrested in 1981 for each of the following offences: homicide, rape and indecent assault, other assaults, armed robbery, unarmed robbery, break and enter, motor vehicle theft, theft over $200, theft under $200 and cheque fraud. Due to the dearth of homicides in Ottawa, we found only seven cases of persons arrested for homicide or attempted homicide. For all the other offence classifications, we selected the 20 cases in such a way as to obtain as close to an equal distribution throughout the year as possible, as the exploration of seasonal variations in mobility was one aspect of the study. Thus, if 200 persons were arrested for a given offence during the year, we selected every tenth arrestee rather than merely the first 20 arrestees for the year.

The city of Ottawa (pop. 300,000) is located within a metropolitan area of one-half million people. On the opposite side of the Ottawa River and within easy commuting distance is the city of Hull and a number of other Quebec communities. Bordering directly on Ottawa are several sizeable suburban communities.

The definition and measurement of our dependent variable, offender mobility, involved two dimensions. First, we distinguished between offenders residing in Ottawa or communities bordering directly on it (the in-towners), those residing outside this area (the out-of-towners), those with no fixed address and those for whom no information existed in the police files.

Secondly, we measured the distances between the location of an offence and the suspect's residence for all offences committed by in-towners. Specifically, through the use of a map, we measured the aerial distance between the two relevant points. We recognize that this is a minimum distance travelled by the offender, as he must confine himself to available vehicular or pedestrian routes. More sophisticated estimation procedures are available.[38,41] However, without conferring with the offender, we have no real way of knowing the distance he actually travelled because the route he selects to arrive at the crime site is unknown. He may also visit friends or tend to other matters en route. Thus, he may have several preliminary destinations before arriving at the crime site. Despite those unknowns, a knowledge of an offender's radius of activity is important. Given those unknowns, the use of aerial distances in measurement may be more appropriate than sophisticated methods because it is a systematically biased estimator of distance travelled – i.e., we know it underestimates this distance.

Our explantory or independent variables were as follows:

Age – This variable was dichotomized into the categories of "under 25 years" and "25 years and over" for some of the analyses.

Sex – The natural dichotomy of male and female was used here.

Season – Seasonal differences in mobility attributable to climate were gauged by bisecting the year according to temperature. Offences committed from May through October were classified as summer offences and those occurring before May and after October of 1981 were classified as winter offences.

Accomplices – It is unclear whether having accomplices reflects greater planning and experience in crime or simply youthfullness. It was felt that, for this reason, this factor should be examined for its possible impact on mobility. The variable was dichotomized into "yes" and "no" categories.

Prior Record – This variable reflects criminal experience and was dichotomized into "yes" and "no" categories. The existence of a prior record was ascertained through checking the Canadian Police Information Centre (CPIC) reports for any previous arrest.

Marital Status – This variable was dichotomized into the categories of "single" and "married". Separated or divorced persons were considered as single. There were sonic problems with missing information for this variable.

Results

Table 3.1 illustrates the status of the different types of Ottawa offenders on the independent and dependent variables.

The average age for all offenders in the sample was 25.1 years.[1] The mean ages vary from those arrested for break and enter (less than 20 years) to those arrested for homicide or attempted homocide, rape or indecent assault and cheque fraud (all averaging over 30 years).

Males accounted for over 90% of the sample. Homicide, sex offence, unarmed robbery, motor vehicle theft and break and enter were exclusively male offences. Only in cheque fraud was there a noticeable female participation (25%).

Slightly over one-half of the offences occurred in what we have called the summer season. These ranged from armed robbery and break and enter, where just less than one-half occurred in the summer, to sex offences, where almost three-fourths occurred during the summer.

Accomplices were involved in one-third of all the offences. The presence of accomplices was rare for the more expressive crimes of assault or those of a sexual nature. This was also true for cheque fraud. Accomplices were by far most likely to be found in cases of armed robbery.

Table 3.1   The characteristics and spatial mobility of diverse types of Ottawa offenders

Offences	Average Age	% Male	Summer Season	% with Accom- plices	% with Prior Record	% Unmarried	% Out-of- Towners	% In- Towners	% No fixed Address	Mean distance travelled by in- towners (in miles)
Homicide	31.2	100	57	57	71	71	0	71	14	.54
Sex Offences	30.9	100	70	20	35	78	10	90	0	1.43
Assault	28.6	90	60	10	45	67	5	90	5	1.33
Robbery Armed	21.5	95	45	85	70	83	5	80	15	1.22
Robbery Unarmed	22.4	100	60	30	80	95	15	55	25	.62
Auto Theft	23.1	100	60	40	70	100	10	70	20	1.24
Theft under $200	23.1	90	50	25	50	100	15	60	5	1.19
Theft over $200	24.0	85	50	25	50	79	5	90	5	1.74
Break and Enter	19.1	100	45	35	65	100	20	65	5	.35
Cheque Fraud	30.8	75	50	15	90	64	25	35	25	1.74
Total	25.1	93	54.5	33	62	81.8	11.8	70.5	11.8	1.22

Over one-half of the offenders had at least one previous arrest. Sex offenders and assaulters were least likely to have a criminal record, while those arrested for homicide, cheque fraud, robbery and auto theft were most likely to have such a record.

More than four-fifths of the entire sample were not married at the time of arrest, where this information was available. Those least likely to be married were those engaging in the crimes of profit of robbery, break and enter, auto theft and theft tinder $200. Most likely to be married were cheque fraud, assault and homicide offenders.

The mobility patterns varied greatly across the different types of offences. Almost three-fourths of all offenders could be classified as in-towners, with over 10% being out-of-towners, a similar proportion having no fixed address and the remainder being unknown. Most likely to be in-towners were those arrested for sex offences, assault, theft over $200 and armed robbery. Most likely to be out-of-towners were those committing cheque fraud, break and enter, unarmed robbery and theft under $200. Most likely to be transient were those committing unarmed robbery and cheque fraud.

The average distance between the offender's residence and the crime site for all in-towners was 1.22 miles. The least mobile were homicide, unarmed robbery and

Table 3.2   Factors associated with offender mobility and transiency

		In-Towners	Out-of-Towners	No Fixed Address	χ^2	P<
Age	under 25 years	85	12	12	1.31	.70
	25 years and over	47	10	10		
Sex	male	124	19	20	1.67	.50
	female	8	3	2		
Season	summer	75	13	10	1.07	.70
	winter	57	9	12		
Accomplices	Yes	44	7	9	.52	.80
	No	88	15	13		
Prior Record	Yes	77	13	19	6.44	.05
	No	55	9	3		
Marital Status	single	98	14	18	.36	.90
	married	16	2	2		

Table 3.3   Factors associated with distances travelled by in-town offenders

		Number of cases	Total Miles	Average Mileage
Age	under 25 years	85	77.48	.91
	25 years and over	47	81.58	1.73
Sex	male	124	152.7	11.23
	female	8	9.16	1.14
Season	summer	75	83.52	1.11
	winter	57	75.54	1.32
Accomplices	Yes	44	74.42	1.69
	No	88	84.64	.96
Prior Record	Yes	77	89.74	1.19
	No	55	69.32	1.26
Marital Status	single	98	100.44	1.02
	married	16	29.28	1.83

break and enter offenders. The most highly mobile were those committing thefts over $200, cheque fraud and sex offences.

Table 3.2 illustrates the relationship between our selected independent variables and offender mobility for the sample as a whole. Chi-square tests of independence were performed to determine whether a statistically significant relationship existed between any of the independent variables and mobility. The only variable related to mobility (according to a criterion significance level of .05) is that of prior record. The proportion of persons with a criminal record who are in-towners and out-of-towners is not unexpected. What is instrumental in producing the significant relationship is the proportion of persons with a prior record who have no fixed address. Although only slightly over one-half of the entire sample has a prior record, close to nine-tenths of persons without a fixed address have a criminal record. Looking at this another way, a felon with a prior record is almost five times as likely to be a transient than one with no record, taking into consideration the proportion of persons in the sample with a record.

Table 3.3 illustrates the relationships between our independent variables and distances travelled by in-towners to commit their offences. It is evident that these variables possess far greater power in explaining differences in the mobility of in-towners than in distinguishing between in-towners, out-of-towners and transients. Older and married offenders, as well as those with an accomplice, tended to travel almost twice as far to commit their offences as did offenders who were young, unmarried and operating on their own. Also, males were slightly more mobile than females, first-time offenders slightly more mobile than recidivists and those operating in the winter season were slightly more mobile than those operating in the summer.

Summary and Conclusions

On the whole, this study found a substantial amount of mobility for Ottawa offenders. Close to one quarter of the sample were classified as out-of-towners or transients. For those with fixed residences in Ottawa, the average distance travelled to the crime site, for all offences combined, was over one mile.

The variables that we found to be most potent in determining whether an offence was committed by an in-towner, out-of-towner or transient were the type of offence and prior record. Violent offenders were somewhat more likely to reside in Ottawa, whereas profit-oriented offenders were more likely to be transient or to live outside the city. Those having a criminal record were substantially more likely to be transient than were those not possessing such a record. Our other independent variables – age, sex, season, accomplices and marital status – did not aid in explaining why some offenders are in-towners and others are out-of-towners or transients.

A different combination of variables was found to determine the distances travelled by in-towners to commit their offences. The nature of the offence was once again important, with the distances ranging from a mean of .35 miles for break and enter to 1.74 miles for both theft over $200 and cheque fraud. Contrary to the literature, which indicates that personal, violent offences tend to be committed closer to home than are property crimes, our study found little support for this pattern, as distances travelled for both sex offences and assault were substantial relative to most offences and the distances travelled for unarmed robbery, in particular, tended to be short. However, in keeping with a previous study, 10 the mean distance travelled for armed robbery greatly exceeded that for unarmed robbery (it was about double), indicating that the former involves greater preparation and resources. It is interesting to note that armed robbers tended to be younger and to have a criminal record less often than their unarmed counterparts.

Other variables strongly associated with the mobility of in-town offenders were age, marital status and the presence of accomplices. Older offenders, as suggested by the literature, were likely to travel much farther than the young. Those who were married and had accomplices were more mobile than the unmarried and those without accomplices, respectively. It could be that some of these relationships are spurious. Older offenders are more likely to be married and, perhaps, to have accomplices or at least to commit those types of offences that require accomplices or greater distance travelled. Multivariate analyses should be conducted in the future to determine the effects on mobility of each of these variables when the other variables are controlled.

Methodological problems abound in any study dependent upon data obtained from the criminal justice system. The charges against an offender may not reflect his actual behavior but, rather, that for which a prosecutor feels he has sufficient evidence or which may induce a defendant to enter a guilty plea. The address contained in an offender's file may not have been his residence at the time the offence was committed. Also, it is possible that those offenders who are apprehended and studied do not represent the mobility patterns of those less likely to be caught. If offenders who are less mobile and, hence, operate on more familiar terrain are less likely to be detected or if, conversely, the highly mobile tend to be better prepared and have more resources and experience allowing them to elude detection better than most offenders, then arrested offenders will provide a skewed sample of the offender population. Previous research provides few clues as to this potential source of sampling bias. Finally, our use of aerial measurements of distances travelled by in-towners may have seriously underestimated the mobility of these offenders.

Notwithstanding these and other potential methodological problems, several policy implications derive from this preliminary Canadian study. Preventive strategies must occasionally be offence-specific, as the dynamics of and motivation underlying different offences may vary considerably. Where the distances travelled for an offence are great, as was the case in cheque fraud where only a small proportion of offences were committed near the offender's residence, preventive efforts in an area riddled by this offence must be victim, rather than offender oriented.

The significant proportion of transients in our sample reinforces the importance of suitable housing and community-based support for offenders. The percentage of transients with a prior record and the abundance of transient residents who commit robbery, cheque fraud and auto theft also points to the classic antisocial pattern of career acquisitive offenders.[19]

Finally, the movement of significant numbers of offenders across political boundaries suggests the need for close cooperation among municipalities and law enforcement agencies. Such movements, in the Ottawa area, were far in excess of that reflected by the number of persons in our sample we have designated as out-of-town offenders. Our distinction between in-towners and out-of-towners was based on geographic criteria. There is one federal, one provincial and five municipal police departments operating in the area in which our in-towners were active. When seven departments have jurisdiction in a medium-sized metropolitan area, the problems posed by crime spillover for law enforcement can well be appreciated.

References

1. Since our sample was drawn in such a way as to contain an equal number of cases of different types of offenders rather than to reflect the distribution of

offences in Ottawa, analyses of the sample as a whole are meant only to reflect this sample and not all Ottawa offenders.

2. Amir M. Patterns (1971). *Forcible Rape.* Chicago: University of Chicago Press.
3. Baldwin. J. and Bottoms, A.E. (1976). *The Urban Criminal: A Study in Sheffield.* London: Tavistock.
4. Beasley, R.W. and Antunues, G.E. (1974). The etiology of urban crime. *Criminology*, 11, 1974.
5. Boggs, S. (1965). Urban crime patterns. *American Sociological Review*, 30.
6. Bordua, D.J. (1958). Juvenile delinquency and anomie: An attempt at replication. *Social Problems*, 6.
7. Brantingham, P.J. and Brantingham, P.L. (1975). The spatial patterning of burglary. *Howard Journal of Penology and Crime Prevention*, 14.
8. Brantingham, P.J. and Brantingham, P.L. (eds) (1981). *Environmental Criminology.* Beverly Hills: Sage.
9. Bullock, H.A. (1955). "Urban Homicide in Theory and Fact", *Journal of Criminal Law, Criminology and Police Science*, 45.
10. Capone, D.L. and Nichols, W.W. (1975). Crime and distance: An analysis of offender behavior in space. *Proceedings, Association of American Geographers*, 7.
11. Carter, R.L. and Hill, K.Q. (1975). *The Criminal's Image of the City.* New York: Pergamon.
12. Chaiken, J.M., Lawless, M.W. and Stevenson, K.A. (1974). *The Impact of Policy Activity on Crime: Robberies on the New York City Subway System.* New York: Rand Institute.
13. Chilton, R. (1964). Continuity in delinquency area research: A comparison of studies for Baltimore, Detroit and Indianapolis. *American Sociological Review*, 29.
14. Ciale, J. and Leroux, J.-P. (1983). *Armed Robbery in Ottawa: A Descriptive Cases Study for Prevention.* Ottawa: Department of Criminology, University of Ottawa.
15. Clarke, R.V.G. and Mayhew, P. (eds) (1980). *Designing Out Crime.* London: Her Majesty's Stationery Office.
16. Connolly, M. (1970). Public goods externalities and international relations. *Journal of Political Economy*, 78.
17. Crow. W. and Bull, J. (1975). *Robbery Deterrence: An Applied Behavioral Science Demonstration.* La Jolla, Cal.: Western Behavioral Science Institute.
18. David, P. and Scott, J. (1973). A cross culture comparison of juvenile offenders, offenses, due process and societies. *Criminology*, 10.
19. Dinitz, S. and Gabor, T. (1980). *Sexual. Aggressive and Acquisitive Offenders in Profile: A Univariate and Multivariare Analysis.* Chicago: Institute of Social and Behavioral Pathology, Department of Psychiatry, University of Chicago.

20. Duffala, D.C. (1976). Convenience stores. Armed robbery and physical environmental features. *American Behavioral Scientists*, 20.

21. Fletcher, J. (1849). Moral statistics of England and Wales. *Journal of the Royal Statistical Society of London*, 12.

22. Gabor, T. (1978). Crime displacement: The literature and strategies for its investigation. *Crime and/et Justice*, 6.

23. Gabor, T. (1981). The crime displacement hypothesis: An empirical examination". *Crime and Delinquency*, 27.

24. Labor, T. and McFarlane, J. (1982). The relationship between urban crowding and crime: A Canadian study. Ottawa: Department of Criminology, University of Ottawa.

25. Hamparian, D., Schuster, R., Dinitz, S. and Conrad, J. (1978). *The Violent Few*. Lexington, Mass.: D.C. Heath.

26. Jeffery, C.R. (1977). *Crime Prevention Through Environmental Design*. Beverly Hills: Sage.

27. Lander, B. (1954). *Towards an Understanding of Juvenile Delinquency: A Study of 8,464 Cases of Juvenile Delinquency in Baltimore*. New York: Columbia University Press.

28. Lateef, B.A. (1974). Helicopter patrol in law enforcement – an evaluation. *Journal of Police Science and Administration*, 2.

29. Luedtke, G. and Associates (1970). *Crime and the Physical City: Neighbourhood Design Technique for Crime Prevention*. Washington, D.C.: National Institute of Law, Enforcement and Criminal Justice.

30. Mayhew, P., Clarke, R.V.G., Sturman, A. and Hough, J.M. (1976). *Crime As Opportunity*. London: Her Majesty's Stationery Office.

31. McIver. J.P. (1980). External effects and the organization of policing in metropolitan areas. Paper presented at the annual meeting of the American Society of Criminology in San Francisco, California, November.

32. Molumby, T. (1976). Patterns of crime in a university housing project. *American Behavioral Scientist*, 20.

33. Newman, O. (1973). *Defensible Space*. New York: Collier.

34. Normandeau, A. (1968). *Trends and Patterns in the Crime of Robbery*. Ph.D. dissertation. Philadelphia, PA: University of Pennsylvania.

35. Orleans, P. (1973). Differential cognition of urban residents: Effects of social scales on mapping. In R. Downs and D. Stea (eds). *Image and Environment*. Chicago: Aldine.

36. Petersilia, J., Greenwood, P. and Lavin, M. (1977). *Criminal Careers of Habitual Felons*. Santa Monica. Cal.: Rand Corporation.

37. Press, S.J. (1971). *Some Effects of An Increase In Police Manpower In the 20th Precinct of New York City*. New York: Rand Institute.

38. Pyle, G.F. (1976). Spatial and temporal aspects of crime in Cleveland, Ohio. *American Behavioral Scientist*, 20.

39. Reppetto, T.A. (1974). *Residential Crime*. Cambridge, Mass.: Ballinger.

40. Reppetto, T.A. (1976). Crime prevention and the displacement phenomenon. *Crime and Delinquency*, 22.

41. Rhodes, W.M. and Conly, C. (1871). Crime and mobility: An empirical study. In P.J. and P.L. Brantingham (eds). *Environmental Criminology*. Beverly Hills: Sage.

42. Ronceck, D. (1975). Density and crime: A methodological critique. *American Behavioral Scientist*, 18.

43. Schmid, C. (1960). Urban crime areas. *American Sociological Review*, 25.

44. Shaw, C.R. and McKay, H.D. (1942). *Juvenile Delinquency and Urban Areas*. Chicago: University of Chicago Press.

45. Singh, A., Celinski, H. and Jayewardene, C.H.S. (1980). Ecological correlates of crime in Ottawa. *Canadian Journal of Criminology*, 22.

46. Touchette, L. (1983). *La délinquance juvénile et sa prévention à Ottawa-Vanier*. Master's thesis. Ottawa: University of Ottawa.

47. Turner, S. (1969). Delinquency and distance. In T. Sellin and M. Wolgang (eds). *Delinquency: Selected Studies*. New York: John Wiley and Sons.

48. Tyrpak, S. (1975). *Newark High-impact Anti-crime Program: Street Lighting Projects Interim Evaluation Report*. Newark, N.J.: Office of Criminal Justice Planning.

49. Waldt, L.G. (1975). *Residential Burglary Prevention Program – Final Report*. Seattle, Wash.: King County Department of Public Safety.

50. Waller, I. and Okihiro, N. (1978). *Burglary: The Victim and the Public*. Toronto: University of Toronto Press.

51. White, R.C. (1932). The relation of felonies to environmental factors in Indianapolis. *Social Forces*, 10.

52. Wolfgang, M.E. (1958). *Patterns of Criminal Homicide*. Philadelphia: University of Pennsylvania Press.

Chapter 4

The Environmental Range of Serial Rapists

David Canter and Paul Larkin

Introduction

Many studies have shown that offenders usually do not travel very far from home to commit crimes (White 1932; Pyle 1974; Repetto 1974; Curtis 1974; Kind 1987). Shaw and McKay illustrated this general trend as long ago as 1942 in their Chicago studies. They established that there is a limited area of zones in which offenders will offend and that these zones were geographically close to the zones in which the offenders lived. However, the majority of the research undertaken to date has involved case studies of, for example, classic crime series like the 'Yorkshire ripper' (Kind 1987). Alternatively they have considered the aggregate pattern of the spatial activity of a sample of criminals (e.g. Pyle 1974). Results from such work has provided useful case and population characteristics. In contrast to previous studies of offender movement that have emphasized the aggregate geographical behaviour of offenders, the present study explores directly the psychological question of the extent to which a general model can be developed that is applicable to any individual offender's spatial activity.

Developing a model of the sequential spatial behaviour of offenders requires tests of the validity of various conceptualisations of the psychological processes which determine where an offender chooses to commit a crime. A robust model would also be of practical value to criminal investigators because it could indicate the likely area of the offender's residence.

The starting point for any theory of an offender's selection of the venue of his[1] crime is the hypothesis that the choice of crime venues relates to some kind of home or base from which the individual operates. This hypothesis is based on the view that the offenders for whom an environmental psychology model is developed will not be random drifters of no fixed abode, but will be residing at one or more locations from which they travel to commit their crimes.

Although the environmental cognition literature is not explicit on the point, there is an implicit assumption throughout such studies that a significant determinant of

---

1   All the offenders presently being studied are male. The male personal pronoun is therefore intended only to refer to male persons throughout this chapter.

representations of places a person develops is the location of a person's e.g. reviewed by Golledge 1987). The proposition is therefore that the 'domocc..ric' locational experiences of law-abiding citizens are a reasonable starting point for building models of criminals movements. The potential validity of such a proposition is supported by Amir's (1971) finding that even individuals who commit the impetuous crime of rape do operate from a fixed point. Amir's account of Philadelphia police file data (1958–1960) draws attention to the value of understanding more about the psychological processes underlying a criminal's spatial behaviour, raising questions about the significance of the 'fixed point' to the offender and the ways in which it might determine the location of his offences.

In contrast to the 'fixed point' having any personal significance to the offender, Shaw and McKay (1942) of the 'Chicago School' proposed that offenders who operate within city centres are reacting to processes beyond their personal experience. They state that behaviour can be explained in terms of the structure of the urban environment. For Shaw and McKay, it is the organizational geometry of cities that gives a pattern to criminal activity. They would thus suggest an arbitrary relationship between the location of offences and between offences and residence other than that the offences are enclosed by a socially recognized 'city centre'.

A somewhat different geographical emphasis is given by Rengert and Wasilchick (1985). They emphasize the importance of the journeys a criminal habitually takes around his home ground. They conducted detailed interviews with 31 burglars, and found a strong likelihood of crime being located on and around the pathways and routes that the burglar habitually used in non-criminal activities. Such journeys through familiar territory are thought to provide information around which an offender could plan his next crime, and that it is this process of information gathering that gives shape to the area in which a person chooses to commit his crimes. They go further to suggest a simple model for offenders' behaviour. The offender in this model is more likely to attack on 'his way home'. Thus the offender will operate within an area which is defined by his home and a base which he frequents; for example, his work, local bar or restaurant.

Brantingham and Brantingham (1981) have proposed more affectively based processes for crimes taking place in the area around a criminal's home. They suggest that the security offered by familiarity with the area would outweigh risks of being recognized in the commission of an offence. However, the avoidance of being recognized near a crime scene would lead to the existence of a minimum distance around the home in which the offender would tend not to offend. Brantingham and Brantingham (1981) do provide some aggregate evidence for such a 'safety zone'. Their arguments therefore lend support to the hypothesis that offenders will tend to offend not only within an area around their home but that there will be a maximum and minimum range of distances from home in which they offend.

Two Models: Commuter or Marauder

In general, then, it seems to be reasonable to assume the existence of a fixed base for men who carry out a number of rapes as for other offenders who commit a series of crimes. There is also some evidence that there will be an area in which the offences are committed that has some non-arbitrary relationship to that base, what might be termed a *criminal range*. The present study tests various models of the relationships there might be between an individual's criminal range and the location of their home base.

Two general models may be proposed to characterize the relationship between base and area of crime, as represented in Figure 4.1. The simplest assumption to make about the geometry of a criminal domain is that it is circular as this only requires the determination of a radius, no other boundary limitations are necessary. In Figure 4.1, therefore, the area around the home (home range) and the area in which the crimes are committed (criminal range) are represented as circles.

The first model is based on what we have called the *commuter hypothesis*. In this case the offender travels from his base into an area to carry out his crimes. This may be determined by the general geometry of the city, as would be consistent with Shaw and McKay's (1942) proposal of the use of the city centre, or it may be an area determined by regular routes that the offender takes as Rengert and Wasilchick (1985) suggest. However, whatever the particular determinants of the specific area of crime, central to this hypothesis that although there will be a domain in which the crimes are committed and this domain will have some distinct relationship to where the offender lives, there will be no clear relationship between size or location of the criminal domain and the distance it is from any given offender's home.

The commuter hypothesis, then, proposes that there is little or no overlap between these two areas and that the offender moves to a district which is outside his home range to offend. This is not to suggest that the criminal range is unfamiliar to the offender, but that it is at an appreciable distance from the area in which he habitually operates as a non-offender.

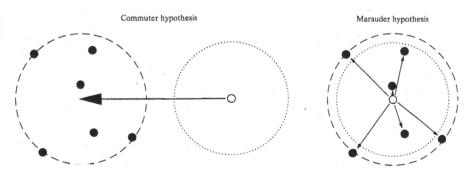

Commuter hypothesis   Marauder hypothesis

Figure 4.1   **Hypothetical models of serial rapists' spatial behaviour; ⊙Criminal range; ●, offences; ⊙, home range; ○, home/base**

A second model may be developed on what we call the *marauder hypothesis*. In this case the base acts as a focus for each particular crime. The offender is assumed to move out from this base to commit his crimes and then return. This relates most directly to the research of Brantingham and Brantingham (1981) who see the home as a focus for the crime locations. This hypothesis implies a much closer relationship between the location of crimes and of a criminal's home, such that the further the distance between crimes the further, on average, the offender must be travelling from home.

In other words, the marauder hypothesis proposes that there is a large or total overlap of the home range and criminal range areas. The offender operates from a home/base definitely located within the boundaries of his safe area for criminal activity.

If either of these hypotheses is strongly supported it has implications for further elaboration of the related model. For simplicity of presentation the development of these implications will be left until after the first test of the two hypotheses.

Sample and Procedure

Although the general arguments above are applicable to any offences, the present study focuses on sexual assaults. These types of crime are a particularly strong test of the essentially rational models that have been outlined. Sexual assault overtly has a profound emotional component to it and may be regarded by many as containing some strongly impulsive aspects (Amir 1971). However, when a rapist does commit a series of assaults on women, with whom he has had no previous contact, some pattern is possible in these offences of which the offender may or may not be aware, just as for burglary or drug abuse. Sexual assaults may therefore be seen as an extreme case that tests the fundamental assumptions that an individual criminal's crime venue has some distinct relationship to his place of residence.

To carry out the study, details of 45 sexual assaulters were made available by British police forces. These included criminals who had been convicted of crimes legally regarded as 'rape', in which vaginal penetration had taken place, as well as other forms of sexual violence. All offenders had been convicted of two or more offences on women they had not known prior to the offence. A total of 251 offences had been committed by these 45 offenders. The mean rape series consisted of 5.6 offences (S.D. = 3.6) with a minimum of 2 and a maximum of 14 offences. The offenders had a mean age of 26.6 years (S.D. = 8.7) ranging from 15 to 59 years. Twenty-one offenders were broadly classified by the police as 'white' in ethnicity and the other 24 as 'black'. All the offenders operated within the Greater London area and/or the South East of England during the 1980s.

Test of Hypotheses

The basic information available to test the hypotheses above is the geographical distribution of the offences in relation to the location of the offender's residence at the time of the offences. For each offender, a separate map was produced indicating the locations of offences and his residence. A further summary of this without the underlying base map was produced, as illustrated in Figure 4.2.

The most direct test of the two hypotheses is whether the region covered by the crimes encompasses the location of the residence. In the commuter hypotheses this would not be common, whereas it would be typical of the 'marauder'. A simple test of these possibilities is to examine the area covered by the offences and see whether the residence is within that area.

In order to define the area of the offences, the two offences furthest from each other were identified and the distance between them taken as the diameter of a circle that was drawn. Such a circle is likely to encompass all the offences, except for rather unusual spatial distributions. There are therefore more precise geometrical aspects that can be derived from the marauder model, circle hypotheses. These hypotheses have two aspects:

(a) the offence of a single offender will be encompassed within a circle that is drawn with its diameter as the two offences that are furthest from each other;
(b) the residence of the offender at the time of the offences will be within the same circle.

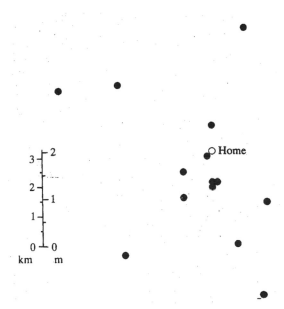

Figure 4.2 **Example rape series. White, 31-year-old, inside serial rapist. ○, Home/base; ●, offences**

Clearly such hypotheses make no allowances for variations in local topography, transport routes and so on. They relate to a generalized mental representation of the broad geographical relationships between locations. As such these hypotheses are similar to those relating to the study of distance estimation in cities (Canter and Tagg 1975). In those studies 'crow flight' direct line estimates of distances around cities were found to have important relationships to actual direct line distances. This was found to be true even independently of travel time between those points (Canter 1977). The circle hypotheses therefore reflect an assumption about a criminal's mental representations about the area in which he commits his crimes. This assumption is that it is the schematic representation of the location of the crimes that is primary rather than very particular topographical details of those locations. Such details may play a role in addition to the schematic 'image', but the present research explores models that do not include such details.

Capone and Nicholas (1975) provide evidence that for robbery, there may indeed be some sort of criminal range. They argue that the offender's goal in crimes of this type is focused on personal gain. Thus the robber will operate within an area which yields the greatest profit and will be looking to identify those areas which have the best opportunities for success. The generality of these findings across different types of crime is an important question. It assumes that an offender in a robbery is maximizing his gain for minimum effort and will therefore travel the minimum safe distance that will offer the prospect of a successful crime. Can the same assumption of economic logic be applied to crimes that may have a more overtly emotional nature such as rape, or crimes in which there is a more considered overt risk for larger scale gain, such as armed bank robbery? Capone and Nicholas show that there is a significant difference in the lengths of armed and non-armed robbery trips, with armed trips having a greater mean distance. The present study focuses on rape, leaving robbery for future research.

There is some evidence that rapists do have similar geographical patterns to burglars. LeBeau (1987a) used centrography (originally developed by Sviatlovsky and Eells 1937) to defend the idea of a structure to the spatial offence behaviour of the individual rapist. Centrography 'allows one to assess and measure the average location, dispersion, movements and directional change of a phenomenon through time' (LeBeau 1987c). The sample of offenders used was 'all the lone-assistant rapes reported in the San Diego police department in 1971 to 1975'. He suggests that the offender may operate from a clear home or base, presenting evidence for a general geographical pattern of rapes around the home of the rapist.

In a further elaboration of these suggestions LeBeau (1987b) points out that although the chronic serial rapists in San Diego that he studied do vary considerably in the distance they travel from their homes, they restrict their 'attacks to within one-half of a mile from his previous attacks' (p. 325). LeBeau (1987b) supports this conclusion with year on year aggregate figures so it is difficult to establish exactly how individual offenders fit into this picture. Furthermore, there is the possibility that many offences are localized in areas that provide special types of target and opportunity. LeBeau's results therefore do raise important questions about the spatial relationships between the residential location of serial rapists and the locations in which they commit their crimes.

Results of the Tests of the Circle Hypotheses

(a) It was found that 41 of the 45 offenders had circles which encompassed all their known offences. That is 91% of offenders had all their crimes located within the circular region. Of the 30 offences, within the four cases that did not co-accord, 23 were located within the circle hypothesis area.

(b) When the residential location was considered it was found that the large majority of the offenders, 39 (87%), had a base within the circle hypothesis prediction area. There were six cases of offenders operating from a base outside the circular region. All of the six spatial patterns showed that the offender commuted to the offence area. Two of the cases involved picking-up victims and assaulting them in a motor vehicle some distance from home. Two others cases involved the offenders targeting a specific street far away from their home area.

The very high proportions of offenders whose crimes are located in accordance with the circle hypotheses provides strong support for the general marauder hypothesis as being the most applicable to these sets of offenders. The commuter hypothesis therefore does not seem tenable for this sample of sexual offenders, although it may have application where very specific types of targeting, for example on prostitutes, was taking place.

Development of the Marauder Hypothesis

If offenders are operating within a circular region that also houses their base, the question arises as to the relative location of their base within their offence domain. In particular, as the size of their criminal range grows does this change the relative relationship to the domestic focus? One way of understanding and developing this argument is to make the simplifying assumption that the home is at the centre of the offence circle. If this is so then those crimes that are committed far away from each other are more likely to be further from the home than those that are nearer to each other. Such a relationship would hold true for any position that the home had in relation to the crime circle, provided the crimes were distributed around it. This more precise specification of relationships between distances is therefore an arithmetic elaboration of the geometric circle model. It can be summarized as a *Range Hypothesis*: the distance between a criminal's offences will correlate directly with the distance those offences are from his home.

A further development of this hypothesis is that if it is supported, the largest distances between offences will be greater than the largest distance between any offence and the offender's home, otherwise the home would be outside of the circle created from a diameter based on the largest distance between offences. Furthermore, if the home was at the centre of the circle then the distance from home to the furthest offence would be half of the maximum distance between offences. In other words, it is hypothesized that regression of maximum distance between offences on maximum distance from home will have a gradient that is less than 1.00 and close to 0.50. A value of less than 0.5 would only be possible if the circle hypothesis was invalid. A gradient greater than 0.5 but less than 1.00 would suggest that the home tended to be eccentrically placed within the crime circle.

The proposition by Brantingham and Brantingham (1981) that there is a safe range round the home in which crimes would not be committed would be supported in the regression equation by a constant value that was positive, but less than the average minimum distance of crimes to home.

Test of the Range Hypothesis

The scatterplot showing the relationship between the maximum distance between crimes and the maximum distance each crime is from the offender's home is given in Figure 4.3.

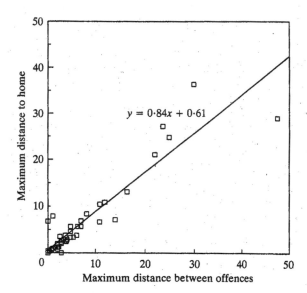

Figure 4.3   Maximum criminal range: relationship between maximum distance between crimes and maximum distance to home. $n = 45$; $r = 0.93$; $p < 0.001$

The correlation for this plot is 0.93 (highly significant at $p < 0.001$). The regression equation is $y = 0.84x + 0.61$. The gradient, at 0.84, does indicate a location within the crime circle, but suggests that it is unlikely to be close to the centre of that circle. This is a finding of some interest which will be discussed later.

The constant is also as predicted. The average minimum distance of crime to home for these offenders was 1.53 miles. The constant of 0.61 miles is well below this. There is, therefore, strong evidence for a minimum distance that the sexual offender is willing to travel from home, in accordance with the hypothesized desire to be at a safe distance away from home.

The criminal's 'safe area' for activity, as defined by this regression equation, is at least 0.61 miles from home but within an area away from all offences which is less than 84% of the maximum distance between offences.

Discussion

The clarity of these mathematical results is little short of remarkable for what is regarded as an impetuous, emotional violent crime. They show that, whatever the rapist's experience of committing the crime, there is a basis to his choice of locations that can be modelled from relatively simple environmental psychology principles.

The relationship that a rapist's home has to the location of his crimes has been established for 45 rapists in the South East of Britain who attacked more than one woman; all of the women being unknown to the offenders before the assaults. The indications are that most offenders move out from their home base in a region around that base to carry out their attacks. However the gradient of 0.84 does suggest that there is some bias to commit a number of offences rather closer to home than would be predicted from a simple circular model. In other words, the base is not at the centre of the circle of crimes.

This eccentricity is important because it may reflect a developmental process in which offenders travel further from home at some stages of their offending career than at other stages. The present data set is not large enough to test this possibility thoroughly although there are certainly anecdotal examples of individuals that illustrate it. Such a development process could interact with the commuter and marauder models proposed. For although the marauder model was clearly the strongest candidate for describing the present sample there were a few individuals who illustrated a strong commuter process. It seems feasible that the differences between 'commuting' and 'marauding' rapists could be a function of the stages in their developments as criminals. With a larger sample this could be tested by the relationship between regression gradient and criminal experience.

The representation of the ranges as circles is, of course, a simplification. The research of both Rengert and Wasilchick (1985) and Capone and Nichols (1975) indicate the possibility that, for North America at least, the expansion of cities from a central down-town may lead to the generation of more eliptical or even sectoral patterns to the geography of serial offending. The grid-pattern of North American cities may also mean that examination of distances between offences is more appropriately carried using city-block metrics rather than the crow-flight measures that were found fruitful for British data.

There are also arguments against the use of more specific models and concrete metrics for the data examined here. The number of offences per offender was relatively small in the current sample. As a consequence very detailed models of the geographical distribution of the offences is difficult to substantiate. Furthermore, it seems very likely that the offences recorded are not all those perpetrated by the offender so models that were very restrictive in the spatial structure could be very misleading.

One further consideration is the psychological question of what exactly is being modelled in the study. If the view is taken that the model is an approximation to the internal representation of the environment that forms the basis of the criminal's actions, then there is research evidence to suggest that for large complex cities crow-flight distances do capture important aspects of a person's 'cognitive map' (Canter and Tagg 1975). Indeed, Canter (1977, p. 90) reports that crow-flight distance estimates correlate better with both actual distance and actual time to travel around London than do time estimates, suggesting that crow-flight distances may be psychologically more primary than other forms of direct experience. This is an important issue which future research, with more data than the present, will need to explore.

The fact that rapists reveal strong democentric behaviour serves to further strengthen the general power of the location of the home in structuring people's lives. It is a process that is worthy of test in may other 'areas of activity, such as shopping behaviour, recreational activities, search for work, or even search for new homes. In the criminal arena it offers direct prospects for practical application in the solving of crimes.

For although the area in which an offender may be living, covered by the circle in the present model, may be very large, nonetheless where detectives are attempting to assign priorities to a long list of suspects the limitations of the circle may still be of utility. It may be possible to reduce the area of the circle by introducing further refinements into the sub-samples of offenders on which the models are based, for example more impulsive offenders may travel shorter distances, or offenders in rural areas may travel further and so on. Research exploring these possibilities has already produced some encouraging results. Investigative suggestions derived from specific studies have also been made available to police investigations with considerable success.

Acknowledgement

We are grateful to Ellen Tsang and Helen Hughes for their assistance on the studies described.

References

Amir, M. (1971). *Patterns in Forcible Rape*. Chicago: University of Chicago Press.

Brantingham, P.J. and Brantingham, P.L. (1981). Notes on the geometry of crime. In P.J. Brantingham and P.L. Brantingham, (eds), *Environmental Criminology*. Beverly Hills, CA: Sage, pp. 27–54.

Capone, D.L. and Nicholas, W. (1975). Crime and distance: an analysis of offender behaviour in space. *Proceedings of the Association of American Geographers*, pp. 45–49.

Canter, D. (1977). *The Psychology of Place*. London: Architectural Press.

Canter, D. and Tagg, S. (1975). Distance estimation in cities. *Environment and Behaviour*, 7, 58–80.

Curtis, L.A. (1974). *Criminal Violence*. Lexington, MA: Lexington Books.

Golledge, R.G. (1987). Environmental cognition. In D. Stokols and I. Altman (eds), *Handbook of Environmental Psychology*. New York, NY: John Wiley, vol. 1, 131–174.

Kind, S.S. (1987). Navigational ideas and the Yorkshire Ripper investigation. *Journal of Navigation*, 40, 385–393.

LeBeau, J.L. (1987a). The methods and measures of centrography and the spatial dynamics of rape. *Journal of Quantitative Criminology*, 3, 125–141.

LeBeau, J.L. (1987b). Patterns of stranger and serial rape offending: factors distinguishing apprehended and at large offenders. *Journal of Criminal Law and Criminology*, 78.

LeBeau, J.L. (1987c). The journey to rape: geographic distance and the rapist's method of approaching the victim. *Journal of Police Science and Administration*, 15, 129–161.

Pyle, G.F. et al. (1974). *The Spatial Dynamics of Crime*. Department of Geography Research Monograph No. 159. Chicago: The University of Chicago.

Repetto, T.A. (1974). *Residential Crime*. Cambridge, MA: Ballinger.

Rengert, G. and Wasilchick, J. (1985). *Suburban Burglary: A Time and Place for Everything*. Springfield, IL: C.C. Thomas Publishing.

Shaw, C.R. and McKay, H.D. (1942). *Juvenile Delinquency and Urban Areas*. Chicago: University of Chicago Press.

Sviatlovsky, E.E. and Eells, W.C. (1937). The centrographical method and regional analysis. *Geographical Review*, 27, 240–254.

White, R.C. (1932). The relation of felonies to environmental factors in Indianapolis. *Social Forces*, 10, 459–467.

Chapter 5

The Road to the Robbery: Travel Patterns in Commercial Robberies

Peter J. Van Koppen and Robert W.J. Jansen*

Previous research suggests that the distance travelled from home to the scene of the crime is related to both the characteristics of the offender and of the offence. In a study on robberies in the Netherlands, the relation between distance travelled and characteristics of robbers and robbery was studied. The data set consisted of robberies for which the perpetrators were convicted in 1992. The cases (434 robberies on commercial targets committed by 585 robbers) were drawn from case files provided by the Dutch police to the courts.

Results show that greater distances from the residences of the robbers to the target of the robbery are travelled by robbers who are more professional, who attack more difficult targets, in more rural areas. Far away robberies are not more successful than those nearby, but if successful generate more proceeds. The results suggest that robbers travel further because they expect more money in specific targets.

Commercial robberies seem a uniform crime: the robbers go in, extort money from the victims with threat of violence and leave as quickly as possible. In practice robberies show quite a lot of variation. Some robbers, for instance, come alone on a bicycle, do not wear any disguise, and flee at the first sign of resistance. Other robbers come in well-organized groups, use considerable violence, and only rob after extensive preparations.

One of the aspects in which robberies vary considerably is the distance travelled from home to the target of the robbery. In this article we examine the relationships between variations in travel patterns and characteristics of robbers and robberies.

Travel Distance

Since the 1960s the spatial distribution of crime has been a growing field in criminology (e.g., Brantingham and Brantingham 1984; Evans and Herbert 1989; Figlio et al. 1986; Georges-Abeyie and Harries 1980; Harries 1980; Herbert 1982).

*We thank two anonymous reviewers for their comments on an earlier draft. Gerard Klay, Nathalie Vriezelaar, Max Wildschut and Miranda Kronenburg gave invaluable contributions to the coding of casefiles.

Little research, however, has been done on how robbers choose their robbery target (an exception is Duffala 1976), and why some travel further than others.

Criminals prefer to operate, in areas they are familiar with (Brantingham and Brantingham 1984). Thus, travelling into unknown territories to locate crime sites is very rare (Reppetto 1974). This is usually explained by the cost in time, money and energy that is necessary to overcome distance (Baldwin and Bottoms 1976; Bullock 1955; Capone and Nichols 1976; Turner 1969). The journey-to-crime literature suggests that criminals combine effort minimization and opportunity maximization (Harries 1980). Since criminals in general prefer easily available targets (Gottfredson and Hirschi 1990), they tend to choose targets close to home, provided they are available there. This pattern of travel to the sites of crime results in the so-called distance-decay function (see Figure 5.1): many crimes occur close to the criminals' homes and the further away from home, the fewer crimes are committed.

The distance-decay function is widely supported in research (Capone and Nichols 1976; Rengert 1989). Capone and Nichols, for instance, found that 33 per cent of trips from home to the place where the robbery was committed were less than one mile (23 per cent for fixed premises); over 50 per cent were less than two miles (41 per cent for fixed premises) (Phillips 1980). The distance-decay function, however, does not decline monotonically. Very close to home, criminals commit few crimes, apparently because there the risk of recognition and thus of apprehension is much larger. Targets close to home are just bad targets (Brantingham and Brantingham 1984).

The distance travelled from home to the scene of the crime is related to both characteristics of the offender and of the offence. To commit a crime, a motivated criminal must come into contact, in time and space, with a victim without the benefit of adequate guardianship (Cohen and Felson 1979). If potential targets are

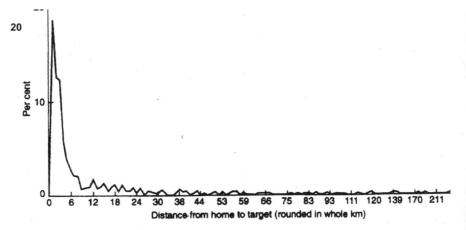

Figure 5.1   Distribution of distances travelled from home to target of robberies, rounded to whole kilometres (876 units of analysis)

dispersed, obviously the criminal has to travel further. Thus criminals committing armed robberies on fixed targets travel further than other kinds of criminals (Capone and Nichols 1976; Rengert 1989), while rapists stay closer to home (LeBeau 1987; Rhodes and Conly 1981).

Although most crimes are committed close to home, there is still a substantial number of criminals who travel greater distances. Their crimes must involve some incentive to leave known territory; some crime targets are attractive enough to do so. Those typically are crimes which are more profitable, but more difficult to commit. Examples may be kidnapping or attacking a strongly protected bank. These are usually also crimes which require much more planning (Capone and Nichols 1976).

The distance travelled also varies with the characteristics of the offender, such as gender (Rengert 1975), race (Nichols 1980; Pettiway 1982), and age (Baldwin and Bottoms 1976; Nichols 1980; Phillips 1980). Nichols (1980), for instance, found that the average distance travelled by older offenders was 4.98 miles, while for younger offenders it was 2.02 miles. Whites travelled further (6.67 miles) than blacks (2.29 miles).

Commercial Robbery

Robbers of commercial targets in general travel further than other kinds of criminals (Capone and Nichols 1976; Rengert 1989), though one can still expect variation. In our analysis we adopt the so-called routine activity approach; which states that to commit a crime, a motivated criminal must come into contact, in time and space, with a victim without the benefit of adequate guardianship (Cohen and Felson 1979). In a densely populated country like the Netherlands, suitable targets can be robbed relatively close to home. There is no need to travel far for a robbery. This effect is augmented by the fact that criminals have a preference for easy available targets (Gottfredson and Hirschi 1990). Thus, criminals stay close to home, unless they have incentives to travel further. One incentive may be that they expect more money at a far away target. It is assumed that the distance travelled to the target of the robbery depends on the distribution of suitable targets, the type of offence, and characteristics of the offender.

Distribution of Targets

The major determinant of the distance travelled is the availability of suitable targets. In rural areas targets for commercial robberies are more widely dispersed than in densely populated areas and thus the robbers need to travel further. The distribution of various types of commercial target also differs; there are simply fewer banks to rob than there are, for instance, shops.

Type of Robbery

Types of target also vary in the amount of planning which is necessary for a robbery. Banks are more difficult to rob than petrol stations, usually because banks have more personnel and a higher level of security. On the other hand the level of security is positively related to the money available. This incentive for robbers may encourage them to skip the relatively easy shops and petrol stations, and rob a bank. To overcome the security measures, however, they have to put more energy into preparations, have to plan more carefully, and divide up tasks. That, in turn, can make the robbers more target selective which may necessitate a longer journey before a suitable bank is found. As a consequence, more professional robbers can be expected to travel further to their target.

In the present study various measures of professionalism were available: the level of security at the target, level of disguise, kind of weapon, the preparations for the robbery, the number of robbers, and the division of tasks during the robbery. All these variables can be considered approximations of the level of professionalism of the robbers. One additional distinct sign of being a beginner in the robbery community is starting the robbery with shouting 'This is a robbery'. A robbery which starts by passing a note, on the other hand, is considered much more professional (Kroese and Staring 1993). In general, however, more professional robberies can be expected to be performed further away from robbers' homes than amateur robberies.

We did not include the mode of transportation among these variables, because the choice in part depends on environmental circumstance. A car may seem the best option to get away quickly after the robbery, but for some targets they are unsuitable. In an old inner city, for instance, riding a bicycle is often much faster. A few years ago some highly successful robberies – from the point of view of the robbers – were committed using boats in Amsterdam. Boats apparently were a better option in Amsterdam, with its many canals, than any other means of transport.

The number of robbers is not a straightforward measure of professionalism. A single robber has more problems in executing a complicated robbery, but extra hands during the robbery risk errors in execution or too much talk afterwards. Given these problems, three seems to be an optimum number. One robber collects the money, a second can restrain bystanders, the third can either be on the look-out and/or drive the car. The robbers, then, must divide the tasks to take advantage of their greater number.

The causal relations between the factors mentioned above and the distance travelled are not always clear. A robber may, for instance, rob a target further away because he has a car that cannot be connected to him, for instance because it is stolen. On the other hand robbers may steal a car or have a car stolen with the express purpose of robbing a distant target. The same problem holds for the availability of firearms.

Robbers

One typical group of robbers is drug addicts. They often need quick and easy money to sustain their addiction (Åkerstrom 1985). As a consequence they choose easy targets: cafeterias and shops which have few security measures and are located close to the robber's home. Robbers who are not addicted are able to attack more difficult targets.

A common explanation for the fact that criminals tend not to commit crimes far away from home is their unfamiliarity with the area. Robberies in unfamiliar areas are more difficult to commit for several reasons. First, more energy has to be put into picking a suitable target. Secondly, preparations for the robbery are more difficult. If robbers, for instance, want to observe the target for an extended period before the robbery, they have to travel to the target repeatedly. Thirdly, an essential part of a robbery is the getaway. Unfamiliarity with the area can cause major problems here. In the present study, for instance, several robbers got lost when fleeing. In a small country like the Netherlands unfamiliarity with the area may cause fewer problems for native Dutchmen than for people who were born abroad. It was therefore expected that people of foreign descent stay closer to home than Dutchmen.

From One Robbery to the Other

We argued above that more professional robberies are committed further away from the robbers' residences than less professional ones. If that is true, it can not only be expected that more professional robbers travel greater distances, but also that individual robbers tend to travel further with every next robbery they commit. Robbers learn from each robbery and thus in a series of robberies become more and more professional.

Method

The data for this study came from official court records. The records consisted both of evidence gathered by the police and the subsequent trial. These cases were robberies for which one or more of the robbers were convicted by the criminal division of a Dutch trial court in 1992. Only robberies of commercial targets were included in the study, excluding robberies of dwellings and street mugging.

In the Netherlands, almost all criminal trials are conducted using documented evidence, mainly produced by the police; witnesses rarely appear in court. The police therefore put much energy into preparing the case files. Both witness and suspect statements are recorded extensively. The disadvantage of using case files, however, was that we could not interview the witnesses or suspects ourselves, but had to rely on the work done by the police officers who took their statements.

The study included 434 different robberies in which 585 different robbers were involved. Since not all robbers were apprehended, we only knew the addresses of the homes of 524 robbers.

For our study we needed court files. Consequently we could not draw a sample of the robberies *committed* in a certain year, but had to turn to cases in which suspects had been *convicted* for robbery in a particular year. For that reason we cannot give exact figures on how large a proportion of robberies and robbers are included in the study compared to all robberies. An estimate, however, is possible based on police figures for all Dutch robberies (CRI 1993). Since there is often a delay between the robbery and the arrest of the robber and always a delay between arrest and conviction, we compare the number of robberies committed in 1991 and 1992. On average, 1,829 robberies were committed per year, of which 32 per cent were solved by the apprehension of one or more of the robbers. Almost all apprehended robbers are convicted, producing an expected conviction rate for 585 *robberies* in 1992.[1] Our sample can thus be estimated to consist of 74 per cent (i.e., 434 robberies) of the population of robberies. There are no data available to estimate the relative size of our sample in terms of *robbers*.

The robberies most commonly involved two offenders (38 per cent of the robberies), 35 per cent were committed by a single robber, and the remainder by more than two offenders, with a maximum of seven robbers in a single robbery. The robberies took place all across the country and included the whole range of possible commercial targets: e.g., banks, post offices, 28 per cent, catering industry, 21 per cent, shops, 30 per cent, petrol stations, 10 per cent, offices, 3 per cent, and an additional 8 per cent in other premises, which included taxis and public transport.

The values of variables in the present study were based on a multitude of sources in the case files: on statements made by the suspects and witnesses and on findings of the police. If sources contradicted, we used the statements made by the suspect as source, then the police, then witnesses. Most of the robbers in the sample (75 per cent) were convicted for a single robbery in 1992; the others for more than one robbery, with a maximum of 13 robberies.

The unit of analysis is a robber involved in a robbery. Thus, robbers were counted for each robbery they committed and were convicted for in 1992. Additionally, robberies were counted for each robber whose home address was known at the time of the robbery. This produced 876 units of analysis.

Professionalism

The measures of professionalism identified above were almost *all* strongly related with each other (see Table 5.1). The relationship may be strong, but there did not emerge a pattern of what might constitute a typical professional or a typical

---

1   The number of 585 robberies for which perpetrators are convicted equals the number of robbers in our sample purely by chance.

non-professional *modus operandi* of a robbery. Therefore, we refrained from combining these variables into a single index of professionalism.

Comparison with all Robberies

For the present study we could of course only use robberies which had been solved by the police, otherwise we would not have known the home addresses of the robbers. There is, therefore, the hazard of drawing conclusions that only hold for the less successful robberies and robbers. In part we could check this.

The criminal intelligence division of the Dutch national police force routinely collects data on all robberies committed in the country since 1988. That enables the police to compare the *modus operandi* of robberies, which in turn may help in solving robberies. The data collected by the national police are not as extensive as the data we collected in the present study on each robbery, but the database of the police allowed for comparison of our data on some variables to all other robberies committed in 1991 through 1992 (N=3,657), namely on type of target, number of robbers, district in which the robberies occurred, success of the robbery, and type of transport. The robberies in the present study only differed significantly on number of robbers (robberies with a single robber are undersampled; $\chi^2 = 90.9$, df = 3, p < .001) and on district (the most rural district, Leeuwarden, and one of the two most urban districts, The Hague, are oversampled; $\chi^2 = 49.2$, df = 4, p < .001).

Journey Travelled

The X and Y coordinates of both the residences of the robbers and the targets were based on postal codes. In the Netherlands a postal code covers about 40 houses. The resulting X and Y coordinates have a precision of about half a kilometre. Although we knew the residential address of each robber and target of the journey, we did not know the route travelled. The Dutch scenery gives the additional problem that cities are not built on a grid system, as is common for many American cities. Therefore, we decided to use the crow-flight approach. The distance D between home and target was computed by Pythagoras's theorem, thus:

$$D\sqrt{(X_{target} - X_{home})^2 + (Y_{target} - Y_{home})^2}$$

Offender Characteristics

Most case files included information on whether the robbers were drug addicts or not. Some of the robbers were addicted to a multitude of drugs. It should be noted that many of the non-addicted robbers use some form of drugs (alcohol or other) prior to a robbery to control their nerves (Kroese and Staring 1993).

Table 5.1 Cross-tabulations of measures of professionalism§

		Security in target		Level of disguise				Weapon used					Preparation for robbery			Number of robbers				Division of tasks
		No	Yes	None	<50%	50–80%	>80%	No	'Other'	Knife	Light gun	Heavy gun	None	Already familiar	Specially prepared	1	2	3	>3	No
Level of disguise	None	9	16																	
	<50%	5	18																	
	50–80%	2	11																	
	>80%	7	32																	
	χ^2	12.5**; N=403																		
Weapon used	No	1	2	4	1	0	0													
	'Other'	5	7	3	1	1	1													
	Knife	8	12	5	5	3	5													
	Light gun	1	4	2	0	1	1													
	Heavy gun	8	51	11	16	10	25													
	χ^2	47.7***; N=550		62.6***; N=596																
Preparation for robbery	None	7	27	12	7	6	3		5	7	3	19								
	Already familiar	6	17	7	3	3	2		3	4	1	15								
	Specially prepared	4	39	8	11	7	14		4	8	2	25								
	χ^2	17.4••; N=426		17.6••; N=491					14.0••; N=671											

Number of robbers					
1	3 *12*	4 *9*	3 *11*	7 *17*	6 *12*
2	5 *29*	9 *11*	2 *22*	17 *10*	12 *24*
3	9 *17*	5 *5*	2 *5*	7 *5*	10 *15*
>3	7 *18*	7 *4*	4 *3*	5 *6*	13 *16*
χ²	18.2***; N=552	17.1***; N=643	57.8***; N=865	31.8***; N=678	

Divisions of tasks (robberies with multiple robbers only)					
No	4 *11*	6 *20*	3 *7*	3 *7*	8 *26*	6 *35*
Yes	21 *64*	2 *22*	3 *14*	1 *4*	5 *20*	
χ²	0.04; N=470	9.8*; N=488	58.5***; N=749	6.7*; N=573	8.5*; N=755	

Type of target						
Bank, post office	0 *40*	6 *13*	3 *3*	4 *11*	7 *3*	10 *13*	3 *22*
Catering	12 *12*	8 *10*	3 *3*	2 *7*	6 *10*	6 *7*	5 *22*
Shop	9 *10*	8 *8*	1 *8*	5 *10*	7 *6*	11 *5*	4 *22*
Petrol station	0 *10*	2 *3*	1 *3*	5 *1*	1 *1*	2 *4*	2 *7*
Company office	1 *3*	0 *1*	0 *1*	0 *1*	1 *2*	2 *1*	0 *2*
Other	1 *0*	1 *3*	2 *2*	0 *4*	2 *2*	3 *4*	3 *7*
χ²	185.4***; N=552	37.9***; N=598	160.7***; N=865	100.6***; N=876	37.9***; N=678	15.5**;

N=755

**p < 0.01; ***p < 0.001

§ Cell-entries are percentages of total; italic type = observed frequency greater than expected.

In the Netherlands the race or ethnicity of offenders is not recorded. We doubt whether race in itself would be of any relevance in the present study, since race has another meaning in the Netherlands than, for instance, in the United States. Differences between races in travel distance are often explained by the slum structure of large cities (Pettiway 1982), which necessitates robbers having to travel from one community to the other. There are no slums in the Netherlands, so we expect that differences between Dutch robbers and robbers who were born abroad stem from their familiarity with the country, rather than from racial differences.

As an approximation to familiarity with the Netherlands we used the country of birth. The Netherlands have some large ethnic communities. In the 1970s and 1980s many people from the former colonies the Dutch Antilles and Surinam emigrated to the Netherlands. A decade earlier many came from both Turkey and Northern Africa (especially Morocco) to work here.

Robbery Characteristics

In the present study the number of robbers varied between one and seven for each robbery. Robberies with more than four robbers, however, were quite rare. Therefore we recorded all larger groups of robbers to the category four or more.

Robbers use all kinds of means of disguise. No disguise is unprofessional, but too much disguise (such as balaclavas) attracts attention during flight. Experience shows that some simple means, as for instance a combination of baseball caps, sunglasses, and a false moustache, are quite effective in preventing recognition, both by witnesses (Penrod and Cutler 1995) and by cameras in the targets. We estimated the percentage of the face and hair of each robber that was covered by disguise using statements of eyewitnesses to the robbery. This estimation is fully explained elsewhere (Van Koppen and Lochun 1997).

We also divided the weapons used into five categories. Some robbers go into the target without the benefit of any weapon. The most common are real guns and knives. But a distinct number of robbers use imitation guns (toy guns etc.), alarm guns and air guns. All others we put into the category 'Diverse weapons'. Most of the weapons in that category were explosive devices – in this study all imitation – but also included baseball bats, etc. One robber in this study even committed a robbery using a bottle of 4711 Eau de Cologne to imitate a weapon.

As mode of transportation we took the transportation used by the robbers to go to the site of the robbery. Some robbers are caught during or right after the robbery, so their escape plans are unknown. Of those we know, however, almost all used the same mode of getaway transport as for arriving.

The Site of the Robbery

The Netherlands are a densely populated country (452 inhabitants/km^2; 1171 inhabitants/sq. mile). We assumed that commercial targets are evenly distributed over the country, but are more dense in populated parts. We divided the country into the five districts of the five appellate courts. The districts of Leeuwarden and Arnhem are the most rural (respectively 193 and 322 inhabitants/km^2), while the districts of The Hague and Amsterdam cover the densely populated west of the country (respectively 792 and 874 per km^2). The district of 's-Hertogenbosch has an intermediate position (476 per km^2). Dividing the country into only five areas may seem a bit crude, but analyses using the 12 provinces or the 25 police districts did not produce any different conclusions.

The variable type of target could have been divided into more categories. Preliminary analyses showed that robberies of banks and post offices hardly differ – at least in the Netherlands. The category for catering includes some hotels, restaurants and a brothel, but most catering targets were either cafeterias or cafes. The category for shops include all kinds of shops, among which tobacco and fashion shops are the most popular. There were no robberies of jewellers in the study.

Results

Travel Distance

The robbers differed considerably in the distance travelled. One robber robbed the shop across the street from his house, but robberies were also committed more than 200 km from home. The longest trip was 267.4 km (166.2 miles). The distribution of the distance between residence and target was heavily skewed: although the mean distance was 19.2 km (sd = 37.5; N = 876), the median was 3.5 km (see Figure 5.1 above).

When considering the distribution in Figure 5.1, we decided to divide the distances travelled into five distinct categories: less than 2 km (N = 270), from 2 to 6 km (the distance one can walk in an hour; N = 255), from 6 to 20 km (the distance one can ride on a bicycle in an hour; N = 154), 20–60 km (the distance one can drive in a car in an hour in traffic; N = 115), and everything above 60 km (N = 82).

Drug users travel less than non-addicts, multi-users especially stay close to home (see Table 5.2). Travel patterns differed depending on the country of birth. Robbers born in Turkey, in other European countries (outside the Netherlands), and in the category 'elsewhere' stayed close to home compared to native Dutchmen. Contrary to expectations, however, robbers from the Dutch Antilles and Surinam committed more robberies a little further away from home, while a group of both Turks and other Europeans fell into the highest category.

The Robbery

As predicted, single robbers stayed close to home. Those who committed robberies in pairs travelled further, and trios travelled even further. Robbers who operated in

Table 5.2   Distance travelled by robbers for each robbery§

	Distance between home and target in km					
	<2	*2–6*	*6–20*	*20–60*	*>60*	*N*
Use of drugs (χ^2=33,55835, df=8, p<0.001)						
No drugs	28	*31*	20	11	*10*	503
Drug user	*33*	25	14	*21*	7	198
Multi user	*54*	*42*	0	4	0	26
Country of birth (χ^2=72,56127, df=20, p<0.001)						
Netherlands	29	*30*	15	*18*	8	352
Rest of Europe	*49*	18	3	*15*	*15*	33
Dutch Antilles, Surinam	27	*30*	23	9	9	344
Northern Africa	28	25	18	*21*	9	57
Turkey	*46*	18	4	4	29	28
Elsewhere	*46*	33	5	7	10	61
Number of robbers (χ^2=51,33511 df=12,p<0.001)						
Single robber	*48*	20	11	*17*	4	119
Two	24	*30*	20	*17*	9	327
Three	28	*34*	14	9	*15*	212
Four or more	35	28	*21*	9	7	218
Moment decided to commit robbery (χ^2=3,63974, df=4, ns)						
Day of robbery	*34*	24	19	13	10	302
Prior to day of robbery	28	*27*	17	*15*	*13*	196
Preparations for robbery (χ^2=8,98177, df=8, ns)						
No preparations	27	*27*	17	*15*	*13*	242
Already familiar with target	*33*	28	*21*	12	6	162
Special preparations	*33*	25	16	*15*	*12*	274
Division of tasks during robbery (χ^2=36,32858, df=8, p<0.001)						
No division	*38*	*32*	16	8	6	124
Division	26	30	*19*	*13*	*11*	631
Single robber	*48*	20	11	*17*	4	119
Mode of transport to robbery site (χ^2=101,82648, df=16, p<0.001)						
Car	19	27	20	*20*	*15*	411
Motorcycle	*52*	24	12	4	8	25
Bicycle	*47*	*31*	10	11	2	94
Walking	*42*	*30*	*19*	5	5	230
Public transport, taxi	12	*24*	32	24	8	25

Table 5.2 *continued*

	Distance between home and target in km					
	<2	*2–6*	*6–20*	*20–60*	*>60*	*N*
Level of disguise (χ^2=17,60351, df=12, n.s)						
No disguise	32	23	16	17	13	151
<50% face covered	27	32	24	13	4	136
50–80% face covered	29	36	12	16	7	89
>80% face covered	32	27	20	14	7	222
Weapon used (χ^2=39,04078, df=16, p<0.001)						
No weapon	*37*	*33*	17	9	4	46
Various weapons	*34*	28	15	*16*	7	98
Knife	*45*	25	14	12	4	153
Alarm gun, air gun	*34*	26	*32*	3	5	38
Revolvers and other heavy guns	26	*30*	*18*	*14*	*12*	530
Type of target (χ^2=111,16609 df=20, p <0.001)						
Bank, post office	18	25	16	*20*	21	223
Catering	29	*37*	20	7	7	217
Shops	*38*	*30*	*19*	9	5	240
Petrol station	*50*	19	9	18	5	80
Company office	18	*38*	*21*	*21*	3	34
Other targets	*39*	23	18'	15	5	82
Security in target (χ^2=32,73722, df=4, p<0.001)						
No	*37*	*41*	14	7	2	132
Yes	27	26	*17*	*16*	*15*	420
Counter in target (χ^2=55,57647, df=8, p<0.001)						
No counter	22	28	*24*	15	11	46
Open counter	*35*	*31*	17	11	6	572
Counter enclosed with security glass	18	26	17	19	20	202
District of robbery (χ^2=106,24237, df=16, p<0.001)						
Leeuwarden	26	19	9	7	*40*	43
Arnhem	*40*	4	*19*	*21*	*17*	53
Amsterdam	*32*	*32*	16	*15*	6	263
The Hague	30	*34*	*22*	10	4	366
's Hertogenbosch	30	24	13	*17*	*17*	151

[§] 876 units of analysis; cell entries are percentages of row total; italic type = observed frequency higher than expected frequency.

larger groups, however, stayed closer to home (see Table 5.2). This suggests that, as hypothesized, the more professional the robber the further he/she travels.

A number of other variables were also used as indicators of professionalism. For most of these variables we found that the less professional, the closer to home the robberies are committed. Robbers who committed the robbery within a day of making the decision, stayed close to home. Robbers who robbed familiar targets (and took the risk that the victims would be familiar with them too) stayed very close to home. Robbers who robbed without a division of tasks and the single robbers stayed closer to home than the robbers who divided tasks. The heavier the weapons used, the further robbers travelled. Robbers travelled further for targets with security measures (see Table 5.2).

The mode of transportation shows that distant robberies are done almost exclusively by car (see Table 5.2). That is not a surprising result. One would, however, expect that the slower the mode of transport, the closer to home the robbery would be committed. That was not the case. First, robberies on motorcycles (both the heavier type and the light motorcycle known in the Netherlands as a *brommer*) are mainly used close to home. A post-hoc explanation might be that robbers use motorbikes not just to overcome the distance to the target, but also choose a motorbike for a robbery to get away fast even in heavy traffic. Secondly, we found that robberies done on foot are committed further away than robberies on bicycle. Probably, this counter-intuitive result is caused by the manner in which we gathered the data. In some cases we took witness statements as source. In some cases witnesses may have reported that the robbers were on foot, while in reality the robbers came with a car that they parked around the corner.

The Target

As expected, the more difficult a target is to rob, the longer trips the robbers travel. Banks were on the one extreme, petrol stations on the other (see Table 5.2). The same pattern was shown by the presence and absence of security: longer trips were taken to rob targets with security. The same was found for the counter variable: targets with a counter (usually shops and cafes) were robbed close by, target with counter with security glass (usually banks, post offices and some petrol stations) were robbed far away, and targets without a counter (usually offices and companies) were in between.

The trip travelled was also related to the density of targets. We took the population density as an approximation of the density of targets. In the most rural district, Leeuwarden, the longest trips were taken; in the most densely populated district, Amsterdam, the shortest. The others are in between in sequence of the population density.

Table 5.3   Parameters of robber and robbery characteristics in HOMALS result[§]

Categories in HOMALS analysis	Units of analysis	Dimension 1	Dimension 2
Travel distance <2 km	270	−0.22	−0.54
District: Amsterdam (urban)	802	−0.58	−0.58
Weapon knife	162	−0.80	−1.03
Target shop	260	−0.73	−0.30
Other targets	89	0.02	−0.85
Walking	254	−0.80	−0.17
Born in North Africa	61	−0.10	−0.25
Travel distance 2–20 km	409	−0.31	0.25
The Hague district (mostly urban)	388	−0.41	0.61
Weapon real gun	579	0.19	0.40
Weapon bomb, etc.	102	0.01	0.35
Target catering	240	−0.54	0.58
Target company office	40	−0.06	0.03
Born in Surinam or Dutch Antilles	350	−0.85	0.19
Travel distance 20–00 km	115	, 0.67	−0.19
Arnhem district (medium rural)	54	1.08	−0.91
's-Hertogenbosch district (medium rural)	159	1.16	−0.47
Bicycle	101	0.82	−0.17
Born in the Netherlands	856	0.81	−0.42
Travel distance >60 km	82	1.87	0.78
Leeuwarden district (rural)	45	1.18	1.01
Target bank, post office	237	0.99	0.53
Not grouped near categories of distance (and not depicted in Figure 2)			
No weapon	54	−1.54	−0.68
Weapon starting pistol, etc.	40	0.05	−1.52
Born in rest of Europe	52	0.22	0.07
Born in Turkey	28	1.91	−0.35
Born elsewhere	62	−0.65	1.78
Target petrol station	82	0.78	−1.41
Car	442	0.49	0.18
Motorbike	26	1.32	−1.14
Public transport	29	−0.94	0.28

[§] Rows are ordered according to groupings in Figure 5.2.

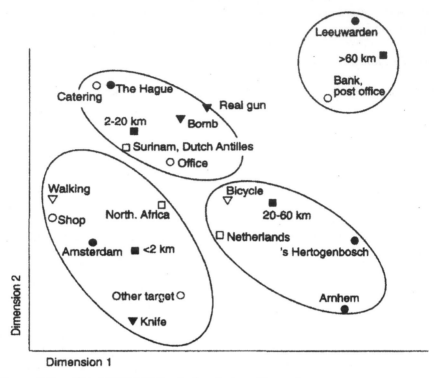

Figure 5.2   Final HOMALS solution in two dimensions

Data Reduction

The data were analysed using HOMALS (Gifi 1983). HOMALS is a homogeneity analysis by means of alternating least squares. In consecutive steps, we eliminated the variables which proved redundant, leaving the variables mentioned in Table 5.3. In this process we collapsed two categories of the dependent variable, the length of the trip, namely 2–6 km and 6–20 km, because these consistently stayed very close together in the analyses.

In the final analysis (see Table 5.3 and Figure 5.2) robberies in the most rural district, Leeuwarden, and robberies on banks came together with the longest trips, above 60 km, namely 2–6 km and 6–20 km, because these consistently stayed very close together in the analyses.

The shortest trips, less than 2 km, were related to robberies in the most densely populated district, Amsterdam, committed on shops and the other category of targets, using a knife, robberies done by North Africans, and in which the robbers came on foot. In between are two distinct groups of characteristics which come together. One was around the 2–20 km category, into which robberies in offices and catering fall, robberies in The Hague district, robberies committed by people from the Dutch Antilles and Surinam, robberies with heavy guns and the other category of:

From One Robbery to the Next

We hypothesized that robbers would learn from their robberies and as they become more professional, would travel further with each robbery. This was not supported in the present study: there were 127 individuals who were convicted of more than one robbery in 1992. Ignoring each first robbery, they together produced 364 units of analysis. Of these robberies 54 (15 per cent) had the same trip distance as the previous robbery, 153 (42 per cent) were closer to home, and 157 (43 per cent) further away from home. These frequencies suggest that in the limited series of robberies in this study there is no tendency to commit each consecutive robbery either closer to or further away from the robbers' residences.

This is further supported by the distribution of individual trips to the site of the robbery. For each individual robber we determined the individual range of operation by simply taking the longest robbery trip. Next, we converted the length of each trip to a percentage of the robber's individual range of operation. Ignoring the longest trip of each robber, percentages resulted which were evenly distributed between 0 and 100 per cent (mean=46.94; modus=46.98; sd=32.8; N=283). This distribution shows that, although Figure 5.1 seems to suggest the contrary, there is no individual distance decay. Rather, the robberies of each robber are dispersed almost randomly within each individual range of operation. The distribution depicted in Figure 5.1, then, stems from each robber, percentages resulted which were evenly distributed between 0 and 100 per cent (mean=46.94; modus=46.98; sd=32.8; N=283). This

Table 5.4   Relation between robbery loot in successful robberies and distance travelled[§] (738 units of analysis)

Distance travelled	Units of analysis	Index loot[§§]
Less than 2 km	234	100
2–6 km	212	160
6–20 km	132	233
20–60 km	94	1183
More than 60 km	66	1639

[§] $F_{(4,733)}=4.73$, $p<0.001$; computed on common logarithm of loot, because of skewedness of variable.

[§§] For security reasons, the Ministry of Justice does not allow us to publish the actual value of the loot. Therefore we present an index figure, with the mean loot in category 'less than 2 km' set to 100.

distribution shows that, although Figure 5.1 seems to suggest the contrary, there is no individual distance decay. Rather, the robberies of each robber are dispersed almost randomly within each individual range of operation. The distribution depicted in Figure 5.1, then, stems from the aggregation of trips made by robbers with different individual ranges of operation (see Van Koppen and De Keijser, 1997 for an extensive discussion of this issue).

For each individual robber we computed the distance to the robbery performed closest to home and the one furthest away. Robberies committed closer to home than the middle between these two distances were compared to the other robberies. These two groups of robberies differed only on two variables significantly (the type of weapon used and on the target), again suggesting that individual robbers do not tend to travel further for certain kinds of robberies and stay closer to home for others.

Discussion

In the present study strong support was found for the distance-decay function: the further from the criminal's residence, the fewer the crimes committed. Half the robberies were committed within 3.5 km of the robber's home. In that sense the results of this study do not deviate from earlier studies (Capone and Nichols 1976; Phillips 1980).

The distance travelled from home to the robbery site is related to characteristics of the robberies, characteristics of the robbers, and characteristics of the targets. In general robbers travel further if they perform more professional robberies. The results support the hypothesis that criminals in committing robberies combine effort minimization and opportunity maximization (Harries 1980): they do not travel far, unless there is an incentive to do so. The most important incentive to travel far for a robbery seems to be, following the well-known robber Willie Sutton, because 'That's where they keep the money' (Sutton 1976). Indeed, the data in the present study partly show that money is the incentive. We were able to assess the relationship between distance travelled and success of the robbery. Of course none of the robbers was robberies above 60 km is more than 16 times the average loot of robberies closer than 2 km to the robbers' residences.

Again, as with other variables in this study, the causal relation is not clear here. We do not know whether robbers organize themselves more to commit a far away but lucrative robbery or that only the more professional kinds of robbers are able to leave known territories to attack profitable targets.

Only studies which give insight into the decision processes of robbers may produce insight into the causal relations involved in committing robberies. Studies in which robbers are interviewed afterwards can only in part shed light on causal relations, because afterwards robbers tend to give a much more rational and balanced account of their decision making than actually took place (Conklin 1972; Haran and Martin 1984; Katz 1991; Kroese and Staring 1993). Probably the only way to discover the causal relations governing target choice and travel distance of robberies is by participatory observation, and that may have some ethical problems.

References

Åkerström, M. (1985). *Crooks and Squares: Lifestyle of Thieves and Addicts in Comparison to Conventional People*. New Brunswick, NJ: Transaction.

Baldwin, J. and Bottoms, A.E. (1976). *The Urban Criminal: A Study in Sheffield*. London: Tavistock.

Brantingham, P.J. and Brantingham, P.L. (1984). *Patterns in Crime*. London: Macmillan.

Bullock, H.A. (1955). 'Urban homicide in theory and fact', *Journal of Criminal Law, Criminology, and Police Studies*, 45, 56–575.

Capone, D.L. and Nichols, W.W. (1976). 'Urban structure and criminal mobility', *American Behavioral Scientist*, 20, 199–213.

Cohen, L.E. and Felson, M. (1979). 'Social change and crime rate trends: A routine activity approach', *American Sociological Review*, 44, 588–608.

Conklin, J.E. (1972). *Robbery and the Criminal Justice System*. Philadelphia: Lippincott.

CRI (1993). *Overvallen in Nederland, jaarcijfers 1992*. Zoetermeer: Korps Landelijke Politiediensten, divisie Centrale Recherche Informatie.

Duffala, D. (1976). 'Convenience stores, armed robbery, and physical environment features', *American Behavioral Scientist*, 20, 227–46.

Evans, D.J. and Herbert, D.T. (1989). *The Geography of Crime*. London: Routledge.

Figlio, R., Hakim, S. and Rengert, G.F. (1986). *Metropolitan Crime Patterns*. Monsey, NY: Criminal Justice Press.

Georges-Abeyie, D.E. and Harries, K.D. (1980). *Crime: A Spatial Perspective*. New York: Columbia University Press.

Gifi, A. (1983). *HOMALS User's Guide*. Leiden: Department of Data Theory, Faculty of Social Sciences, University of Leiden.

Gottfredson, M.R. and Hirschi, T. (1990). *A General Theory of Crime*. Stanford, CA: Stanford University Press.

Haran, J.F. and Martin, J.M. (1984). 'The armed urban bank robber: A profile', *Federal Probation*, 48, 47–53.

Harries, K.D. (1980). *The Geography of Crime and Justice*. New York: McGraw-Hill.

Herbert, D.T. (1982). *The Geography of Urban Crime*. London: Longman.

Katz, J. (1991). 'The motivation of the persistent robber', in M. Tonry, ed., *Crime and Justice: A Review of Research*, 277–306. Chicago: University of Chicago Press.

Kroese, G.J. and Staring, R.H.J.M. (1993). *Prestige, professie en wanhoop: Een onderzoek onder gedetineerde overvallers* [Prestige, Profession, and Despair: A Study among Robbers in Prison]. Arnhem: Gouda Quint.

LeBeau, J.L. (1987). 'The journey to rape: Geographical distance and the rapist's method of approaching the victim', *Journal of Police Science and Administration*, 15, 129–36.

Nichols, W.W. (1980). 'Mental maps, social characteristics, and criminal mobility', in D.E. Georges-Abeyie and K.D. Harries, (eds), *Crime: A Spatial Perspective*, 156–66. New York: Columbia University Press.

Penrod, S.D. and Cutler, B.L. (1995). 'Witness confidence and witness accuracy: Assessing their forensic relation', *Psychology, Public Policy, and Law*, 1, 817–45.

Pettiway, L.E. (1982). 'Mobility of robbery and burglary offenders: Ghetto and non ghetto spaces', *Urban Affairs Quarterly*, 18, 255–70.

Phillips, D.P. (1980). 'Characteristics and typology of the journey to crime', in D.E. Georges-Abeyie and K.D. Harries, (eds), *Crime: A Spatial Perspective*, 167–80. New York: Columbia University Press.

Rengert, G.F. (1975). 'Some effects of being female on criminal spatial behavior', *Pennsylvania Geographer*, 13, 10–18.

Rengert, G.F. (1989). 'Behavioral geography and criminal behaviour', in D. J. Evans and D.T. Herbert, (eds), *The Geography of Crime*, 161–75. London: Routledge.

Reppetto, T. (1974). *Residential Crime*. Cambridge, MA: Ballinger.

Rhodes, W.M. and Conly, C.H. (1981). 'Crime and mobility: An empirical study', in P.J. Brantingham and P.L Brantingham, (eds), *Environmental Criminology*, 167–88. Beverly Hills, CA: Sage.

Sutton, W. (1976). *Where the Money Was*. New York: Viking.

Turner, S. (1969). 'Delinquency and Distance', in T. Sellin and M. Wolfgang (eds), *Delinquency: Selected Studies*, 11–26. New York: Wiley.

Van Koppen, P.J. and De Keijser. J.W. (1997). 'Desisting distance-decay: On the aggregation of individual crime-trips', *Criminology*, 35, 301–10.

Van Koppen, P.J. and Lochun, S.K. (1997). 'Portraying perpetrators: The validity of offender descriptions by witnesses', *Law and Human Behaviour*, 21, 663–87.

PART 2
Stylistic Variations

Chapter 6

Crime Scene and Distance Correlates of Serial Rape

Janet Warren, Roland Reboussin, Robert R. Hazelwood,
Andrea Cummings, Natalie Gibbs, and Susan Trumbetta

1. Introduction

Research demonstrates that a large number of sexual crimes against strangers are committed by a relatively small number of serial offenders (Abel et al. 1987; Hazelwood and Warren 1990; Grubin and Gunn 1990; Jackson et al. 1995). This observation, coupled with the potential for studying patterns of events in terms of their usefulness in predicting future events, has given rise to a growing interest in studying the behavior of serial or career criminals. The patterning of their criminal behavior over time in terms of the types of crime perpetrated, the *modus operandi* manifest in categorically similar crimes, and the temporal and geographical constellations created by a crime series allows for empirical and investigative inquiry not possible with crimes that are studied either individually or in the conglomerate.

One area of inquiry that has evolved out of this perspective involves the behavior of the serial rapist. Known to offend primarily against strangers (Hazelwood and Warren 1990), the serial rapist's involvement in rather startling numbers of sexual assaults has led to study of this phenomenon by law enforcement in the United States and elsewhere (Davies and Dale 1995 ; Jackson et al. 1995). Hazelwood and Warren (1990) reported on the study of 41 serial rapists who were responsible for 837 rapes and 400 attempted rapes. Further research using this same data set indicated that the behavior of the serial rapists could be quantified using behavioral scales that summarized the interaction between the rapist and his victim during each of his successive rapes. The behavior demonstrated during the first rape was found to be useful in determining which of the rapists in that particular data set would escalate in violence and the motivational type that they would manifest over the course of their series of offenses (Warren et al. 1991). These findings motivated the current study of serial rape that sought to explore the relationship between this quantifiable crime scene behavior (i.e., what the rapist did and said to the victim during the rape) and the geographical sequencing of successive rapes by the same offender (i.e., the distance traveled to offend and the location of the rapist's residence in relation to his series of crimes).

Intrinsic to this type of inquiry was the attempt to define the cognitive decision-making that determined these disparate aspects of serial sexual crime (i.e., the where, when, and why of the criminal behavior) and to determine if one known component of it (i.e., the crime scene behavior of the rapist as described by the victim) could be used to determine a yet unknown component of the offender's crime behavior (i.e., the locations in which the offender might live or reoffend). This conceptual framework hypothesizes that serial rapists may rape different types of victims, for different reasons, and that these differences might manifest in differing search patterns for victims in relation to the offender's place of residence. The applied value of this type of inquiry lies in its potential predictive and investigatory relevance to law enforcement in its attempts to apprehend serial sexual offenders. The origins of the current, study lie in the development by the FBI of an investigative adjunct termed criminal investigative analysis (CIA). Criminal investigative analysis or "profiling" was developed by the FBI in the late seventies to aid local law enforcement in the investigation of hard-to-solve, serial violent crimes. Originally evolving out of the investigatory experience of a handful of individuals, over the past 5 years it has become the focus of empirical study in Canada, England, The Netherlands, and the United States. One of these areas of inquiry has focused on the geographical patternings of offenses by a single offender and has, in its development, looked to preexistent bodies of theory and research contained in environmental criminology, geographical ethnography, journey to crime literature, and geographical profiling or targeting. Unique to the current research is the use of detailed crime scene information in the individualized study of the "hunting patterns" (Rossmo 1995b) of a large sample of serial sexual offenders.

Criminal Investigative Analysis

Ault and Reese (1980), in the first written piece on offender profiling, define profiling as a process designed to identify and interpret certain items of evidence at the crime scene as it may inform a description of the personality type or motivation of the perpetrator. Douglas et al. (1986) subsequently described "criminal profiling" as a six-stage process that ideally results in the apprehension of a serial criminal. Stage 1, the profiling input stage, involves the careful review of all pertinent case information, including a complete description of the crime and the crime scene, the background of the victim, forensic information pertaining to all aspects of the crime, photographs of the crime, and autopsy reports if relevant. Stage 2, the decision process stage, involves the arranging of the information into meaningful patterns. These patterns involve the type of murder (e.g., mass, spree, and serial) or rape (e.g., power-reassurance or power-assertive), victim risk factors, offense risk level, the potential for escalation, the timing of different aspects of the crime, and location characteristics. Stage 3, the criminal assessment stage, involves the possible reconstruction of the sequence of events and behaviors occurring between the victim and the perpetrator and the motivation as best estimated from the constellation of crime scene dynamics. Stage 4, the criminal profile stage, involves an assessment of the type of person likely to have committed the crime given the motivation themes derived from the previous analysis of the crime scene. In stage 5, the investigation stage, suspects fitting the general profile are evaluated and further information generated regarding them, while in Stage 6, the perpetrator is identified and apprehended.

Following case descriptions of the process by Hazelwood et al. (1987) and an outline for a profiling interview to be used with victims of rape by Hazelwood and Burgess (1987), Pinizzotto and Finkel (1990) undertook an empirical study of the process as performed by profilers, detectives and psychologists. Finding the profilers able to create a richer, more comprehensive description of the perpetrator in the case of rape, Pinizzotto and Finkel comment on the complexity of the profiling process and suggest that it is not simply an unilevel process that links the what, why, and who of a crime in a linear fashion but, rather, a complex multilevel series of attributions, correlations, and predictions that encompass the "what"-to-"who" loop. In 1992, Douglas and Munn described three aspects of asexual crime: the *modus operandi* (i.e., the means of locating a victim, perpetrating the crime and escaping without being apprehended), the signature (i.e., aspects of the sexual encounter that convey the sexual fantasy underlying the crime), and the staging of the crime (i.e., altering of evidence at the scene of the crime) and suggest that these three aspects have different developmental processes and hence different significance in linking offenses by the same offender. Most recently, Jackson et al. (1995) examined the process of creating profiles using an expert/novice paradigm and found that a profiler, compared to an experienced detective, used more probabilistic thinking and reasoning processes that evolved out of the extensive study of a large number of solved crimes of a similar type.

This set of writings seeks to provide conceptual and, more recently, empirical substance to a subjective process of investigation that has been found useful in the apprehension of particularly violent, serial offenders. The present study, building on this applied foundation, attempts to inform this process regarding suppositions about the location of the offender as potentially implied by his behavior in the context of his actual crimes.

Environmental Criminology

Brantingham and Brantingham (1984) were the first to develop the concepts of "cognitive mapping" and "opportunity space" as they apply to criminal behavior. Citing the work of Tolman (1948), they defined cognitive mapping as "the process by which individuals learn about, remember and use knowledge about an area" (p. 358). They observe that an individual's cognitive map has many dimensions (i.e., color, sounds, and symbols) and reflects the individual's (or in this particular case, the offender's) "overall geographic ... knowledge of an area." In defining the concept of "opportunity space," they suggest that potential crime victims are not distributed uniformly in space. Rather, it is "the interaction of the location of potential targets and the perpetrator's awareness or activity space that culminates in particular patterns of crime occurrence" (p. 362). From this perspective, Brantingham and Brantingham emphasize that crime occurrence in a city is highly patterned and can be understood only if the "subjective environment" of the perpetrator is appreciated, They emphasized that "potential criminals do not search through a whole city for targets, they look for targets within their more restricted awareness space" (p. 365).

Of relevance to law enforcement is the Brantinghams' (1981) conception of a buffer around the offender's place of residence; as they hypothesize: "While criminals know more of the area close to home and are more likely to locate a target easily, they are also more likely to *be* known and increase their risks close to home. One would expect that there would be an area right around the home base where offenses would become less likely" (p. 32). In developing this search model, Brantingham and Brantingham reference research by Turner (1969), who used a distance decay model to explore burglaries perpetrated by Philadelphia delinquents. He found a peak in burglaries approximately a block distant from the offender's home, with little delinquent activity in the intervening block area.

Brantingham (1978) and Brantingham and Brantingham (1981) also discuss the cognitive processing which accompanies the offender's decisions regarding crime site selection. They suggest that offenders learn through experience or social transmission cues or clusters of cues that are associated with "good" victims or targets. These cues constitute a template against which potential targets are evaluated and, as such, represents a "search process [which] may be consciously conducted, or ... [which] may occur in an unconscious, cybernetic fashion so that the individual cannot articulate how [it is] done" (Brantingham and Brantingham 1981, p.29). Brantingham and Brantingham postulate that once this template is formulated, it becomes relatively fixed and eventually self-reinforcing.

These tenets of environmental criminology provide probabilistic assumptions that combine the offender with his potential criminal targets according to basic premises of human behavior. As such, they provide a theoretical basis for the consistency and predictability in the offender/ victim/environment paradigm that constitutes the basis of the geographical analysis underlying this extension of criminal investigative analysis.

Ethnographic Geography

Coucelis et al. (1987) examined various templates of cognitive space and the role of certain points in organizing spatial cognitive information and structuring mental maps. Highlighting the potential significance of particular "anchor points" in a person's life and movement, they discuss the perceptual or symbolic salience of these locations; their rational-spatial properties, such as location within daily activity space; and relational-nonspatial properties, such as their actual or potential significance in a person's life. Reporting on the mental maps of 57 subjects in Goleta, California, the authors note that major anchor points tend to define associated regions of the mental map and that "cues associated with a particular anchor point will be displaced (distorted) in the same direction as the anchor point itself, so that the whole corresponding region will 'move' in piece, relative to the regions defined by the other anchor points" (p. 107).

In a final report submitted to the U.S. Department of Justice, Rengert and Wasilchick (1990) examined six statistical models that define the spatial patterns of individual burglars. Developing the models based in part upon the work of Huff (1984) and Coucelis et al. (1987), they commented upon the ubiquitousness of criminal opportunities, a "distance bias," which motivates a burglar to stay close to important "anchor points," and a "directional preference," wherein a burglar tends to operate in "more familiar rather than less familiar areas" (p. 50). Taking into consideration these factors as well as the behavior of the drug-free and drug-dependent burglar, they proposed six resultant patterns of offending but found that one or two models generally resulted in the most correct predictions for each burglar, suggesting that burglars tend to follow replicable decision-rules as they choreograph offenses.

Journey-to-Crime Literature

Journey-to-crime studies indicate that the distances traveled by offenders to commit offenses vary according to demographic characteristics of the offender such as age (Nichols 1980), sex (Rengert 1975), and race (Pettiway 1982), The nature of the crime itself also influences this distance factor. Pyle (1974) found that rapists in Akron, Ohio, traveled shorter distances than did robbers and burglars, a finding confirmed a few years later by Rhodes and Conly (1981) in Washington, DC. These authors also found that rape tended to occur in areas characterized by construction, urban renewal, and temporary lodgings.

In a study that looked specifically at rapes over a four-year period, LeBeau (1985) found that serial offenders tended to "use repeatedly the same geographic and ecological space" (p. 397). He reported that this geographically specific pattern of offending contributed significantly to changes in the numerical, geographical, and ecological descriptions of rape from one year to the next in various areas throughout San Diego. In subsequent research, LeBeau (1987a) attempted to differentiate among single, serial, and open (unapprehended) rapists. LeBeau found that while serial rapists tended to vary in the distance that they traveled from home to rape, they consistently seemed to restrict their attacks to within one-half mile of their previous attacks.

Five years later, LeBeau (1993) presented four case studies from the same sample that looked at the "spatial-temporal analysis of serial rapists." Focusing on the patterning of offenses in terms of both their geographical patterning and their temporal sequencing, he suggests that the choice of crime location evolves out of four distinct factors: spatial knowledge, time, distance, and type of area. In reviewing his four cases, LeBeau descriptively outlines the relative importance of these factors in producing the different spatial patterns created by four serial rapists of different ages and ethnic backgrounds. In so doing, he identifies a pattern by which each of the rapists eventually backtracked to the area of an earlier offense. Hypothesizing that this tendency may derive from time pressures, rewarding memories, or the exhaustion of spatial knowledge, he emphasizes the need for further study of this pattern in order to facilitate the investigation of unapprehended offenders.

Drawing upon the work of Brantingham and Brantingham (1981) and Rengert and Wasilchick (1985), Canter and Larkin (1993) explored the spatial activity of 45 British offenders charged with two or more sexual offenses. They hypothesized that two general models could be used to describe the relationship between an offender's area of offending and his home base. The "commuter model" assumes that the offender travels away from his home to perpetrate his crimes, with his "criminal range" being independent of and an appreciable distance from his home base. The "marauder model" assumes a closer relationship between an offender's home and his criminal range and hypothesizes that the offender moves out in a random pattern from his home base to commit crimes.

In examining the spatial activity of these 45 sexual offenders who were responsible for 251 sexual offenses, Canter and Larkin found that 91% of the offenders did, in fact, have their crimes located within a precise, circular region and that 87% of the offenders lived within the circular area. According to Canter and Larkin, further analysis revealed that the offenders maintained a "safe area" of at least 0.61 miles around their home, with the average minimum distance from crime to home being 1.53 miles. In discussing these findings, Canter and Larkin (1993) suggested that "the clarity of these mathematical results is a little short of remarkable for what is regarded as an impetuous, emotional violent crime ..." (p. 18). They emphasize that "whatever the rapist's experience of committing the crime, there is a basis to his choice of location that can be modeled from relatively logical environmental psychology principles" (p. 18). In a subsequent set of analyses, Canter and Gregory (1994) examined certain offender and offense characteristics to see if they could be used to reduce the area covered by their circle hypothesis. They computed chi-squares on four variables: race, venue (indoors or outdoors), day of the week, and age at arrest. Race and venue were significant. Black offenders offended closer to their residence than white offenders and those offenders who raped out of doors traveled 2.7 times farther than those who raped indoors.

Davies and Dale (1995) studied the distances traveled by 111 serial rapists using information obtained from the national identification records maintained by police departments throughout Britain. They observed that 22% of the offenders "were known to be itinerant to a greater or less extent" and referenced Farrington's (1993) observation that "convicted offenders move home more often than non-offenders" (p. 6). Regarding the distanced traveled by the rapist, Davies and Dale report that 29% of 299 rapes occurred within a mile of the rapist's residence, 51% within 2 miles of the rapist's residence, and 76% within 5 miles (Table 6.1, p. 8). The authors found "no evidence" of the buffer zone discussed by Brantingham and Brantingham (1984), Canter and Larkin (1993), and Rossmo (1995a); they observe, however, that many of their cases were from the densely populated London area and that a buffer zone might not be observable given the 0.5 mile intervals used in their research.

These studies offer empirical support to the theoretical premises discussed above, specifically that rapists manifest distinct travel patterns in their search for victims, that these appear to be relatively consistent over time, and that different patterned relationships between the cluster of the offenses and the offender's home can be observed for groups of offenders.

Criminal Geographical Targeting/Profiling

Rossmo (1995b) defines geographical profiling as the process through which target location patterns of serial violent offenders are used to determine spatial information about the offender, most often the location of future offenses or the offender's residence. In discussing the implementation of this type of process, Rossmo suggests that it is best undertaken after a criminal investigative profile has been completed both to inform investigators about the personality and lifestyle of the offender and to inform decision-making about whether a series of offenses have been perpetrated by the same offender.

Drawing from the Brantingham and Brantingham model for crime selection (1981) and the routine activities approach of Felson (1986), Rossmo developed an applied system of spatial analysis which integrates target backdrop information with crime location characteristics. Used with cases of serial murder, arson, and rape, the "criminal geographical targeting model" derives from a four-step process: (1) a delineation of the offender's hunting area calculated from the offender's crime locations; (2) the calculation of "Manhattan"[8] distances from every point on the map to each crime location; (3) the use of the Manhattan distance in a function that assigns each point a value based upon a distance-decay assessment of whether or not the point lies inside a buffer safety zone; and (4) the addition of these multiple values to create a score for each map grid wherein the higher the resultant score, the greater the probability that the grid contains the offender's home or workplace. The derivation of these values creates a three dimensional probability surface that can be overlaid on a city map to direct investigatory efforts as they relate to suspect prioritization, patrol saturation, alternative information system access (e.g., postal code access), and Task Force integration.

Criminal geographical targeting represents the first attempt to apply many of the theoretical tenets of environmental criminology to the actual investigation of violent serial offenders. Its success is encouraging and supports further inquiry into detailed

---

8   The Manhattan distance is the actual distance traveled between points using the street grid, as opposed to the straight-line distance.

information on the travel patterns of serial offenders in order to add specificity to this deductive, applied process.

The present study builds upon these theoretical tenets and empirical bodies of research to further explore the cognitive symmetry that combines crime scene behavior with decisions about crime site selection. Drawing on the FBI's format for "profiling" cases of serial crime, the current study uses variables describing the offender and his *modus operandi* to explore correlational or predictive relationships with the distance and directionality the offender travels in order to offend. As such, it examines the relationship between the "how" and the "where" of the criminal behavior manifested by a single offender in a way that is designed to inform the investigative efforts of law enforcement.

Implicit to this inquiry is the assumption that some kind of cognitive symmetry can be determined in the offense decision making of an offender, so that one known parameter of a rapist's offending (i.e., how he commits his offenses) can be used to better predict or estimate a yet unascertained component of his activity (i.e., the offender's location).

In so doing, the study will contribute to the journey to crime literature as it pertains to the behavior of serial rapists while also informing certain tenets of environmental criminology. While environmental criminology posits that crime occurs when a potential offender interacts with a potential victim in a situation that makes a crime profitable and easy, the current study suggests that racial, motivational, and historical characteristics of the individual offender also interact with these tenets to create identifiable spatial patterns of crime that are determined, to some extent, by the anchor point of the offender's residence. As such, the results can be used to refine further the estimative accuracy of the travel predictions utilized when these premises are translated into criminal geographical targeting. Finally, the current study explores the concept of a buffer zone presented by Brantingham and Brantingham (1984), and referenced by Canter and Larkin (1993), Rossmo (1995a), and Davies and Dale (1995), and offers empirical support for this theoretical proposition.

2. Method

The study involves a nonrandom sample of 565 rapes perpetrated by 108 serial rapists. The cases were collected from participants in a course offered four times a year to middle-management police officers from around the country by the FBI. The participants obtained these cases in most instances from their own departments, although, on occasion, they procured a case from a neighboring jurisdiction. Included in the submission of these cases were (1) a detailed victim statement for each rape, (2) the police report detailing the series of crimes, and (3) a map showing the location of each rape as well as the home and place of employment of the rapist. This resulted in the identification of 108 serial rapists with a mean of 5.3 rapes (SD=3.5) and a range of 2–17 rapes.

The crime scene behavior manifest during each of the 565 rapes was quantified by two coders using a 30-page protocol developed by the authors. Part A of the protocol contained 52 multiple-choice items which described the relationship of the victim to the offender; the encounter, rape contact and dropoff locations; the type of approach used by the rapist to gain proximity to the victim; the use or presence of bindings, weapons, and fetishistic items; the use of alcohol and drugs by the rapist; the sexual acts performed and sexual dysfunctions displayed; victim characteristics; the presence or use of a vehicle; and the types of articles removed from the rape site by the perpetrator. Many of these items included subparts and, when coded, produced 123 variables. Modal variables were also created to describe the behavior manifest by an offender across his series of offenses and were used in many of the analyses reported below.

Part B of the protocol contained 58 five-point scales that described the verbal, sexual, and physical interactions that occurred between the rapist and his victim during the rape. Of these, 49 were revisions and expansions of a previous set of scales, described by Warren et al. (1991). The remaining nine scales were retained from the previous study (Warren et al. 1991) in their identical form.

Reliability coding was obtained for 100 of the rapes over the course of the coding. On the first section of the protocol, which contained the multiple choice items describing the rape and its context, k's could be computed for 106 of the 123 variables. The mean k was 0.78; for the 10 k's below 0.40 the median percentage agreement was 95. For the behavioral scales, the second section of the protocol, the median of the correlations was 0.76; the median percentage agreement for the 10 lowest correlations (0.57 and below) was 79.

The geographical data were generated using MapInfo software. The geocoding included, for every case, the latitudes and longitudes of each of the rape incidents, the rapist's residence, and his place of employment (if the rapist was employed). When the rapist had lived at several locations during the case, all of the residences were entered into the geographical database and later analyzed according to the temporally determined rape residence spatial relationship. In these cases with multiple residences, only the rape-residence pattern with the largest number of rapes was included in the larger data set.

The geographical database was subsequently integrated with the crime scene database that summarized the rapist's behavior on each of the rapes for which there was geographical data. Sixteen cases were removed from the main data analyses, as they involved rapes occurring over 20 miles (i.e., 21 to 620 miles) from the rapist's residence; these cases represented travel patterns between cities or across states that were thought to confound the local patterns being explored in the current study. Two distance variables were computed in addition to the mean (i.e., closest and farthest distance). The closest (shortest) distance represented the distance from the rapist's residence to the rape closest to the residence regardless of its placement in the sequence of rapes. Similarly, the farthest distance represented the longest distance the offender traveled to commit an offense. These were computed to estimate the extent of the search behavior manifested by serial offenders.

Two shapes were also designed to examine the relational patternings of the crimes to the residence: the convex hull polygon (CHP) and the Marauder/Commuter model. The area of the convex hull polygon was determined by drawing a boundary around the outermost rape points in each case so as to include all of the rape points in that particular case. The Marauder/Commuter model (Canter and Larkin 1993) was drawn by joining as the diameter the two rapes that were the farthest distance from each other in each case and determining whether the residence of the offender lay inside or outside the area. The offenders whose residence lay inside the circle were designated Marauders, and those outside, Commuters. These shapes were used to explore the relationship between the offenses and the location of the offender's residence.

Results

As summarized in Table 6.1, the 83 local serial rapists (i.e., those rapists who traveled less than 20 miles) in this sample traveled, on average, 3.14 miles to commit their rapes. Their closest distance was, on average, 1.7 miles, while their farthest distance traveled was, on average, 4.9 miles. Interestingly, while the mean closest distance was 1.7 miles, almost one-half (40 rapists) of the rapists raped at least once within 0.5 mile of their home.

Given the frequency at which offenders raped within 0.5 mile of their home, an attempt was made to explore the applicability of the buffer zone discussed in the

Table 6.1   Distances traveled by serial rapists: Complete sample and locally-based rapists

Distance	N	Mean	SD	Range
1. Closest distance				
Complete	99	8.18	31.16	0–242.48
Local	83	1.66	0.48	0–13.90
2. Mean distance				
Complete	99	14.54	43.88	0.03–310.24
Local	83	3.14	3.04	0.03–16.40
3. Farthest distance				
Complete	99	22.03	70.69	0.05–620.22
Local	83	4.93	4.22	0.05–18.40
4. Area				
Complete	76	55.38	227.00	0–1628.60
Local	64	9.27	26.71	0–192.50

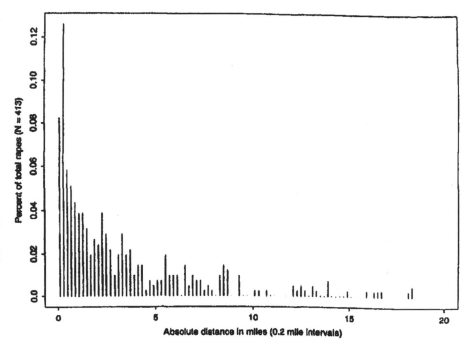

Figure 6.1   Proportion of rapes by distance from residence to rape location

environmental criminology literature referenced above. Data relevant to this inquiry are summarized in Figures 6.1 and 6.2. Figure 6.1 contains data on the absolute distance traveled by each of the local rapists with three or more rapes. Figure 6.2 contains data for each case with five or more rapes, standardized relative to the mean of that case.[9] Five or more rapes were used in the configuration of Figure 6.2 to provide a more continuous distribution for each case. The data in Figure 6.1 suggest a fairly consistent distance decay function with the exception of the first distance interval, which contains 8% (n = 34), in contrast to 13% (n = 52), of the overall rapes which are contained in the second distance interval.[10] The relatively small distance encapsulated in thcsc two distance intervals (approximately 0.4 miles) suggests that a significant number of rapes (over 20%) occur in areas that have a rather striking proximity to the offender's home. Following this interval, the expected distance decay function is demonstrated.

---

9   Distances were standardized to take into account differences in local geography and offender perceptions of distance.

10   In part, the relatively small number of cases in the first interval may be an artifact since there are fewer targets between 0 and 0.2 miles from home than between 1.0 and 1.2 miles from home. Because of street grids and the Manhattan distance, this relationship is not quadratic (Larson 1972).

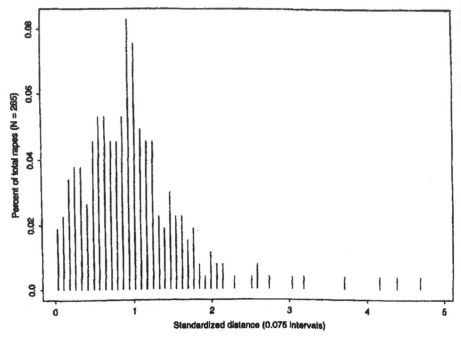

Figure 6.2   Proportion of rapes by standardized distance from residence to rape location. Cases with five or more rapes

A more explicit pattern is seen in the context of the standardized distances (interval = 0.075) displayed in Figure 6.2. As demonstrated, there is no interval around the home where no rapes occur. In the first interval of 0.075 of the mean distance traveled, 6 (1.8%) rapes are recorded. Brantingham and Brantingham (1984), however, define their concept of the buffer zone as representing the part of the individual's journey to crime distribution that does not follow a distance decay function. This construct, represented by the modal crime trip distance, equals 0.975 in the current study, only slightly less than the mean distance.

In an attempt to explore these travel patterns further, the relationship of the distance traveled to the demographic characteristics of the offender, his crime scene behavior, and his criminal history was explored. The shortest, mean, and farthest distance traveled as well as the area covered by the polygon created by the cluster of each offender's rapes are presented in Table 6.2. Mean distances and confidence intervals for variables that obtained the 0.10 level of significance are shown in Figure 6.3. Median areas of the polygons created by the cluster of each offender's rapes, with interquartile ranges, are shown in Figure 6.4 (the interquartile ranges were used to avoid having to show negative values for the standard deviations, which were produced by the skewed distributions). This manner of presenting the data was chosen for two reasons. First, the nonrepresentative nature of the data

Table 6.2   Distance traveled (miles) and area covered by modal demographic, criminal history, crime scene behavior, and geographical pattern of serial rapists

Factors	N	Shortest	Mean	Farthest	N	Area of polygon
I. Rapist's race						
White	26	2.70**	4.32***	6.24**	20	9.52"
Other	43	1.24	2.46	3.97	32	3.45
Unknown	14	–	–	–	–	-
2. Clinical type						
Type 1	33	2.16	3.36	4.81	29	7.06
Type 2	42	1.43	3.17	5.32	30	12.67
Types 3 and 4	8	0.83	2.12	3.37	5	1.63
3. Increaser status						
Increaser	21	0.81*	2.59	5.10	18	5.45
Nonincreaser	62	1.95	3.33	4.86	46	10.76
4. Indoors/outdoors						
Indoors	49	1.61	3.38	5.44	43	11.91
Outdoors	29	1.55	2.69	4.22	19	4.20
5. Victim race						
White	60	1.91	3.61**	5.55**	46	11.61
Other	23	1.00	1.93	3.31	18	3.28
6. Approach						
Con	11	1.05	2.49	3.96	7	2.10
Surprise	59	1.55	3.20	5.20	52	10.86
7. Ritual						
No	31	1.27	2.30**	3.90*	24	4.78
Yes	52	1.89	3.64	5.54	40	11.96
8. Restraints						
No	61	1.31**	2.61***	4.22***	45	4.57**
Yes	22	2.62	4.63	6.89	19	20.39
9. Bindings obtained						
At scene	10	2.35	5.37**	0.82*	9	38.26
Brought	8	0.99	2.39	4.41	6	6.22
10. Gun presence or use						
No	73	1.74	3.17	4.80	56	9.84
Yes	10	1.08	2.93	5.84	8	5.22
11. Knife presence or use						
No	37	1.75	3.38	5.31	32	11.79
Yes	46	1.59	2.95	4.62	32	6.75
12. Day or night						
Daytime	11	3.12**	3.88	4.86	8	0.80
Nighttime	65	1.44	3.09	5.11	53	10.85

continued over

Table 6.2 *continued*

Factors	N	Shortest	Mean	Farthest	N	Area of polygon
13. Time of week						
Weekdays	46	1.74*	2.87	4.31	32	3.82
Weekend	23	0.86	2.85	5.49	21	15.37
14. Victim						
Child	5	2.86	3.90	5.18	5	1.31
Adult	61	1.66	3.21	5.09	49	9.64
Aged	5	0.85	2.05	3.96	4	1.94
15. Offender age						
<20	11	0.59*	1.61	2.64*	5	1.25
20-29	53	1.55	3.10	5.01	46	11.22
>29	19	2.58	4.13	6.02	13	5.43
16. Community						
Rural	2	1.97	3.58	4.19	1	1.51
Suburban	55	1.97	3.58	5.33	44	11.75
Urban	13	0.67	1.49	3.72	12	4.06
17. Entry						
Not forced	46	1.67	3.04	4.70	31	3.97
Forced	37	1.64	3.26	5.21	33	14.24
18. Sexual dysfunction					'	
No	65	1.49	2.96	4.76	53	9.13
Yes	18	2.27	3.78	5.53	11	9.92
19. Substance abuse						
No	73	1.76	3.21	5.00	58	10.19
Yes	10	0.92	2.61	4.39	6	0.33
20. Burglary						
No	40	1.36	2.54*	4.02**	30	2.49*
Yes	42	1.96	3.73	5.82	34	15.24
21. Presence of other person						
No	73	1.67	3.11	4.88	59	9.12
Yes	10	1.60	3.39	5.30	5	11.01
22. Convex hull polygon						
Res./inside	16	1.08	3.20	5.51	16	23.54***
Res./outside	48	1.66	3.06	4.92	48	4.51
23. Marauder/commuter						
Marauder	36	0.74***	2.36**	4.55	36	7.62
Commuter	28	2.51	4.03	5.73	28	11.38

*P<0.10.
**P < 0.05.
***P<0.01.
****P< 0.001.

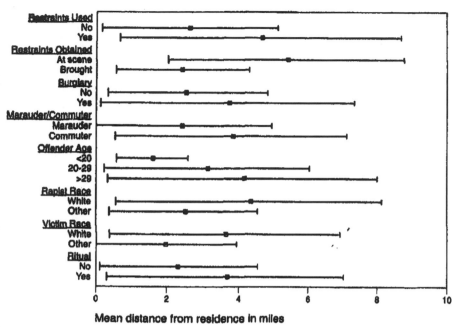

Figure 6.3   Mean distance from residence. Confidence interval (2 SD)

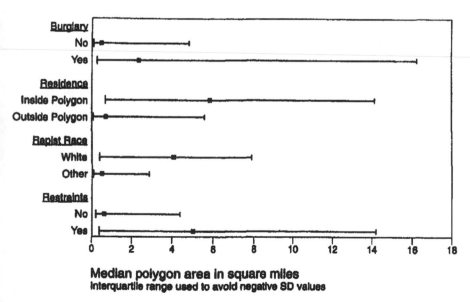

Figure 6.4   Median area of polygon. Lines show interquartile range

diminishes the meaningfulness of significance levels. Second, the applied purpose of the paper heightened the need to present the data in a visually clear and practically interpretable form. Distance was found to vary with the demographic characteristics of the offender as well as certain "signature" and *"modus operandi"* aspects of his crime scene behavior. Elements of his criminal history also showed consistent variability with his journey to crime behavior.

As shown in Table 6.2, white rapists traveled farther than their minority counterparts, as did minority rapists who raped white women (the rate of racial crossover was 2% for white rapists and 69% for minority offenders). White rapists had larger shortest (2.70 miles compared to 1.23 miles), mean (4.32 miles compared to 2.46 miles), and farthest (6.24 miles compared to 3.97 miles) distances. As illustrated in Figure 6.3, the minority rapists showed less variability in mean distance traveled, with 98% of the minority rapists raping within a mean distance of 4.75 miles from their home. Alternatively, rapists who traveled more than a mean of 4.75 miles were almost always white in the current sample. Older rapists also traveled farther than younger rapists. As summarized in Table 6.2, the shortest (P=0.09), mean (P=0.09), and farthest (P= 0.10) distance traveled varied across the three age categories. As illustrated in Figure 6.3, unlike their older counterparts, 98% of the rapists under the age of 20 years raped within a mean of 2.75 miles of their homes.

As referenced earlier in the paper, Douglas and Munn (1992) describe certain "signature" aspects of sexual crimes that contain the fantasy substrate of the sexual crime and which, as a result, are expected to remain fairly consistent over a series of sexual assaults. As indicated in Table 6.2, three of these signature components vary significantly with the distance traveled by the offender (i.e., the presence of ritual in the majority of the rapes, the use of bindings in the majority of the rapes, and the manner in which the bindings were obtained for the majority of the rapes). As shown in Table 6.2, rapists who demonstrated a "ritualized" behavior in the majority of their offenses tended, on average, to travel farther than rapists who did not (on average 3.64 miles, as contrasted to 2.30 miles; $P<0.05$). In the current study, "ritual" was coded if the rape included verbal or behavioral scripting, sexual bondage, or any type of fantasy-based behavior that was not directly concerned with obtaining a victim, protecting the rapist's identity, and/or facilitating the rapist's escape. Similarly, rapists who used bindings or restraints in the context of their offenses tended to travel farther (on average 4.63 miles, as contrasted to 2.61 miles; $P<0.01$) and raped over a significantly larger area than those who did not (20.39 miles^2, as contrasted to 4.57 miles^2; $P < 0.05$). These two variables may be capturing the same behavior or different gradations of the use of restraints in enacting sexual bondage.

As indicated in Table 6.2, the *manner* in which the restraints were obtained also was related to the mean distance traveled by the offender. Those who brought restraints to the scene of their rapes traveled, on average, 2.39 miles, while those who obtained their restraints at the scene of the crime traveled, on average, 5.37 miles ($P< 0.05$). The use of restraints was also related to whether the offender's first or last rape was closest to his home. Those rapist's whose first rape was closest to home tended to use bindings significantly more often than those whose latter offenses were closest to home. These variables, as illustrated in Figure 6.3, suggest that 98% of these rapists who did not manifest a ritualized type of rape behavior, who did not use restraints, and/or who did not fashion restraints at the scene of the crime tended to offend on average no farther than 4 to 4.5 miles from their residences. Those who manifest the more ritualized aspects of rape behavior showed greater variability and tended as a group to travel, on average, longer distances to locate their victim. This pattern may reflect greater specificity in terms of the type of victim being sought or alternatively more complex, methodical behavior patterns in general. The aspects of the offender's *modus operandi* (i.e., the means of locating a victim, perpetrating the crime, and escaping without detection) that varied with the distance traveled focused on the timing of the offense and the association between the rape and the burglarizing of the victim. As shown in Table 6.2, the shortest distance traveled is longer for rapists who rape predominantly during the day than for those who rape predominantly at night (3.12 miles, as contrasted to 1.44 miles; $P<0.05$). Burglarizing victims in the majority of the rapes was also related to the offender's mean ($P<0.08$) and farthest distance ($P<0.05$) traveled as well as the overall area covered ($P<0.06$). These components of the crime suggest that the offender has had experience with other types of property crime and that his motivation for the crime encompasses both a sexual and a nonsexual component. This hypothesis was confirmed with subsequent analysis of the criminal history information obtained for each offender. This analysis showed significant positive correlations among the size of the nonoffending area, the average distance traveled, the general area covered by the rapist, and the number of property crimes contained in the rapist's computerized criminal history. The number of previous rapes reported on the rapist's computerized criminal history also correlated with the area variable, suggesting that rapists who have been convicted of previous rapes tend to travel farther when implementing a subsequent series of sexual assaults.

Finally, the overall geographical pattern of rapes manifested by each rapist appears to be related to the distance traveled by the rapist. Specifically, the area of the rapes perpetrated by those rapists whose residences lie within the convex hull polygon is significantly larger ($P<0.05$) than the area of rapists who residences lie outside the convex hull polygon, (23.53 miles², as contrasted to 4.51 miles²). This finding, if replicated, may prove useful in determining location of a serial offender's residence (i.e., if the area of a rapist's offenses is less than 4 miles², the probability is greatest that he lives somewhere outside the pattern created by his crimes). In contrast, if the area of the offenses is greater than 5 or 6 miles², the probability is greater that the offender lives inside the pattern created by his offenses. The variables related to the polygon area at a significance level of 0.10 or less are summarized in Figure 6.4. As indicated, the race of the rapist and whether he burglarized his victims and/or used restraints were all related to a larger area covered. Interestingly, a larger polygon area did not necessarily reflect larger distances traveled but, in may cases, represented more multidirectional search patterns. Marauders as defined by Canter and Larkin

Table 6.3   Multiple regression of distances traveled and area covered by demographic, crime scene behavior, and geographical patterns of serial rape

Dependent variable	Close distance	Average distance	Farthest distance	Area
1. Offender race	0.07	0.05	0.02	−0.004
2. Offender age	0.21	0.22	0.22	0.02
3. Victim race	0.04	0.06	0.10	0.09
4. Ritual	0.04	0.12	0.10	−0.02
5. Restraints	0.35	0.31	0.28	0.29
6. Increaser status	0.22	0.14*	0.005	−0.06
7. Forced entry	0.03	0.02	0.004	0.08
8. Burglary	0.06	0.13	0.15	0.19
9. Day/night	0.01	0.09	0.10	0.04
10. Day of week	0.12	0.11	0.08	0.25
11. Convex hull	0.10	0.04	0.04	−0.35'
12. Commuter/Marauder	0.46*	0.28	0.08	0.03
$R2$	0.30	0.18	0.06	0.15
F value	2.93**	1.99"	1.29	1.78

*$P<0.05$.
**$P<0.01$.

(1993), rapists whose residence lay within the circle formed by the two distances in their series that are a greatest distance from each other, were also found to travel, on average, less distance than Commuters, whose residence lay outside the cluster of their offenses. The shortest distance traveled was also significantly different for the two groups ($P<0.01$). For Marauders, the shortest distance traveled was 0.74 miles, while for Commuters, it was 2.51 miles. Interestingly, the area covered by the two groups over the course of their rapes was not substantially different, suggesting that different conceptualizations of space rather than size of space defines the victim search pattern of these two groups.

To assess the relative importance of the variables found to be significantly related to the distances traveled by the serial rapists in the current study, a multiple regression was run for each of the distance variables described above (see Table 6.3). The offender's race, the victim's race, the presence or absence of "ritual," the use or non-use of restraints, whether the rapist escalated in violence over, the course of his rape career (i.e., increaser/ nonincreaser status), the presence or absence of forced entry, the coocurrence of burglary, the offender's age, the timing of the rape, the weekday/weekend designation of the rape, and whether the residence was inside or outside the convex hull and the Marauder/Commuter model were entered (stepwise) as the dependent variables. Each of these variables was found to be significant or close to significant in the bivariate analysis and reflect either demographic or crime scene information believed by criminal investigative analysts to be relevant in the investigation of serial crime. Significant models were obtained for the shortest and average distance. A correlation matrix revealed no problems of multicollinearity in the data. The highest correlation in the matrix was 0.53 (reflecting the tending of whites to use restraints more than blacks), well below the 0.70 level at which Tabachnik and Fidell (1989, p. 87) admonish the analyst to "think carefully" before including both variables in the analysis.

The model for shortest distance ($P<0.01$) accounted for 30% of the variance; the only significant variable was Marauder/Commuter status ($P<0.01$); as illustrated in Table 6.2 and Figure 6.3, Marauders rape closer to home than do Commuters. The model for average distance ($P<0.05$) explained 18% of the variance; those rapists who escalated in violence tended to travel shorter mean distances than those rapists who did not escalate in violence.

4. Discussion

The results of the current study must be considered in terms of the nonrandom nature of the sample. The cases analyzed represent a sample of solved cases that may be overrepresentative of the more "interesting" cases investigated by various departments across the country. Less "interesting" or complex series of rapes might not have been included in this sample and thus biased the sample in terms of larger geographical dispersion. Unsolved cases might also involve more complex victim selection or travel patterns that contribute to the difficulty investigators have in identifying and apprehending the offender.

Of relevance to journey-to-crime literature is the finding that local serial rapists travel on average 3.14 miles to rape but that the average shortest/closest distance is 1.66 miles. More important to investigators was the finding that half of the serial rapists in the study raped at least once within 0.5 miles from their residence. This suggests that rapists tend, at least on occasion, to rape in areas that seem to put them at risk because of the proximity of their offense behavior to their home. As shown in Figures 6.1 and 6.2, there does, however, also appear to be an area around the important anchor point of the offender's home that contains a lower probability of rape behavior.

In terms of the Brantinghams' (1984) conceptualization of the buffer zone (i.e., the space over which offending becomes more probable as the distance from home increases), this distance for the current sample of serial rapists was 0.975 of their mean crime trip distance. This finding suggests that the factors pertinent to defining the individual search patterns of these serial rapists vary in their individual and cumulative effect as the distance from home varies. The small number of rapes in the intervals most proximate to the homes of the offenders suggest that the wish to avoid recognition supersedes, significantly, the wish to procure a victim with the least temporal and geographical effort. This wish is not as absolute as one might expect, however, as at least a small number of rapes occur in the same complex as the offender's residence. It seems likely that the travel patterns away from home also allow the offenders increased access to an ever-widening pool of potential victims and, for some offenders, reflect movement toward other significant anchor points (e.g., place of work, red light district, etc.).

As theorized by the Brantinghams, this centrifugal movement, however, eventually begins to wane; the offender's apparent wish to avoid recognition and find an ever-widening pool of potential targets diminishes and the distance decay function that determines many aspects of human spatial behavior begins to dominate. Brantingham and Brantingham (1984, p. 344) observe, "People interact more with people and things that are close to their home location than with people and things that are far away." They ascribe this tendency to the costs of farther travel as well spatial familiarity with the area proximate to a person's home. The pervasiveness of this pattern is quite remarkable given that it clearly contradicts the objective reality of their being an increasing pool of targets as the radius of the offender's crime pattern increases. This increase is, however, further influenced and/or diminished by the realities of actual travel time.

The results further suggest that the rapist's geographical decisions in terms of the distance he travels to rape vary systematically with certain of his demographic characteristics, his crime scene behaviors, and aspects of his criminal history. This suggests some degree of cognitive symmetry that may be of value in the investigation of serial crime. Of particular importance to investigation is the finding that white rapists travel on average farther than minority rapists, as may older offenders, to locate their victims. The finding regarding race is similar to that found by Canter and Gregory (1994) in their study of 45 British offenders charged with sexual assault. In the current sample, these racial differences may reflect class distinctions and therefore lesser and greater mobility, the smaller area covered by exclusively minority neighborhoods, or cultural differences in the cognitive structuring of space. The differences in the distance traveled by younger and older rapists may reflect greater impulsivity in the offense behavior of younger offenders, greater access to vehicles by older offenders, or, as mentioned above, differences in age-related development of geographically determined cognitive space.

Somewhat more unexpected was the relationship between ritualized behavior and the use of restraints and the distance traveled by the rapist. It appears that the rapist who is enacting a more scripted, ritualized type of rape tends to travel farther to find his victim. The manifestation of ritualized behavior and the use of restraints have been associated with specific sexual fantasies that are driving the sexual assault and, as such, may also be associated with the choice of a more specific victim and/or more sophisticated cognitive processing of all aspects of the crime.

The distance characteristics of the rapes were also found to vary with the criminal history of the rapist and the means he used in gaining access to the victim within her home. Rapists who had more extensive criminal histories, who used forced entry, and who burglarized the victim during the rape tended to travel farther to rape. This seems to reflect both a more generalized criminal motivation for the crime and more experience in perpetuating nonsexual crimes.

Of particular investigative relevance is the significant difference in the area covered by rapists who live inside the convex hull polygon formed by their offenses as contrasted to those who live outside the convex hull polygon. As indicated in Table 6.2 and Figure 6.3, those who reside inside the convex hull polygon cover on average 23.5 miles^2, as contrasted with those who live outside the convex hull polygon, who cover on average 4.5 miles^2. This pattern is manifest regardless of the fact that the two groups show no differences in the closest, average, or farthest distance traveled, demonstrating that the difference lies in the patterning of the offenses in relationship to the residence rather than the actual distance traveled. This finding might be used by investigators to inform their prediction of whether or not any particular offender lives inside the polygon (i.e., the area covered is equal to or less than 4.5 miles). This patterning may emanate from the fact that rapists who rape in the area around their home have a more intimate knowledge of a broader area than those who commute to a more unknown area. Conversely, those rapists who commute may also be targeting a particular, specific type of victim or situation that is contained in a more precise geographical locale.

These findings are obviously not conclusive given the nonrandom nature of the sampling. However, the relationships discussed above do point toward some degree of cognitive symmetry between what the rapist does during his rape and the decisions he makes regarding the means he uses to locate his victims. This manifestation of cognitive symmetry is not surprising given other aspects of human decision-making. This symmetry may not, however, be part of the offender's conscious decision-making. It may represent an unconscious synthesis of cues that are not apparent to the perpetrator and, in fact, represent a geographical fingerprint which he inadvertently leaves behind as he perpetrates his crimes.

Obviously, further study of and replication of these findings could be of great value to the investigator or criminal investigative analyst. For example, the current data suggest that younger rapists will be living closer to their offenses than older rapists; alternatively, those who manifest a more complex, ritualized form of crime scene behavior are more likely to have traveled farther to locate their victims. These findings may also serve to help structure empirical attempts to determine the most probable location of the rapist's residence. Even in this preliminary form, they can help to inform the deductive reasoning that lies at the heart of criminal targeting analysis (Rossmo 1995). Already being introduced into standardized software, this technique makes use of general journey to crime estimates of the travel patterns of different types of offenders. More detailed estimates of travel patterns related to observable crime scene behavior and demographics of offenders can only help to increase the predictability and applicability of these evolving spatially oriented investigative processes.

Acknowledgements

This research was supported by transfer of funds 91-IJ-RO27 awarded by the National Institute of Justice, Office of Justice Programs, U.S. Department of Justice, to the Federal Bureau of Investigation. Points of view in this document are those of the authors and do not necessarily represent the official position or policies of the U.S. Department of Justice. The authors wish to thank Dr. David Reboussin for statistical assistance and many useful comments in the preparation of the manuscript and our anonymous reviewers for their invaluable suggestions.

References

Abel, G., Becker, J., Cunningham-Rathner, J., Mittelman, M., Rouleau, J., and Murphy, W. (1987). Self-reported sex crimes of nonincarcerated paraphiliacs. *J. Interpers. Violence*, 2(6), 3–25.

Ault, R.L. and Reese, J.T. (1980). A psychological assessment of crime profiling. *FBI Law Enforce. Bull.*, 49(3), 22–25.

Brantingham, P.J. (1978). A theoretical model of crime site selection. In Kuohn, M., and Akers, R.L. (eds.), *Crime, Law and Sanction*, Sage, Beverly Hills, CA, pp. 105–118.

Brantingham, P. and Brantingham, P. (1981). *Environmental Criminology*, Sage, Beverly Hills, CA.

Brantingham, P. and Brantingham, P. (1984). *Patterns in Crime*, Macmillan, New York.

Canter, D. and Gregory, P. (1994). Identifying the residential location of rapists. *J. Forens. Sci. Soc.*, 34, 169–175.

Canter, D. and Larkin, P. (1993). The environmental range of serial rapists. *J. Environ. Psychol.*, 13, 63–69.

Coucelis, H., Golledge, R., Gale, N. and Tobler, W. (1987). Exploring the anchor point hypothesis of spatial cognition. *J. Environ. Psychol.*, 7, 99–122.

Davies, A. and Dale, A. (1995). *Locating the Stranger Rapist*, Police Research Group Special Interest Series: Paper 3, Home Office Police Department, London.

Douglas, J.E. and Munn, C. (1992). Violent crime scene analysis: *Modus operandi*, signature, and staging. *FBI Law Enforce. Bull.* Feb.: 1–10.

Douglas, J.E., Ressler, R.K., Burgess, A.W. and Hartman, C.R. (1986). Criminal profiling from crime scene analysis. Special issue: Psychology in Law Enforcement. *Behav. Sci. Law*, 4, 401–421.

Farrington, D. (1993). Have any individual, family, or neighbourhood influences on offending been demonstrated conclusively. In Farrington, D., Sampson, R. and Wikstrom, P. (eds), *Integrating Individual and Ecological Aspects of Crime*, National Council for Crime Prevention, Sweden.

Felson, M. (1986). Routine activities and crime prevention in the developing metropolis. *Criminology*, 25, 911–931.

Grubin, D. and Gunn, I, (1990). *The Imprisoned Rapist and Rape,* Institute of Psychiatry, Department of Forensic Psychiatry, London.

Hazelwood, R. and Burgess, A.W. (1987). *Practical Aspects of Rape Investigation: A Multidisciplinary Approach,* Elsevier, New York.

Hazelwood, R. and Warren, J. (1990). The criminal behavior of the serial rapist. *FBI Law Enforce. Bull.* Feb., 11–17.

Hazelwood, R., Ressler, R.K., Depue, R.L. and Douglas, J.E. (1987). Criminal personality profiling: An overview. In Hazelwood, R. and Burgess, A.W. (eds), *Practical Aspects of Rape Investigation: A Multidisciplinary Approach,* Elsevier, New York, pp. 137–150.

Huff, J. (1984). Spatial aspects of residential search. In Clark, W. (ed.), *Modelling Housing Market Search,* St. Martin's Press, New York, pp. 169–199.

Jackson, J., Van den Eshof, P. and De Kleuver, E. (1995). In Bekerian, D. and Dennett, J. (ed.), *Offender Profiling – Apprehending the Serial Criminal,* John Wiley & Sons, Chichester.

Larson, R.C. (1972). *Urban Police Patrol Analysis,* MIT Press, Cambridge, MA.

LeBeau, J. (1985). Some problems with measuring and describing rape presented by the serial offender. *Just. Q.,* 2, 385–398.

LeBeau, J. (1987). Patterns of stranger and serial rape offending: Factors distinguishing apprehended and at large offenders. *J. Crim. Law Criminol.,* 78, 309–326.

LeBeau, J. (1993). Four case studies illustrating the spatial-temporal analysis of serial rapists. *Police Stud.,* 15(3), 124–145.

Nichols, W. (1980). Mental maps, social characteristics and criminal mobility. In GeorgesAbeyie, D. and Harries, K. (eds), *Crime, A Spatial Perspective,* Columbia University Press, New York, pp. 156–166.

Pettiway, L. (1982). Mobility of robbery and burglary offenders: Ghetto and nonghetto spaces. *Urban Affairs Q.,* 18, 255–270.

Pinizotto, A.J. and Finkel, N.J. (1990). Criminal personality profiling: An outcome and process study. *Law Hum. Behav.,* 14(3), 215–233.

Pyle, G. (1974). *The Spatial Dynamic of Crime* (Research Paper No. 159), Department of Geography, University of Chicago, Chicago.

Rengert, G. (1975). Some effects of being female on criminal spatial behavior. *Pa. Geographer,* 13(2), 10–18.

Rengert, G. and Wasilchick, J. (1985). *Suburban Burglary: A Time and Place for Everything,* Charles C Thomas, Springfield. IL.

Rengert, G. and Wasilchick, J. (1990). *Space, Time and Crime: Ethnographic Insights into Residential Burglary.* Report submitted to U.S. Department of Justice, National Institute of Justice, Office of Justice Programs.

Rhodes, W. and Conly, C. (1981). Crime and mobility: An empirical study. In Brantingham, P. and Brantingham, P. (eds), *Environmental Criminology,* Sage, Beverly Hills, CA, pp. 167–188.

Rossmo, D. (1995a). Overview: Multivariate spatial profiles as a tool in crime investigation. In Block, C.R., Dabdoub, M. and Fregley, S. (eds), *Crime Analysis*

Through Computer Mapping, Police Executive Research Forum, Washington, DC, pp. 65–97.

Rossmo, D. (1995b). Place, space, and police investigations: Hunting serial violent criminals. In Eck, J.E. and Weisburd, D. (eds). *Crime and Place,* Criminal Justice Press, New York, pp. 217–235.

Tabachnik, B.G. and Fidell, L.S. (1989). *Using Multivariate Statistics,* 2nd ed., Harper Collins, New York.

Tolman, E.C. (1948). Cognitive maps in rats and man. *Psychol. Rev.,* 55, 189–208.

Turner, S. (1969). Delinquency and distance. In Wolfgang, M. E. and Sevin, T. (eds), *Delinquency, Selected Studies,* John Wiley, New York.

Warren, J., Reboussin, R., Hazelwood, R. and Wright, J. (1991). Prediction of rape type and violence from verbal, physical and sexual scales. *J. Interpers. Violence,* 6(1), 55–67.

Chapter 7

An Examination of the Relationship Between Distance Travelled and Motivational Aspects of Firesetting Behaviour

Katarina Fritzon

Introduction: Geographical Issues in Arson Research

Compared to other offences such as burglary (Rengert and Wasilchick 1985) and rape (Amir 1971), there have been few studies examining the spatial behaviour of arsonists. However, studies of these other crime types have shown that it is possible to model offender spatial choices. These studies, which draw on ideas from the fields of Environmental Criminology and Environmental Psychology, have focused on the relationship between where an offender lives and the location of his/her offences.

What this research has tended to find is that, generally, criminals do not travel very far from home to commit their crimes (e.g. Stephenson 1974) and the frequency of criminal activity decreases as the distance from home increases (e.g. Lowe and Moryadas 1975). The most frequently cited research within this field is that conducted by Brantingham and Brantingham (1981) who proposed a theoretical model for explaining offender's spatial behaviour. This model has a number of components which offer up specific testable hypotheses about the location of an offender's crimes in relation to his home. One of the most important of these is the concept of familiarity as a determining factor of where offenders will tend to commit their crimes. Areas where criminals conduct routine activities such as work, shopping and recreation, combine to form what the Brantingham's term 'activity space'. These are the areas where crimes are most likely to be committed. Another significant concept is that of a 'buffer zone' existing around the offender's home in which he/she is less likely to commit crimes due to the risk of recognition.

The influence of concepts such as these on the spatial behaviour of arsonists, however, remain untested as research in this area has tended to focus simply on identifying areas within a city where incidences of arson are most frequent (e.g. Brady 1983; Bennett et al. 1987). Furthermore, this research appears to be relevant to only certain forms of arson. For example, Brady (1983) identified areas of Boston, Massachusetts, where the incidence of arson was particularly high, predominantly those populated by ethnic minorities. Brady argued that these areas were particularly vulnerable to arson because they have a high proportion of abandoned properties. Similarly, Bennett et al. (1987) studied arson in Springfield, another town in Massachusetts, and again explained the identification of certain 'hot-spots' in terms of a variety of social, economic and housing conditions.

Taken together, then, these two studies are a first step towards highlighting a possible causal link between socio-economic factors and arson. However, beyond these instrumentally motivated arsons, they do not offer broader psychological insight into how the existence of these 'natural areas for crime' actually translates to firesetting behaviour at an individual level.

One possibility is that the people who live in these areas may be more likely to use arson because of a perceived lack of alternative methods for achieving goals (Fannin and Clinard 1965). This has been examined by Pettiway (1987) who found that the rate of retaliative (revenge) arson in so-called 'natural' crime areas was higher than in other areas. However, this study still only deals with one form of arson and has a predominantly socio-economic focus.

In summary, then, these studies have all focused on the geographical distribution of arson at a macro level, i.e. across a given city, rather than examining spatial patterns operating at the individual, micro, level. The Environmental Psychology perspective contributes a more individual-focused psychological approach to concepts of offender spatial behaviour. Therefore, it is useful to examine findings from research conducted within this field of study in order to find a model for understanding the spatial behaviour of arsonists. The journey to crime, according to environmental psychologists, can be explained as a complex interaction between aspects of the offender's personal characteristics and factors relating to the offence itself.

Previous research has shown that criminals tend to travel further to commit property offences than crimes against people (e.g. White 1932). A similar distinction exists between arson that is targeted against people and that which targets properties (e.g. Canter and Fritzon 1998), and it may therefore be proposed that the former would involve travelling greater distances.

Within property crimes themselves, greater distances are travelled when the value of the property is larger (Baldwin and Bottoms 1976). Similarly Capone and Nichols (1975) found that robbers travel further if they are armed than if not. It has been suggested that this is linked to the level of planning required by armed robbers (Gabor and Gottheil 1984). Therefore, this may be a factor which would affect the spatial behaviour of offenders committing other crimes involving planning, such as arson.

These studies have tended to focus on property offences, where there is an underlying assumption that an offender is acting to maximize his personal gain from the crime, and minimize the effort involved in committing it. Research on more person-focused offences, such as rape, however, have indicated that here offenders are seeking to minimize the amount of effort required to commit the assault. For example, Le Beau (1987) looked at the method of approach used by rapists and found that those who used methods that required the most effort (illegal entry, kidnap-attack and meeting at a party) tended to travel shorter distances from home. Recent research on serial arsonists has suggested that these are similar to rapists in relation to both their criminal range and the relationship this has to their home (Kocsis and Irwin 1997). It was found that in 79 per cent of rape, 82 per cent of arson and 70 per cent of burglary cases a circle drawn around the two farthest crimes in a series encompassed all the offences committed by that individual. Furthermore, in 71 per cent of rape, 82 per cent of arson and 48 per cent of burglary cases the offender's base was located within the circle. As these results suggest, the ability to encompass both the range of offences and the home of the offender within a circular area defined by the two farthest offences is not a logical necessity; but does indicate that the home serves as a focal point for offending behaviour (Canter and Larkin 1993).

The similarities observed by Kocsis and Irwin (1997) between rape and arson is possibly due to the importance of the target or victim in both of these offences. It could be argued that the spatial behaviour of burglars is more random because essentially the opportunity to commit burglary exists everywhere. The location of their crime-sites, therefore, might be expected to be more dependent on concerns about detection or opportunistic factors such as coming across a house which is unoccupied, and does not present environmental psychological obstacles against being burgled (Shaw and Gifford 1994). Rapists on the other hand, do not have such a widely available choice of targets and so victim selection may be the primary factor which affects the location of their crimes. Based on previous research on arson (e.g. Canter and Fritzon 1998; Harris and Rice 1998) it might be expected that certain forms of arson will be target focused, like rapists, whereas others will be more opportunistic, like burglars. Although the above research was based on serial offenders, these hypotheses can also be tested in relation to single offenders.

As well as the findings which show a relationship between the nature of the offence and distance travelled, there has also been research showing that offender characteristics appear to affect the journey to crime distance. For example, Repetto (1974) found that younger offenders tend to travel shorter distances than older ones. Also, female offenders are more likely to commit offences within their own residential area than males (Rengert 1975). Finally, Nichols (1980) noted that white offenders travelled almost three times as far as black offenders.

Taken together, the above research findings raise a number of empirical questions in relation to the spatial behaviour of arsonists. The first is whether differences in styles of firesetting behaviour will reflect the general principles found for other crime types. It is important to test whether arson is a crime in which level of emotional commitment leads to travelling shorter distances as has been shown for other crimes (e.g. White 1932). This is an interesting question which relates to the function that arson represents to the individual who uses this as a method of achieving goals. The distances that such individuals are prepared to travel reflect their commitment to the firesetting activity with shorter distances revealing a more limited level of functioning.

This distinction between emotional vs goal-directed acts of arson is also expected to be revealed by examining relationships between arsonists' personal characteristics and distances travelled. For example, age has often been cited as relevant in other crime types with younger offenders generally travelling shorter distances than older (e.g. Repetto 1974). However, it is also possible that in arson a more important determining factor is behavioural motivation rather than there being a direct relationship with age or other personal characteristics *per se*. Underlying all of these research questions is the opposite possibility that if arson is a product of psychological disorder, patterns relating to external issues such as distances travelled may not be distinguishable.

The results of the study have both theoretical and practical implications. Clearly, the finding that certain forms of arson are associated with offenders travelling particular distances would be of considerable investigative importance. Equally important, however, is an increased understanding of the relationship between spatial behaviour and psychological motivating factors. The results of this study can be seen as a first step towards such an understanding, with the identification of links between certain crime-scene behaviours and distances travelled suggesting the nature of decisions made by arsonists as to how far they are prepared to travel to achieve particular firesetting goals, whilst operating on a 'least effort' principle.

Method

The hypotheses were tested by examining the distances travelled by a sample of arsonists and examining associations with both individual variables and groups of variables, specifically those that reflect distinctions found for other crime types. The rationale for this is that different styles of arson can be compared to particular crime types which have been found to differ geographically.

A total of 156 cases involving a single crime-scene which was set on fire by either a single offender or multiple offenders were examined. The data came from solved police files of arson and, as such, a number of methodological issues are raised. On the one hand such a source of data is arguably more objective and reliable than, for example, asking offenders to explain their motivations for setting fires, and estimates of distances travelled. Although it would be of interest to supplement archival data with in-depth interviews to explore the subjective cognitive or emotional factors that may influence the spatial behaviour of arsonists, this would be beyond the scope of the present study which is intended as a first step towards a model of how motivational factors relate to distances travelled to set fires.

It is also important to note, however, that the nature of police data is that cases that are harder to solve, for example, arson for profit, will tend to be under-represented and conversely those that are easier, for example, ones where the offender is known to the victim, will probably be over-represented. In terms of actual coding reliability of the information present in the files, this is less of an issue for the geographical analysis, as it can be assumed with a fairly high degree of confidence that both the address of the offence location and the address of the offender residence will have been recorded accurately in the file. However, the verity of other information, such as behaviour by the offender before, during and after the offence as reported by the offender him/herself and/or witnesses, is less certain. It is also equally possible that behaviours occurred that were not reported or recorded. In order to overcome this limitation, data was coded dichotomously and analysed using Jaccard's coefficient which does not take account of negative co-occurence, and has been found to demonstrate reliable results in other studies using police data (e.g. Canter and Heritage 1990; Canter and Fritzon 1998).

For the single offenders, the measurement of distance was between the offender's home and the location of his/her offence. Where there were multiple offenders, the average distance from each of the offender's home bases to the location of the fire, was taken to provide the overall distance travelled.

A number of the arsons had been coded as involving the offender's own home. However, there were a few cases where the fire was actually set in the garden of the home, or in the stairwell of a flat, but not actually inside it. This distance is not measurable on a map, but was fixed 0.1 km so as not to lose an important distinction.

Results

Overall Distance Travelled

The mean distance travelled from home for all arsonists was 2.06 km. The minimum was 0 km and the maximum was 116.19 km. This shows that, generally speaking, arsonists do not travel very far to commit offences. Other research on criminal mobility has shown that the distances travelled from hone to commit crimes tend to be quite short (Brantingham and Brantingham 1981). White (1932) gave an average of 1.66 miles (2.67 km) for all offenders, a finding which has subsequently been supported (Barker 1989). Other research has found that there are differences in the distances travelled according to the type of crime committed. In a summary of American studies, Harling (1972) showed that for drugs offences the distance was 2.17 miles (3.49 km), for theft it was 1.83 miles (2.94 km), burglary 0.77 miles (1.24 km) and vandalism 0.62 miles (1 km). Rhodes and Conly (1981) additionally found that for robbery the mean was 2.10 miles (3.38 km) and for rape it was 1.15 miles (1.85 km). Again, the similarity between arsonists and rapists is suggested by the fact that the mean of the current sample is closest to that for rape.

The following analysis is broken down into three separate sections to reflect the different factors that are hypothesized to affect distances travelled. The first analysis focuses on specific features of the acts of arson and relates distance travelled to the different forms of arson described by those features. The second examines the hypothesis that distance travelled exists as an empirically observable dimension to arsonists' behaviour, as revealed by Smallest Space Analysis; the third examines associations between distance travelled and characteristics of the offender. These results are compared to research findings on distances travelled by other sorts of offenders to address to issue of whether or not arson is similar to other crimes in this respect.

Distance Travelled Related to Styles of Arson

A recent study by Canter and Fritzon (1998) identified four main styles of arson behaviour. These related to the target of the attack being either a person or an object, and its motivational category being either instrumental or expressive. These distinctions are also reflected in the literature previously outlined (e.g. White 1932; Rhodes and Conly 1981) and therefore this is considered to be a useful framework in terms of modeling arsonist spatial behaviour. The four styles identified by Canter and Fritzon (1998) reflected different underlying psychological processes which Fritzon (1998) subsequently labelled Despair, Display, Damage and Destroy. Despair represents an expressive act directed at a person, usually the arsonist him/herself, in an attempt to draw attention to emotional distress. Display was also expressive and attention-seeking but directed at an object, usually a large public building or institution. Occasionally, the arsonist would attempt to gain recognition for 'discovering' the fire, and these were often serial cases. Damage arsons were targeted at properties where there was some instrumental gain involved, such as concealing another crime or peer acceptance. Finally, Destroy arsons represented targeted and planned attacks against a specific person, sometimes an ex-partner or another known person, and these were also instrumental in the sense that the arsonist wished to gain revenge for some real or imagined wrongdoing. These styles of firesetting were also found to have particular offender characteristics associated with them. Because of the very different psychological nature of these arson types, this model is applied to the current study in order to examine whether individuals display different patterns of spatial behaviour depending on which of the four types of arson they commit.

The overall mean of 2.06 km travelled to commit arson indicates a strong bias towards committing offences close to home. Such a bias would be expected to exist to a lesser or greater degree for each of the four styles of arson outlined above. In other words, the more emotional forms of arson would be expected to be highly constrained by the home base, whereas those cases where a specific instrumental gain was sought would be expected to conform to a more rational targeting pattern.

Method

The 156 cases in the current study were classified according to the Canter and Fritzon (1998) framework in the following way. Each case was given a score consisting of the number of variables present for each of the four behavioural themes, Damage, Display, Destroy and Despair. The variables that make up each of the themes are listed in Appendix A. Because the four themes contained unequal numbers of variables, these raw scores were converted into proportions, i.e. the number of variables present divided by the number of variables possible. Any individual case was then classified as exhibiting predominantly Damage, Display Destroy or Despair crime-scene features if the proportional score for that theme was at least equal to, or greater than the cumulative score for the other three themes. This method of classification has also been used in recent studies by Salfati and Canter (1999) and Fritzon et al. (in press).

For each of the four offence types, the distance travelled from home was broken down into a series of steps and the number of offences occurring at each of those distance steps was plotted on a bar graph. This allows for an examination of the distance decay patterns found for different styles of arson.

Results

Damage

The mean distance travelled for this type of offence was 2.11 km (S.D. = 4.07). The minimum distance from home was 0.08 km, i.e. 8 m, which demonstrates the existence of what is known as a 'buffer zone' effect, in other words an area immediately surrounding an offender's home base where he is unlikely to commit offences (Brantingham and Brantingham 1981). Only two offenders who set the Damage type of fire travelled less than 0.1 km from home. The vast majority, however, did not travel very much further than 1 km which is still a very short distance. This reflects the opportunistic nature of this form of arson. Two Damage arsonists were prepared to travel distances in excess of 15 km, with the greatest distance travelled in this category being 18.5 km (see Figure 7.1).

Display

Figure 7.2 shows that Display arsonists have a very limited pattern of spatial behaviour, in that none travel further than 2 km from home (mean = 0.54 km, S.D. = 0.55 km). It is also interesting to note that even though those individuals who set fire to their own home were not included in this analysis, the graph shows that a substantial proportion of the Display arsonists set fire very close to home. This is revealing of the expressive nature of this form of arson which supports the finding in previous literature that these types of offences involve minimal travelling (e.g. White 1932).

Destroy

This form of arson showed the greatest variety in distances travelled by offenders, with a minimum distance of 0.02 km and a maximum of 116.26 km (mean = 6.24,

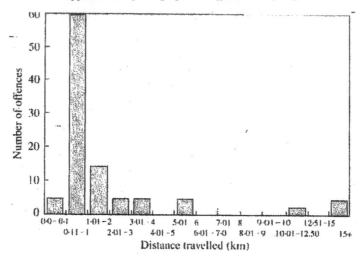

Figure 7.1   Distances travelled to Damage (*n* = 42)

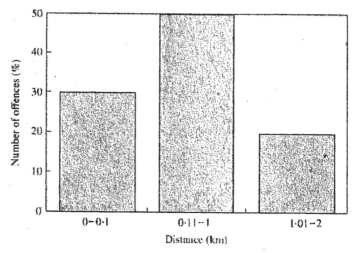

Figure 7.2   Distances travelled to Display (*n* = 10)

S.D. = 18.27) (see Figure 7.3). There is also a noticeable difference between this form of arson and the others in the pattern of 'distance decay', which is the name given to describe the generally observed phenomenon that as the distance from home increases, fewer offenders are found who travel those distances. Although with Destroy arson there is a general trend towards fewer offenders travelling over greater distances, there are various smaller peaks occurring for certain distance ranges. For example, 15 per cent of offenders travelled between 4 and 6 km, which is a larger

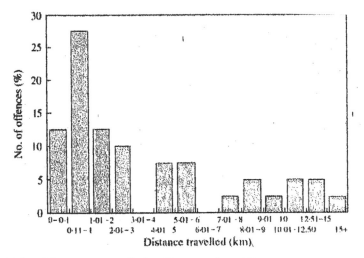

Figure 7.3   Distances travelled to Destroy (*n* = 40)

number than those who travelled between 2 and 4 km (10%). Again, the offenders who set fire to their own home were not included in this analysis, but the graph nevertheless shows that the majority of Destroy arson occurs very close to home. There were a number of cases, for instance, where a partners clothing was taken outside and made into a bonfire in the back garden.

Overall this graph shows that this form of arson is very much dependent on the location of the target; and that offenders will travel the required distance in order to burn the intended property.

Despair

Figure 7.4 shows that the vast majority of these arsonists set fire to their own home or an area immediately surrounding it (mean = 0.56 km, S.D. = 1.69). However, a few individuals did travel further (max. 8.05 km); these were mainly cases where they returned to an ex-partner's residence, or travelled back to their own home from temporary accommodation. This pattern of distance decay, where there is a disproportionately high level of activity close to the home base, is described in the literature as a Pareto function. The Despair graph emphasizes the psychological tie of the home to these individuals, indicating that they are highly constrained in their spatial activity.

Overall, these four graphs support the hypothesis that the instrumentally motivated arsonists would be prepared to travel greater distances from home. None of the expressive cases involved travelling further than 8 km and the vast majority of these fires occurred less than one km from home. The instrumental cases, however, showed a less limited pattern of travelling with some cases involving distances in excess of 100 km.

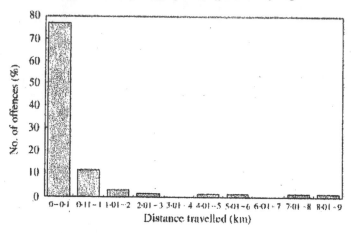

Figure 7.4   Distances travelled in Despair (*n* = 60)

Distance as a Dimension of Criminal Behaviour

The differences found in the distances associated with certain crime-scene variables suggest an interesting possibility, namely that these relationships could be observed empirically as an additional dimension of criminal behaviour, which could be revealed by a procedure known as Smallest Space Analysis. Smallest Space Analysis converts the associations among variables into distances plotted on a geometric map so that groups of thematically similar variables can be represented visually. It is also possible to examine the effects of additional external variables, such as distances travelled or the age of offenders associated with each of the behavioural variables. This is done by calculating the mean value of the external variable in all the cases where the SSA variable was present, and noting this mean value on the SSA plot. It is then possible to examine whether an additional thematic dimension relating to this external variable can be identified on the original SSA plot.

The hypothesized structure of such a representation would be that those variables for whom the mean distance travelled was greatest would exist on a different plane in the geometric space from variables associated with shorter mean distances.

The two-dimensional projection of the SSA of arson actions is shown in Figure 7.5 with the numbers corresponding to the variables listed in Appendix A. Figure 7.6 shows the same diagram but with distance plotted as an external variable, in other words each variable is shown with the mean distance travelled in cases containing that variable. This plot can be partitioned into two halves, as shown in Figure 7.6, such that the lower half contains all the variables associated with travelling less than 1 km, whereas the upper half contains variables associated with travelling farther than 1 km.

Comparing this plot with Figure 7.7 we can see that distance maps onto the thematic similarities among the variables in that almost all of the < 1 km variables

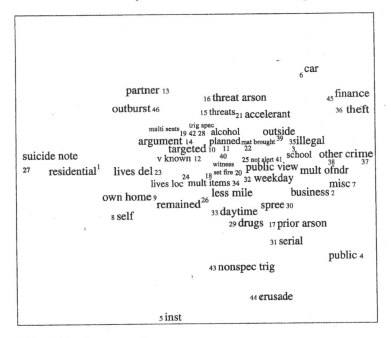

Figure 7.5   SSA of arson actions

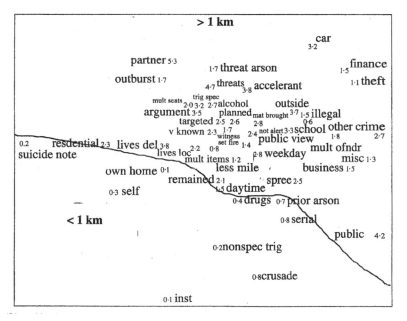

Figure 7.6   SSA partitioned according to distance travelled

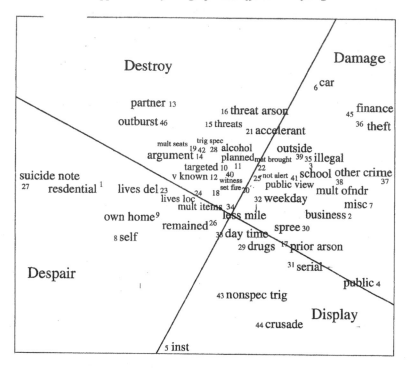

Figure 7.7   SSA partitioned into thematic behavioural regions

are those that describe the Display and Despair forms of arson (Fritzon 1998) which together reflect the Expressive motivation for firesetting (Canter and Fritzon 1998). These fires have a strong emotional component and often involve an element of attention-seeking. Many of these fires occur in the arsonists' *own home,* and therefore involve minimal travelling. The mean distance for this variable is not zero, however, due to a number of offences where the individual had been living elsewhere on a short-term basis (e.g. parent's home) but had returned to their own home to set fire to it.

It is worth noting that *public buildings,* which is one of the variables that is associated with the expressive form of arson, involves travelling greater distances than the other variables in this region. This is probably due to logistical reasons, in other words the individual not being able to locate a public building suitable for burning closer to home. The other two variables that 'belong' in the expressive category but occur farther than 1 km from home are *lives endangered by location* and *lives endangered deliberately.* These are both conceptually associated with arsonists setting fire to their own home or their immediate surroundings in parasuicidal acts. However, they also co-occur with cases involving targeting another victim, often an ex-partner. Since this variable has the highest mean distance (5.3 km), this increases the mean for the associated 'lives endangered' variables.

The other variables that involve travelling distances of over 1 km all indicate an instrumental motive for the offender's actions. For example, *partner argument, threats, accelerant,* and *specific trigger* are all reflective of the revenge motive for arson which serves a clear externally observable function. Similarly *other crime* and *car* indicate that the firesetting occurs as part of other criminal (instrumental) activity. The increased distance from home is particularly pronounced for the variables *public view* and *outside* suggesting a rational explanation, namely that the likelihood of being caught setting fires outdoors is already greatly increased, without adding the possibility of being recognized close to home. Arsonists might therefore be expected not to set fires outdoors (and especially in public view) within a certain range of their local neighbourhood.

These results indicate that particular sorts of arson are associated with different patterns of spatial behaviour, namely that expressive crimes occur close to home than instrumental ones. A *t*-test on the aggregate means for the expressive (0.40 km) and instrumental (2.98 km) variables showed that the difference was statistically significant ($F = 5.15, p < 0.05$) whereas a one-way ANOVA on the means for each of the four separate behavioural types was not significant ($F (3135) = 1.41, p = 0.24$). It seems, therefore, that it is the overall function of the arson that determines distance travelled rather than the specific way that it is carried out. The fact that this dimension of criminal behaviour can be demonstrated empirically and represented visually, is an important finding, with both theoretical and practical implications. These will be discussed in the conclusions.

Having demonstrated that the underlying meaning of an arson offence has an impact on the distance travelled by the offender, it is interesting to examine whether this variable is also affected by aspects of the offender's personal characteristics. Previous research on other crime types has shown, for example, that age and gender have an impact on distances travelled to commit crimes. With arson, an alternative possibility is that this is an offence for which the most significant influence on offender spatial behaviour is determined by the function of the act irrespective of other personal circumstances. Therefore, the following analysis examines associations between offender characteristics and distances travelled.

Distance Travelled Related to Characteristics of Offender

In order to discover whether the presence or absence of certain background characteristics would affect the distances travelled by those arsonists, *t*-tests were calculated on the differences between the mean distances travelled when an offender had a particular characteristic, and the mean distance travelled when he/she did not. Table 7.1 shows these results. The variables are grouped according to Canter and Fritzon's (1998) four distinct offender types, namely Failed Relationship, Psychiatric History, Young Offender, and Repeat Arsonist.

The only significant differences found were in relation to variables whose presence increased the mean distance travelled by an arsonist. These were: age

Table 7.1   Differences in distance travelled related to offender characteristics

Theme	Characteristic (n)	Mean d if present (S.D.)		Mean d if absent (S.D.)		F
Delinquent	No cro (69)	2.93	(14.16)	1.45	(3.02)	3.78
	Caution (12)	2.16	(4.82)	2.05	(9.62)	0.00
	Sch trouble (53)	1.59	(3.80)	2.28	(11.02)	0.60
	Age (<161) (37)	1.48	(4.04)	2.22	(10.38)	0.41
	Pupil (34)	1.41	(4.15)	2.22	(10.27)	0.41
	Social svcs (39)	1.37	(3.95)	2.27	(10.46)	0.54
	Parents (58)	1.12	(2.43)	2.55	(11.41)	3.04
Failed relationship	Child (29)	5.39	(21.57)	1.36	(2.94)	16.49***
	Separated (35)	4.95	(19.57)	1.30	(3.05)	11.16***
	Partner (37)	4.65	(19.16)	1.33	(2.89)	12.62***
	Age (26–35) (43)	3.75	(17.74)	1.48	(3.14)	7.43**
	Alcoholism (46)	3.49	(17.16)	1.52	(3.19)	6.14*
	Alone (59)	3.27	(15.13)	1.40	(3.33)	3.96*
	Age (36–45 (16))	1.37	(3.29)	2.13	(9.78)	0.17
	Manual (18)	1.24	(1.20)	2.16	(9.89)	0.93
	High quals (30)	1.15	(1.48)	2.26	(10.29)	1.36
Repeat arsonist	Inst (12)	1.72	(5.29)	2.08	(9.60)	0.00
	AWOL (13)	1.62	(4.601	2.09	(9.66)	0.04
	Pers dis. (27)	1.16	(3.72)	2.23	(10.08)	0.47
	False alarm (12)	0.87	(2.00)	2.15	(9.69)	0.48
	Prior arson (44)	0.85	(1.62)	2.49	(10.82)	2.47
Psychiartric	Psychosis (15)	9.05	(29.77)	1.37	(3.03)	34.86***
	Female (27)	4.82	(22.29)	1.53	(3.21)	12.60***
	Depression (28)	4.55	(21.91)	1.56	(3.23)	11.65***
	Age (46+) (11)	0.20	(0.39)	2.19	(9.66)	0.95
	Suicide (29)	0.57	(1.53)	2.37	(10.24)	1.85
Central	Left sch < 16 (77)	2.88	(13.40)	1.36	(3.10)	3.5
	Unemployed (101)	2.59	(11.79)	1.27	(3.12)	2.47
	White (156)	2.06	(9.61)	1.99	(5.26)	0.001
	Age (17–25) (59)	1.73	(2.79)	2.24	(11.45)	1.15

*$p = 0.05$, **$p = 001$, ***$p = 0.001$.

26–35, alcoholism, alone, child, depression, female, partner, psychosis, left school before the age of 16, and separated. These are mainly characteristics associated with the Failed Relationship sub-group of arsonists. Canter and Fritzon (1998) showed that these individuals tend to set Destroy fires which the previous analysis found to involve travelling greater distances.

In relation to the Psychiatric History arsonists, a number of slightly surprising findings emerged. These were that female, depressed and psychotic offenders travel longer distances to set fires. The first of these results contradicts research on distances travelled by female offenders generally (e.g. Rengert 1975). However, the number of females in the current sample was relatively small and the results may have been skewed by the fact that the person who travelled the farthest distance for the whole sample (116.19 km) was female. Also surprising was the fact that persons with mental problems (psychosis and depression) travelled longer distances from home. Again, the above individual also had these diagnoses, and when removed from the analysis, the average distance travelled by arsonists with these characteristics decreased to 0.53 km for females, 1.40 km for psychosis and 0.40 km for depression.

Finally, these results supported the findings of previous research that older offenders tend to travel further than younger ones. This was true for this sample of arsonists to the extent that those in the age band 26–35 travelled the farthest distance, although as age increased beyond this the distances travelled became shorter again. This is probably due to the findings by Canter and Fritzon (1998) that older offenders tend to commit the Despair and Display forms of arson, both of which involve minimal travelling.

A separate analysis was conducted on criminal history variables to see whether previous convictions for particular offences were associated with travelling further or shorter distances to set fires.

Table 7.2 shows the results of the *t*-tests on the criminal history variables. These are organized into the Expressive/Instrumental dichotomy used by previous research (e.g. Cornell et al. 1996; Canter and Fritzon 1998).

Table 7.2 shows that having a previous conviction for certain offences affects the distances travelled to commit a subsequent arson. The results for expressive and instrumental offences were mixed, although on the whole offenders with instrumental offences travelled further than those who had committed expressive crimes (1.91 km compared to 1.57 km). This result accords with previous research findings (e.g. White 1932).

Within the instrumental category, those offences associated with travelling the largest distances were robbery, traffic and theft of a car (Taking Without Owner's Consent). People who commit traffic offences and steal cars will be used to the high level of spatial mobility associated with driving a car. The greatest distances were associated with having a previous conviction for robbery. At the more sophisticated end of the range of robbery offences, the use of getaway cars and selecting targets for maximum gain would be expected to be associated with travelling large distances, but even at the level of street robbery, an offender may want to avoid committing

Table 7.2   **Differences in distance travelled related to previous convictions**

Theme	Offence type (n)	Mean d if present (S.D.)		Mean d if absent (S.D.)		F
Instrumental	Robbery (6)	5.03	(7.74)	1.06	(2.38)	37.07**
	Traffic (14)	2.69	(4.79)	1.07	(2.67)	11.39**
	Twoc (18)	1.94	(4.78)	1.17	(2.56)	4.29*
	Theft (57)	1.62	(3.43)	0.78	(2.42)	2.66
	Burglary (39)	1.59	(3.19)	1.13	(3.11)	0.67
	Theft fr. car (13)	1.58	(3.29)	1.29	(3.13)	0.04
	Police/courts (16)	1.30	(3.22)	1.34	(3.14)	0.00
	Deception (14)	0.53	(0.99)	1.49	(3.38)	3.08
	MEAN (i)	1.91				
Expressive	Drugs (12)	3.58	(5.52)	0.97	(2.43)	22.79**
	Crim dam (41)	1.65	(3.70)	1.05	(2.53)	1.54
	Assault (34)	1.74	(3.38)	1.07	(2.97)	2.20
	Weapon (17)	1.37	(3.03)	1.33	(3.18)	0.00
	Publ disrdr (26)	0.92	(2.48)	1.52	(3.39)	1.48
	Drunk (14)	0.19	(0.42)	1.56	(3.38)	5.96*
	MEAN (e)	1.57				
	Arson (16)	0.46	(0.92)	1.54	(3.42)	4.15*
	Prison (26)	1.45	(2.78)	2.17	(10.11)	0.49

$*p = 0.05$; $**p = 0.01$.

these offences close to home for fear of recognition. This might explain, therefore, why arsonists with robbery convictions travel further than those without.

On the other hand, it was found that arsonists who had previously committed offences involving deception travelled shorter distances to set fire. This is probably due the association identified by Fritzon (1998) between this offence history and the Despair form of arson which tended to occur very close to home.

The category of offences which are associated with travelling shorter distances are mainly expressive crimes which do not require a high level of criminal sophistication.

Having a prior conviction for arson is associated with the Display form of arson which was one of the categories that was committed closest to home. The shorter distances travelled by arsonists with alcohol related convictions was somewhat surprising given that the variable alcoholism had the opposite association. As stated in Appendix B, one of the reasons for coding an offender as alcoholic was if he had a number of convictions involving alcohol. However, there were a substantial number who were also described by their partners in the police interview as having a drinking problem, which was a second criteria for coding them as alcoholics. These offenders were also the ones who committed the Destroy form of arson, and were not necessarily the same ones who had convictions for alcohol-related offences. The possibility of two separate groups of individuals with different alcohol-related backgrounds may explain the differences found in the distances travelled by arsonists depending on whether they were described by their partners as alcoholics or had drinking related convictions.

Within the expressive category, however, it was found that people with drugs convictions travelled further. This also supports the finding by Haring (1972) who found that greater distances were travelled in relation to drugs offences.

These results support the value of the distinctions captured in the Canter and Fritzon (1998) and Fritzon (1998) models of both actions and characteristics. It has been shown that each of the four themes of arson and arsonist carried implications for the distances typically travelled by the individuals concerned. The most important factor, however, seems to be the nature of the fires themselves, as most of the results relating to the way that offender features affect distance travelled were best explained by reference to the style of firesetting associated with those background characteristics.

Conclusions

This chapter has tested a number of hypotheses about the relationships between the spatial behaviour of single and serial arsonists and aspects of the Canter and Fritzon (1998) and Fritzon (1998) '4D' model of arson. These relationships support previous research findings, for example in relation to expressive crimes occurring closer to home than instrumental. It was also found that arsonists travel further to target people than to set fire to objects.

In terms of the 4D model it was found that Display and Despair forms of arson both occur very close to home, whereas Damage and Destroy involve the offender travelling slightly further. For example, in relation to Damage, offences which occurred outside were further from home, probably due to concerns about recognition. The distances associated with committing the Destroy form of arson were found to be very much dependent on the location of the victim. This has parallels with the spatial behaviour of rapists, who are also concerned with target selection.

These findings also enrich our understanding of the meaning underlying arson behaviour: Despair and Display arsons are both expressive and as such are concerned with internal processes. This does not require the arsonist to travel very far in order to fulfil the function of setting fires. The Damage form of arson can be seen as fundamentally opportunistic and so the distance travelled relates to the location at which the environmental opportunity for firesetting is found. Generally, the individuals who commit this form of arson have limited resources and so will not travel very far from home. In some cases, however, particularly where the arson is associated with joy-riding, the use of a car will mean that the arson can occur further from home. Finally, the Destroy form of arson involves a reaction to an external source of frustration and so the distance travelled will depend on the location of this source.

The results of this study have particularly important implications for police investigations of arsons in that they can potentially be used to prioritize suspects based on where they live in relation to the crime and its features. Also the study further enriches our understanding of how the psychological processes underlying the motivation for setting a fire relate to the distances that individuals are prepared to travel. The supports previous research indicating that crimes motivated by internal processes tend to involve travelling shorter distances than crimes where the specific external target is important.

Acknowledgements

I would like to thank Professor David Canter for his constructive comments in the preparation and revision of this manuscript.

References

Amir, M. (1971). *Patterns in Forcible Rape.* Chicago: University of Chicago Press.
Baldwin, J. and Bottoms, A.E. (1976). *The Urban Criminal.* Tavistock Publications.
Barker, M. (1989). Criminal Activity and Home Range: A study of the spatial offence patterns of burglars. University of Surrey, M.Sc. dissertation (unpublished).
Bennett, W.D., Merlo, A.V. and Leiker, K.K. (1987). Geographical patterns of incendiary and accidental fires in Springfield, Massachusetts, 1980–1984. *Journal of Quantitative Criminology*, 3(1), 47–64.
Brady, J. (1983). Arson, urban economy and organised crime: The case of Boston. *Social Problems*, 31(1), 1–27.
Brantingham, P.J. and Brantingham, P.L. (eds). (1981). *Environmental Criminology.* Beverly Hills: Sage.
Canter, D. and Fritzon, K. (1998) Differentiating Arsonists: A Model of Firesetting Actions and Characteristics. *Legal and Criminological Psychology*, 3, 73–96.
Canter, D. and Heritage, R. (1990). A multivariate model of sexual offence behaviour: developments in 'offender profiling' I. *The Journal of Forensic Psychiatry*, 1(2), 185–212.
Capone, D.L. and Nichols, W. (1975). Crime and distance: An analysis of offender behaviour in space. *Proceedings of the Association of American Geographers,* pp. 45–49.
Cornell, D.G., Warren, J., Hawk, G., Stafford, E., Oram, G. and Pine, D. (1996). Psychopathy in instrumental and reactive violent offenders. *Journal of Consulting anal Clinical Psychology*, 64(4), 783–790.

Fannin, L.F. and Clinnard, M.B. (1965). Differences in the conception of self as a male among lower and middle class delinquents. *Social Problems*, 12, 205–214.

Fritzon, K., Canter, D. and Wilton, Z. (in press). The application of an action systems model to destructive behaviour: The examples of Arson and Terrorism. *Behavioral Sciences and the Law*.

Fritzon, K. (1998). Differentiating arson: An action systems model of malicious firesetting. Unpublished Ph.D. dissertation, University of Liverpool.

Gabor, T. and Gottheil, E. (1984). Offender characteristics and spatial mobility: An empirical study and some policy implications. *Canadian Journal of Criminology*, 26, 267–281.

Harling, L.L. (Ed.) (1972). Summary report of spatial studies of juvenile delinquency in Phoenix, Arizona. The geography department of Arizona State University In D. Herbert, (ed.), *The Geography of Urban Crime*. Longman.

Harris, G.T. and Rice, M.E. (1996). A typology of mentally disordered firesetters. *Journal of Interpersonal Violence*, 11(3), 351–363.

Kocsis, R.N. and Irwin, H.J. (1997). An analysis of spatial patterns in serial rape, arson and burglary: The utility of the Circle Theory of environmental range for psychological profiling. *Psychiatry, Psychology anal Law*, 4(2), 195–206.

Le Beau, J.L. (1987). The journey to rape: Geographic distance and the rapist's method of approaching the victim. *Journal of Police Science and Administration*, 15, 129–161.

Nichols, W.W. Jr. (1980). Mental maps, social characteristics and criminal mobility. In D.E. Georges-Abeyie and K.D. Harries, (eds), *Crime: A Spatial Perspective*. Columbia University Press.

Pettiway, L.E. (1987). Arson for revenge: The role of environmental situation, age, sex and race. *Journal of Quantitative Criminology*, 3(2), 169–184.

Rengert, G.F (1975). Some effects of being female on criminal spatial behaviour. *The Pennsylvania Geographer*, 13(2).

Rengert, G.F. and Wasilchick, J. (1985). *Suburban Burglary:* Springfield, IL: Charles C. Thomas.

Repetto, T.A. (1974). *Residential Crime*. Cambridge, MA: Ballinger.

Rhodes, W.M. and Conly, C. (1981). Crime and mobility: An empirical study. In P.J. Brantingham and P.L. Brantingham, (eds), *Environmental Criminology*. Beverly Hills, CA: Sage.

Salfati, C.G. and Canter, D.V. (1999). Differentiating stranger murders: Profiling offender characteristics from behavioural styles. *Behavioural Sciences and the Law*, 17, 391–406.

Stephenson, L.K. (1974). Spatial dispersion of intra-urban juvenile delinquency. *Journal of Geography*, 73, 20–26.

Shaw, K.T. and Gifford, R. (1994). Residents' and burglars' assessment of risk from defensible space cues. *Journal of Environmental Psychology*, 14, 177–194.

White, R.C. (1932). The relation of felonies to environmental factors in Indianapolis. *Social Forces*, 10, 459–467.

Appendix A

Offence variables and their classification according to Canter and Fritzon (1998) and Fritzon (1998).

Damage

School: a fire which occurs in any area of an educational establishment would be coded as school. For example, if fire is set to waste bins outside the school, this would be coded as both miscellaneous and school.

Car/vehicle: any type of vehicle which is used for transportation of goods or people, is coded as car/ vehicle, including bicycles and boats.

Misc. /Uninhabited/Derelict property: misc. applies to items burned which were not inside a property; for example a rubbish bin or park bench. However, anything which is burned inside a property will be coded as that property, e.g. a rubbish bin inside a school is coded as school. Uninhabited or derelict properties can be both commercial and residential properties which are currently not in use.

Material brought: anything which the offender brought for the specific purpose of starting or accelerating the fire would be coded as this. It's important that the material is something which he would not normally be carrying, e.g. matches or a cigarette lighter is ambiguous particularly if the individual is a smoker.

Spree: if the offender sets more than one fire with a gap of no more than 24 hours then this is coded as spree firesetting.

Forced/illegal entry: if the offender was required to make some effort to obtain entry to the fired property, then this would be coded as forced/illegal entry. Also, if the offender could be said to be trespassing, e.g. in a hay barn which has open access, this variable would be coded as present.

Theft from premises: this variable would be coded if any property is taken either before or after the firesetting.

Other crimes: If the firesetting occurs in conjunction with any other offence, e.g. vandalism, burglary, theft of a car.

More than one offender: the other individual need not be instrumental in the actual setting of the fire, e.g. they could be acting as a look-out. If another person is present during the firesetting and they do not actually try to stop the offender then they arc counted as a co-offender.

Outside: if the fired object is itself outside, or the individual sets fire to a house by throwing a fire bomb or inserting lighted material through the letter box then this is coded as being outside.

Public View: if the firesetting occurs in a place and time where the offender could potentially be seen by passers-by, then this is coded as being in public view. If the firesetting occurs at a time where there are unlikely to be other people around, but in a place which usually has CCTV, e.g. a car park, then this would also he coded as public view.

Finance: this refers to the offender's belief that he/she will financially or otherwise benefit directly from the fire. The benefit need not be in terms of monetary gain, e.g. persons in council housing who wish to be moved would be coded as 'financial'. This variable does not, however, refer to theft of property during the arson, as the financial gain has to come as a result of the arson, rather than being incidental to it.

Destroy

Targeted property: if there is any evidence to suggest that a specific property was burned for a particular reason, then this is coded as targeted. In other words it must be apparent or readily inferred that the offender(s) would not have set fire to anything other than that object. For example, if the offender travelled any great distance to the target, by-passing other buildings with similar properties. Also, if the victim was known, and the fire followed a dispute, then it can be inferred that the victim was targeted.

Planned: for example, if materials were brought to the scene, like petrol or matches, then this would suggest planning. Also if the individual made an effort to avoid detection, e.g. wearing gloves when handling petrol containers.

Victim (ex-) partner: this variable would also be coded as present if the offender fires property belonging to someone close to his/her (ex-) partner, e.g. a family member or new partner. The rationale for this is that person would not have been targeted were if not for their association with the (ex-) partner. Prior violence/argument with victim: this refers to any dispute, preferably heated, occurring within a reasonable time-frame (usually not more than a month) of the arson.

Prior threats toward victim: this includes verbal or physical threats of an overt or implicit nature.

Prior threat of arson: if the offender has made any threatening remarks with reference to fires, even in an abstract sense such as, 'I once knew someone whose house burned down', or 'be careful you don't leave matches lying around; someone might get hold of them', then these count as threats of arson.

Accelerant used: again, there is usually mention of an accelerant in the fire investigator's report.

Alcohol use: the offender may not state that he has consumed alcohol, but if a police officer or witness mentions that the offender appeared to be drunk or smelled of alcohol then this is coded.

Witness: if the firesetting takes place in front of another person who is not a willing participant, i.e. explicitly or implicitly does not condone the act, then he/she is coded as a witness. It is important that the offender knows that the other person is present, therefore a passerby who happens to see the firesetting would not be coded as a witness.

Trigger specific to victim: if the firesetting occurs immediately following, or within a reasonable time period of an argument or other, usually emotional trigger, and is targeted at a specific person or property, then that is a victim-specific trigger.

Outburst: if the fire contains multiple seats and/or multiple items and takes place: in a 'frenzied' attack, e.g. smashing up the targeted property.

Despair

Residential: this refers to a property which at the time of the fire was being used for residential purposes. If the property was derelict or uninhabited (as opposed to simply unoccupied) at the time, then it would not be coded as residential. An exception to this would be an uninhabited flat contained within a block of flats some of which were inhabited. Also a property which was known to contain 'squatters' would be classified as residential.

Self: if an individual starts a fire in their own home, and then makes no attempt to leave or alert anyone, then this is coded as self.

Own Home: this is coded in addition to residential and/or self.

Multiple items fired: this refers to the objects which have actually ended up on fire, rather than secondary objects used to start that fire. In other words, if multiple waste bins or skips are burned then this variable would be coded as present, but if multiple bits of newspaper are used to set fire to one waste bin, then this variable would not be coded.

Multiple seats of fire: this refers to initial ignition points of the item(s) fired. For example, if a house is burned by pouring petrol in one room and holding a match to a curtain in another room, then the fire would be coded as having multiple seats. The number of seats of a fire are usually stated in the investigating fire officer's report.

Lives endangered deliberately: if the offender knew that the property was occupied at the time of the fire and made no attempt to alert the occupants, then this is coded.

Lives endangered by location: a fire in any residential property, or building attached to a residence which is not completely detached, has the potential to endanger lives.

Suicide note: this is coded not only in the presence of an actual suicide note, but if the offender has alerted any one prior to the fire of their intention or wish to commit suicide.

Remained at/returned to scene: this is where the offender either remains at the scene, or returns while the fire is still burning, or returns to the same property to set another fire.

Display

Business: the property is currently in use as business premises. A disused unit on an industrial estate would not be coded as business. Other exceptions include allotments and pigeon lofts which would be coded as uninhabited.

Public building: this includes any type of building to which the public have access, e.g. library, church, town hall, law courts, police station, etc.

Hospital/Institution: if the fire is set on any part of the institution's grounds then it is coded as institution.

Prior arson: this is coded if the offender has set any fires prior to the current offence. Although this variable is duplicated in the *Offender variable* list, it is included here in order to identify which other actions are associated with prior arson.

Drug use: this refers to any recreational, i.e. nonprescription drug, including solvents.

Serial: if the offender sets more than one fire with a gap of more than 24 hours then this is coded as serial firesetting. However, if the gap is a matter of years rather than weeks or months then this would not be serial, but the offender would be coded as having prior arson in his history.

Nonspecific trigger: if the firesetting occurs immediately following, or within a reasonable time period of an argument or other, usually emotional trigger, and there is no obvious targeting of a specific person or property, then that is a nonspecific trigger.

Crusade: this is coded if the firesetting appears to be attention or recognition seeking, e.g. if the offender him/herself 'discovers' the fire, or exaggerates injuries sustained.

Additional variables (not specifically associated with one of the four styles)

Victim known: this generally goes along with targeting and includes institutions or governing bodies that the offender has been involved with, e.g. school he/she has attended or council-owned properly if he/she is a council tenant.

Set fire: if the offender has actually placed a burning object (e.g. match or lighted piece of paper) to the property he wants to fire, then this is a set fire. If the burning object has been thrown, e.g. a petrol bomb, or burning pieces of paper have been dropped onto an object from above, then this is not coded as a set fire.

Did not alert anyone: if the offender left the scene of the fire without subsequently alerting either the fire brigade or any other person, then this variable is coded.

Weekday: a weekday is classified as being between 0001 h on a Monday and 16 59 h on a Friday.

Daytime: if the offence occurs during daylight hours, this is classified as daytime. Note that this will depend on the time of year: e.g. 21 00 h in July would be daytime whereas in November it would not.

Appendix B

Offender Variables

(1)   No CRO: the offender has no previous convictions of any kind.
(2)   Previous arson: this is the same variable as in the *Offence variables* list.
(3)   False alarm calls: this may be known to the emergency services either because they have traced the offender's number, or because he/she has confessed to making false alarm calls.
(4)   Female.
(5)   Partner.
(6)   Child.
(7)   Recently separated/divorced: under ordinary circumstances, this variable would be coded if the separation has occurred not more than 6 months prior to the arson attack. If, however, circumstances make it clear that the offender still feels acrimony towards the partner or his/her new partner, then this variable would be coded.
(8)   Institution: this is coded if the offender is living in any kind of institution, e.g. hospital or juvenile detention centre.
(9)   Living with parents: the offender is living in the care of his/her parents or legal guardians.
(10) School pupil: if the offender is still of school age (i.e. 16 or under) then this is coded even if he/she is not actually attending a school.
(11) Unemployed: this is only coded if the offender is chronically unemployed. If the offender was employed until just before the arson, or has a history of employment interspersed with short periods of unemployment, then the nature of the main type of employment is coded.
(12) Manual work: either skilled or unskilled manual work, e.g. plumber, labourer, factory worker.
(13) HiQuals: this is coded if the offender has obtained secondary or tertiary qualifications of any kind.
(14) White.
(15) Depression: this is coded if the offender has come to the attention of psychiatric services and been diagnosed as suffering from depression, or if

he/she has attempted or threatened self-harm behaviour. This may also be coded if the offender states that he/she feels depressed or if any person known to the offender has remarked that they seem to be depressed.

(16) Psychosis: again this is coded if the offender has received a psychiatric diagnosis of psychosis. This is also coded if he/she acts in an extremely bizarre way before, during or after the firesetting offence.

(17) Personality disorder: this is coded if the offender appears to be slightly 'abnormal' in any way, for example, has set a large number of fires previously. Juvenile firesetters who have a conduct disorder are also given the generic classification of personality disordered.

(18) Psychiatric treatment: if the offender has ever been in the care of psychiatric services, either as a voluntary or day-care patient, then this is coded.

(19) Alcoholism: this is coded if the offender appears to have a significant alcohol problem, for example if he/she has (had) relationship difficulties because of alcohol, or if he/she has a number of alcohol-related convictions.

(20) Suicide: this is coded if the offender has any history of threatened or actual self-harm.

(21) Caution only: if the offender has come to the attention of police, but not been formally charged with any offence, then this is coded as Caution Only.

(22) School trouble: this is coded if there is any history of behavioural or academic problems at school.

(23) School before 16: if the offender left school before the age of 16.

(24) Social services: if the offender, usually a juvenile, has come to attention of social services, e.g. if they have been taken away from their parents to a juvenile home.

(25) AWOL: at the time of setting the fire, the offender was supposed to be somewhere else, e.g. at school or at work.

Criminal History Variables

(1) Theft: this includes all categories of theft (e.g. theft from a person, shoplifting and during the course of a burglary) except for theft from a car which was coded separately.

(2) Burglary: residential and nonresidential.

(3) TWOC: this includes attempted and actual theft of a car.

(4) Theft from car: this was coded if an offender broke or attempted to break into a car, whether or not any property was actually stolen.

(5) Drugs: this includes convictions for both possession and supply of all categories of illegal drugs.

(6) Criminal damage: this includes all forms of damage to property, except arson which was coded separately.

(7) Assault: any form of assault including common assault, actually bodily harm and grevious bodily harm, as well as assaulting a police officer.

(8)   Public disorder: offences involving an element of violence were combined (e.g. breach of the peace, threatening behaviour).

(9)   Arson.

(10)   Traffic: this includes several traffic violations, e.g. driving while disqualified, no insurance and failing to display tax disc.

(11)   Robbery.

(12)   Weapon: this includes possession and use of an offensive weapon.

(13)   Drunk: this category combines a number of offences, such as found drunk, drunk and disorderly and urinating in a public place.

(14)   Deception: various forms of deception (e.g. obtaining pecuniary advantage by deception and forgery) were combined.

(15)   Police/courts: a number of offences relating to the judicial process, such as failure to appear and nonpayment of fine were subsumed under this category.

Chapter 8

The Journey to Rape: Geographic Distance and the Rapist's Method of Approaching the Victim

James L. LeBeau

Menachem Amir's now classic work, *Patterns in Forcible Rape*, has served as the springboard for many subsequent works on the topic. Amir's labors included extensive and detailed observations, descriptions, and classifications of many facets associated with the offense and its participants. However, three concepts received limited or no attention in his essay. Namely, the method of approach or how does the offender approach his victim; the number of offenses committed by the same offender before he is apprehended by the police; and the distance traveled by the offender from his residence to the location where he first encounters his victim. It is this travel behavior or the journey to rape that is the focus of this article. Moreover, its purpose is to demonstrate how the journey to rape varies with the offender's method of approach and the number of reported rapes committed by the same offender.

Theoretical Concepts

The Method of Approach

Amir, utilizing Philadelphia police file data for the years 1958 and 1960, offers a rather involved discussion of the method of operation of the rapist. One of the concepts Amir attributes to being part of the method of operation is the number of scenes in an incident. A rape incident, according to Amir, can be composed of three separate and distinct scenes, locations, or sites: (1) the initial meeting place; (2) the crime scene; and (3) the after scene (Amir 1971, p. 137). The initial meeting place is essentially the location where the victim meets the offender. The crime scene is the location where the actual rape takes place while the after scene is the location where the offender leaves the victim. A rape can be very immobile (that is, where the initial meeting place fulfils the function of all three scenes), or a rape can be very mobile (that is, where all scenes are separate and distinct locations). Amir suggests that a rapist will meet his victim at a particular type of site and then assess whether he needs to move the victim to a location more conducive to the commission of the crime (1971, p. 38). While Amir developed this elaborate scene typology, he did not measure the geographic distances among and between the scenes.

Other characteristics of the rape discussed within the context of the method of operation by Amir include the degree of planning by the offender; types of locations for the initial meeting place and crime and after scene; types of force used by the offender; and the victim's behavior and response. Yet, Amir does not indicate how the offender approached his prey in the first place. This is unfortunate because in the field of criminal investigation, the offender's method of approach reflects a substantial portion of the information which constitutes his method of operation (Hazelwood 1983).

How the offender obtains access to the victim is the essence of the method of approach. From the literature emerges two different approaches – the blitz or sudden attack rape and the confidence rape (Burgess and Holmstrom 1974; Hazelwood 1983; Schwendinger and Schwendinger 1983). "The blitz rape occurs 'out of the blue' and without prior interaction between assailant and victim" (Burgess and Holmstrom 1974, p. 4). While a majority of the blitz rapists are strangers to their victims, the principal distinguishing characteristic of this approach is that the offender immediately threatens or employs force to neutralize and subdue his victim (Schwendinger and Schwendinger 1983). Typical blitz rapes are those where the offender breaks into the residence of the victim as well as those involving the surprise attack outdoors. Finally, although she does not refer to blitz rapes, Williams asserts that stranger rapes involving blitz-like approaches constitute the classic rape and are more likely to be reported by the victim (1984, pp. 462–463).

At the other extreme is the approach of the confidence rapist. The actual sexual assault is preceded by a range of interaction between the victim and offender (Burgess and Holmstrom 1974; Hazelwood 1983; Schwendinger and Schwendinger 1983). The assault in the confidence rape represents a violation of trust on the part of the offender. The method of how the rapist gains access to the victim dictates two distinct variations of confidence rape (Burgess and Holmstrom 1974).

The first form of confidence rape is where the victim and offender know each other and a relationship exists between the two. The assailant uses the relationship to gain access to the victim and "then deceives the person by not honoring the bounds of that relationship" (Burgess and Holmstrom 1974, p. 8).

Capturing the victim is the second form of confidence rape abstracted by Burgess and Holmstrom (1974). "In this style, there is an effort to strike up a conversation with the victim and to use verbal means to capture her rather than physical force" (Burgess and Holmstrom 1974, p. 6). Rapes where the offender meets the victim in a bar or at a party, as well as those where the victim is hitchhiking or accepts a ride from the offender, are examples of this approach (Nelson and Amir 1977). Amir reveals that third parties looking for a cause for rapes evolving from confidence methods will often blame the victim for the assault or imply that the victim precipitated the event (Amir 1971, p. 261).

Burglary rape has received two designations in the literature. While this method qualifies as a blitz rape, it also has been labeled a felony rape. In other words, the sexual assault might constitute a by-product of another felonious act and thus may have been an unplanned event (Schwendinger and Schwendinger 1983, p. 46). Still, Amir advises that burglary rape depicts a situation where "the rape is not conceived of as emanating from the felony" (1971, p. 178), and each offense is dealt with separately.

This brief review of the method of approach indicates that rape does not emanate from a single type of interaction between the victim and offender. The commission of property offenses such as illegal entry of residence can result in rape; an innocuous meeting between two individuals in a bar, at a party, or in a park can result in rape; and, as might be expected by some the rapist can leap out from behind a bush or parked car and attack an unsuspecting victim. Rape, therefore, can be the very tragic result of a host of different encounters or victim-offender interactions.

The Number

Most law enforcement practitioners have long known that it is seldom appropriate to assume a one-to-one correspondence between the number of offenders and number of offenses. The finding that a minority of delinquents in a birth cohort committed a majority of the reported offenses (Wolfgang, Figlio, and Sellin 1972) is substantial evidence that an offender can commit more than one offense. In the rape literature, number routinely refers to the number of offenders in an incident. Thus, from Amir's writings, one becomes accustomed to thinking of rapes as being perpetrated by one, two (pair), or multiple offenders (Amir 1971, p. 182). However, recidivists and career or serious criminals have also received some consideration in the literature. Recently, there has been considerable attention paid to serial murderers, individuals who commit two or more murders before they are apprehended by the police. However, the literature is rather barren when it comes to discussing the serial rapist or the number of rapes committed by the same person before he is apprehended by the police (Groth, Longo, and McFadin 1982; Ressler, Burgess, and Douglas 1983).

The effects of the serial offender on the assumptions and generalizations about crime can be considerable. For example, LeBeau (1984, 1985) demonstrates how the presence of serial offenders exhibits pronounced numerical, geographical, and ecological variations from year-to-year as well as over- and underestimates the racial representation of offenders. Finally, if a number of illegal-entry-of-residence rapes are committed by the same person, one has to seriously question the assumption that the sexual assaults are unplanned and a mere by-product of a burglary.

The Distance

Police crime analysts, environmental criminologists, and geographers have paid increased attention to the journey to crime statistic or, simply, the distance traveled by the offender from his residence to the location of the crime. This measure, for quite some time, was largely descriptive and not the integral portion for models leading to testable hypotheses (Rhodes and Conly 1981). However, in a relatively short period, the journey to crime statistic has evolved from being a description, to an analogy with the journey to work or shop statistic (Harries 1980), to being a central concept in a model developed by the Brantinghams (1981) for explaining a criminal's search area.

A fairly consistent finding by scholars using the journey to crime statistic is that offenders travel longer distances to commit crimes against property when compared to the distances traversed by those who commit crimes against people (White 1932; Curtis 1974; Pyle 1974; Repetto 1974). There have been exceptions to this finding though. Turner (1969) did not find any significant differences based on offense type and the distances between the offender's residence and crime location for 1960 Philadelphia data. Recently, Pettiway (1982) found that black robbers and not burglars traveled longer distances to their crime sites, which is a complete reversal of what the previous literature indicated.

Within specific types of crime, scholars have examined trip differences according to the offender's age (Nichols 1980; Phillips 1980; Baldwin and Bottoms 1976); sex (Rengert 1975); and race (Pettiway 1982; Nichols 1980). However, Capone and Nichols (1975, 1976) have taken a very novel approach in assessing the distances traveled by robbers. The authors hypthesized (1975, p. 46):

1. The frequency of robbery trips declines as distance from the residence of the offender increases.
2. There is significant difference in the lengths of armed and strong-arm robbery trips with armed trips having a greater mean distance.
3. There is significant variation in the mean distance traveled by offenders to different types of premises.
4. Distance traveled by offenders is directly related to the value of property realized in the robbery.

All four hypotheses were verified, but the importance of the research is that the authors found significant distance differentials according to the characteristics of the offense and not of the offender. These characteristics are the outcomes of a series of decisions made by the offender. Therefore, this study represents and examines the difference in distances by features of the offender's method of operation.

Literature on the distance traveled by rape offenders is not as common or as in-depth as travel studies for other crimes. White found in Indianapolis, that the average distance traveled by violent and property offenders was .85 and 1.72 miles, respectively, while the rapists average 1.52 miles (1932, p. 511). Proceeding on the assumption that Chicago police precincts were the same as neighborhoods, Erlanson found that 87 percent of the rape offenders lived in the neighborhood or precinct of their offense (1946, p. 340). The problem with this work is that the real dimensions of the police precincts are not uniform. Amir, defining "vicinity of crime" as an area of five city blocks, found that 68 percent of the known rape offenders in his sample lived within the vicinity of the victim and the scene of the offense (1971, p. 91). Pyle et al. (1974) found that in Akron, Ohio, the rape offender traveled an average of 1.34 miles, the second shortest distance traveled by offenders for any other crime. Finally, Rhodes and Conly (1981, p. 179) reveal that, based upon their Washington, D.C., data, rapists traveled an average of 1.15 miles, while the average for burglars and robbers was 1.62 and 2.1 miles, respectively. The few and uncomplicated examinations of rapists' travel behavior indicate that they make very short commutes corresponding with the accepted finding that the distances for crime against the person are shorter than crimes against property.

The Problem

The literature review suggests that those responsible for crimes against people travel shorter distances than the offenders responsible for crimes against property. Consequently, the rapist, who commits a crime against a person, should generally travel shorter distances than property offenders. Yet, previous studies indicate that rape is the outcome of a variety of methods. Therefore, one of the important research questions to be addressed is whether the travel distance of rapists varies according to their methods of approaching the victim.

Rapes, where the offender breaks into or illegally enters the residence of the victim, as well as those where the offender immediately attacks and/or kidnaps the victim, are probably the most typical forms of blitz rape. Yet, these approaches are commonplace for the property crime of burglary and the violent crime of armed or strong-armed robbery. Thus, one could hypothesize that the rapist utilizing the illegal entry of residence approach will travel a longer distance than the offender who kidnaps and/or attacks his victim. The position of the confidence rapist on a distance scale compared to the blitz methods cannot be predicted, mainly because these methods are not commonplace for any type of violent or property crime. Thus, there are no conceptual antecedents or grounds for predicting the magnitude of the journeys.

A purely exploratory venture in this article is the distance differentials traveled by the serial as opposed to the single offenders. Therefore, this article examines distance differentials within the context of the method of approach and the number of rapes committed by the same offender.

Method

The Data

The data for this study are all the lone assailant or one offender rapes reported to the San Diego, California, Police Department during the years 1971 to 1975. All the pertinent information for this study was gleaned from the incident case files. The original data set consists of 612 cases but not all the cases are used in this study. First, 201 cases or 32.8 percent of the total cases were open cases where the suspect had not been apprehended; thus, no addresses were available for calculating trip distances. Another 91 cases were excluded because the rapes were between victims and offenders who had intimate interpersonal relationships. In other words, confidence rapes of the knowing-the-victim variety were excluded from this study because it is the rapes between participants of the more anonymous relationships that require the expenditure of more law enforcement resources for identifying and apprehending suspects. After making these omissions, 52.3 percent of the total cases (320 cases) remained, which were the basis of analysis for this study.

Victim-Offender Relationship

The remaining cases were classified according to the victim-offender relationship scheme developed by Amir (1971, p. 233) for his Philadelphia study. Therefore, the victim-offender relationships used are stranger, casual acquaintance, or acquaintance (Table 8.1).

Method of Approach

Six methods for approaching the victim were developed from reading the case files (Table 8.2). Illegal entry of residence and kidnap-attack are the two blitz methods. The remaining four methods are varying forms of confidence rape. The advantage of this classification scheme is that one receives an indication of how the rapist approached his victim as well as the type of place of the encounter (residence versus outdoors).

Offender Type

Finally, the cases were classified according to the number of rapes committed by the same person before he was apprehended by the police. Therefore, two classifications are presented: "single" – an offender commits only one reported rape and is apprehended by the police; and "serial" – an offender commits two or more reported rapes before he is apprehended by the police. Of the 320 rapes included in this study, 156 were single rapes and 164 were serial rapes committed by 39 offenders (LeBeau 1978).

Table 8.1   Victim-offender relationship categories

Stranger	– No previous contact and acquaintanceship established before the offense.
Casual acquaintance	– Offender becomes known to victim just before the offense.
Acquaintance	– Victim has some prior knowledge about her offender's residence, place of work, or nickname, but no specific relationship exists.

Source: M. Amir, *Patterns in Forcible Rape* (Chicago: University of Chicago Press, 1971).

Table 8.2   Methods of approaching the victim

Illegal entry	– Offender breaks into the residence of the victim.
Kidnap-attack	– In an outdoor setting, offender immediately applies force to neutralize the victim.
Accept ride	– Offender offers victim in transit a ride or offender looks for hitchhiking victims.
Meet outdoors	– Offender encounters the victim in an outdoor setting.
Public building	– Offender meets his victim in a public or semi-public building.
Party/bar	– The offender meets the victim at a party or in a bar.

The Journey Distance

The principal locations used in this study were the residence of the offender and the location of the initial meeting place between the victim and offender. Obviously, the "illegal entry of residence" method implies that the initial meeting place was also the location of the crime; while the "accept a ride" method involved movement and different locations during the assault. In essence, the journey to rape measure refers to the offender's travel to the first place he encountered his victim.

Geographic distance throughout the study is expressed in miles, but the distance itself is not the typical straight line distance from point to point. Since access and movement in urban space, in reality, are not based on straight line movement, a more appropriate distance measure would take into account a directional change. Hence, the distance in this study is metropolitan distance or "Manhattan geometry" (Lowe and Moryodas 1976, p. 15). Therefore, the distance between two points assumes a third location or simply a right angle movement.

Table 8.3   Victim-offender relationship frequencies of single and serial offenders

Relationship	Single	Serial	Total
Stranger	77.00 (49.4)	150.00 (91.5)	227.00 (70.9)
Casual acquaintance	52.00 (33.33)	7.00 (4.3)	59.00 (18.4)
Acquaintance	27.00 (17.3)	7.00 (4.3)	34.00 (10.6)
Total	156.00	164.00	320.00

Chi square = 69.4; 2 d.f.; sig. = .0000
Note: ( ) = percentage of column total.

Table 8.4   Methods of approach of the single and serial offenders

Approach	Single	Serial	Total
Illegal entry	31.00 (19.9)	95.00 (57.9)	126.00 (39.4)
Kidnap attack	32.00 (20.5)	37.00 (22.6)	69.00 (21.6)
Accept ride	32.00 (20.5)	12.00 (7.3)	44.00 (13.7)
Meet outdoors	13.00 (8.3)	11.00 (6.7)	24.00 (7.5)
Public building	16.00 (10.3)	8.00 (4.9)	24.00 (7.5)
Party/bar	32.00 (20.5)	1.00 (.6)	33.00 (10.3)
Total	156.00	164.00	320.00

Chi square = 73.7: 5 d. f.: sig. = .0000
Note: ( ) = percentage of column total.

Table 8.5 **Mean journey length (miles) by methods of approach and offender type**

	Illegal Entry	*Kidnap Attack*	*Accept Ride*	*Meet Outdoors*	*Public Bldg.*	*Party Bar*
All offenders						
2.5 miles	1.10	3.38	8.10	6.16	4.57	1.90
(319)	(126)	(69)	(44)	(24)	(24)	(32)
Single offenders						
3.5 miles	1.60	5.29	7.00	5.30	4.20	1.90
(156)	(31)	(32)	(32)	(13)	(16)	(32)
Serial offenders						
1.77 miles	0.98	2.30	11.74	7.25	5.56	–
(163)	(95)	(37)	(12)	(11)	(8)	–

Anova distance by all offenders and methods: d.f. (5,319); F = 10.751; significance = .0000
Anova distance by Single and methods: d.f. (5,150); F = 2.383; significance= .0411
Anova distance by Serial and methods; d.f. (4,158); F = 12.395; significance= .0000
Note: (#) = n

Throughout this research the concept of mean distance does not imply arithmetic average. Actually, the mean distance is the geometric mean. Essentially, the distances are converted to logarithms, summed and divided by the number of observations. The main advantage of this measure is that it is less affected by the extreme quantities and it represents a more typical average (Arkin and Colton 1970). Although the values from this procedure are in logarithmic form, the antilogarithm appears on all tables and within the discussions throughout the text.

Results

As noted in Table 8.3, there is a significant difference in the victim-offender relationship composition between the two offender types. The serial offenders show a strong proclivity to be strangers to their victims, while almost half of the single offenders are strangers. It is quite apparent that the serial offenders attempt to maximize anonymity.

The offender types exhibit a significant difference in the types of methods used to approach their victims (Table 8.4). The serial offenders show a strong preference or bias for the blitz methods since 80 percent of their rapes utilized the illegal entry of residence and the kidnap-attack methods, while only 40 percent of the single rapes involved these methods. An oddity is the almost equal numerical and proportional

Table 8.6   Anova: Journey to rape by method and offender type

Source of Variation	Sum of Squares	DF	Mean Square	F	Signif. of F
Main effects	34.87	6	5.81	9.28	.001
Method	27.84	5	5.57	8.88	.001
Offender Type	99	1	.99	1.57	.211
2 way interactions	2.93	4	.733	1.17	.324
Explained	37.80	10	3.78	6.03	.001
Residual	192.98	308	.627		
Total	230.79	318	.72		

measure of the kidnap-attack method between the two offender types. Still, the serial offenders are more blitz rapists while the singles show a stronger preference for the confidence approaches.

Table 8.5 depicts the results from a series of one-way analysis of variance (ANOVA) tests comparing the mean distances traveled by the offenders. Both serial and single offenders traveled the shortest mean distances to assault their victims when using the illegal entry of residence method. Thus, it appears that offenders travel the shortest distance to commit rapes which involve a method linked to crimes against property (Table 8.5). Serial offenders traveled the second shortest mean distance to commit kidnap-attack rapes. The method with the second shortest mean distance for the single offender is meeting the victim at a party or bar, a confidence method.

A two-way analysis of variance was conducted in order to assess the effects of the method of approach, offender type, and the interaction of those two variables or the mean journey to rape distances. As suggested by the results presented in Table 8.6, method of approach appears to be more significant in accounting for the journey to rape distances than the type of offender responsible for the act. In addition, the interaction between these two factors is very weak.

Discussion and Summary

An examination of the victim-offender relationship and method of approach composition for the serial and single offenders indicates that each offender type was different. The serial offenders are predominantly strangers employing the blitz methods. In contrast, there is a greater likelihood for the single offenders to be nonstrangers using confidence methods. In reality, one must assume that the single offenders are inclined to be serial offenders who have only one assault reported, or the single offender is an easier offender to apprehend because of the way be commits his rape. In other words, this type of offender may relay more information about himself to the victim who in turn conveys it to the police (Skogan and Antunes 1979).

The previous journey to crime studies have suggested that, by and large, offenders travel longer distances to commit crimes against property than crimes against the person. This study examined the variation in the distances traveled by rape offenders controlling for the method of approach and the type of offender (single or serial). It was hypothesized that rapists employing a typical property crime method such as illegal entry of residence would travel longer distances than rapists using a typical violent crime method such as kidnap-attack.

The results clearly indicate that the method of approach is a more significant contributor to rape distance variation than the type of offender. Specifically, the single and serial offenders traveled the shortest distances to commit rapes using the illegal entry of residence method. For the serial offender, the second shortest commute was the kidnap-attack method, but this method accounted for the fourth shortest commute for the single offender. Finally, forms of capturing-the-victim confidence rape accounted for the longest journeys by the single and serial offenders.

Implications and Conclusions

Use of the method of approach and the journey to crime measure have both theoretical and practical implications. The method of approach is an additional factor to be considered in the offender's decision-making process. Specifically, the Brantinghams assert criminals respond to a sequence of cues associated with good victims or targets (1981, p. 29). Therefore, one must assess if there are cues which alert the criminal to the best method of approach to use as well.

The travel distance and method of approach may be important information for inclusion by the police crime analyst or criminal investigator in a *modus operandi* file. There are two possible outcomes emanating from this practice. The first is that the method of approach and travel distance used by an individual in past crimes may help the police link that individual with present crimes. This outcome is associated with targeting and monitoring career criminals. The second outcome is based on the assumption that certain methods are characterized by different travel distances. Therefore, it may be possible for the criminal investigator to calculate from the location where an offender and victim first meet, a minimal search radius for the unknown offender. Of course, additional research and evaluation is needed in order to assess if these possible outcomes are worthy of policy and implementation.

Acknowledgement

The points of view or opinions expressed in this research do not necessarily represent the official position or policy of the San Diego, California, Police Department.

References

Amir, M. (1971). *Patterns in Forcible Rape.* Chicago: University of Chicago Press.
Arkin, H. and Colton, R. R. (1970). *Statistical Methods,* 5th edition. New York: Barnes and Noble.
Baldwin, J. and Bottoms, A. E. (1976). *The Urban Criminal: A study in Sheffield.* London: Tavistock.
Brantingham, P. J. and Brantingham, P. L. (1981). Notes on the geometry of crime. In *Environmental Criminology,* edited by P. J. Brantingham and P. L. Brantingham, pp. 27–54. Beverly Hills: Sage.
Burgess, A. W. and Holmstrom, L. L. (1974). *Rape: Victims of Crisis.* Maryland: Robert J. Brady Company.
Capone, D. L. and Nichols, W. (1976). Urban structure and criminal mobility. *Amer. Beh. Sci.,* 20, 199–214.
—— (1975). Crime and distance: An analysis of offender behavior in space. *Proceedings, Assn. Amer. Geographers,* pp. 45–49.
Curtis, L. A. (1974). *Criminal Violence.* Lexington. MA: Lexington Books.
Erlanson, O. A. (1946). The scene of sex offenses. *J. Crim. L. & Crim.,* 31, 339–342.
Groth, A. N., Longo, R. E. and McFadin, J. B. (1982). Undetected recidivism among rapists and child molesters. *Crime & Del.,* 28, 450–458.
Harries, K. D. (1980). *Crime and the Environment.* Springfield: Charles C. Thomas Press.
Hazelwood, R. R. (1983). The behavior-oriented interview of rape victims: The key to profiling. *FBI L. E. Bul.,* 52, 8–15.
LeBeau, J. L. (1985). Some problems with measuring and describing rape presented by the serial offender. *Jus. Qtrly.* 2 (September), 385–398.
—— (1984). Rape and race. *J. Offender Counseling Services & Rehabilitation,* 9(1–2), 125–148.
—— (1978). The spatial dynamics of rape: The San Diego example. Unpublished Ph.D. dissertation, Department of Geography, Michigan State University.
Lowe, J. C. and Moryodas, S. (1976). *The Geography of Movement.* Boston, MA: Houghton Mifflin Company.
Nelson, S. and Amir, M. (1973). The hitchhike victim of rape: A research report. In *Victimology: A New Focus, volume 5,* edited by Israel Drapkin and Emiliano Viano, pp. 47–64. Lexington, MA: D.C. Heath.
Nichols, W. W. (1980). Mental maps, social characteristics, and criminal mobility. In *Crime: A Spatial Perspective,* edited by Daniel E. Georges-Abeyie and Keith D. Harries, pp. 156–166. New York: Columbia Univ. Press.

Pettiway, L. E. (1982). Mobility of robbery and burglary offenders: Ghetto and nonghetto spaces. *Urban Affairs Qtrly.*, 18(2), 255–270.

Phillips, P. D. (1980). Characteristics and typology of the journey to crime. In *Crime: A spatial perspective*, Daniel E. Georges-Abeyie and Keith D. Harries (eds), pp. 167–180. New York: Columbia Univ. Press.

Pyle, G. F. et al. (1974). *The Spatial Dynamics of Crime*. Department of Geography Research Paper No. 159. Chicago: The University of Chicago.

Rengert, G. F. (1975). Some effects of being female on criminal spatial behavior. *The Pennsylvania Geographer*, 13(2), 10–18.

Repetto, T. A. (1974). *Residential Crime*. Cambridge, NIA: Ballinger.

Ressler, R. K., Burgess, A. W. and Douglas, J. E. (1983). Rape and rape-murder: One offender and twelve victims. *Amer. J Psych.*, 140(January), 36–40.

Rhodes, W. M. and Conly, C. (1981). Crime and mobility: An empirical study. In *Environmental Criminology,* edited by P. J. Brantingham and P. L. Brantingham, pp. 167–188. Beverly Hills: Sage.

Schwendinger, J. R. and Schwendinger, H. (1983). *Rape and Inequality.* Beverly Hills, CA: Sage Publications.

Skogan, W. G. and Antunes, G. F. (1979). Information, apprehension, and deterrence: Exploring the limits of police productivity. *J. Crim. Jus.*, 7, 219–234.

Turner, S. (1969). Delinquency and distance. In *Delinquency: Selected Studies,* M. E. Wolfgang and T. Sellin (eds), pp. 11–26. New York: John C. Wiley.

White, R. C. (1932). The relation of felonies to environmental factors in Indianapolis. *Soc. Forces*, 10(4), 498–509.

Williams, L. S. (1984). The classic rape: When do victims report? *Soc. Probs.* 31 (April), 459–467.

Wolfgang, M. E., Figlio, R. M. and Sellin, T. (1972). *Delinquency in a Birth Cohort.* Chicago: The University of Chicago Press.

Chapter 9

Characteristics of Serial Arsonists and Crime Scene Geography in Japan

Masayuki Tamura and Mamoru Suzuki

Preface

We have been doing research on criminal personality profiling for three years. From the viewpoint of the investigator, profiling is needed in a situation where the community's fears are extremely high and the arrest of the perpetrator is not an easy task. However, from the viewpoint of the researcher, the crimes for which investigators seek profiling data do not always lend themselves to the process of profiling. Profiling is more viable for those crimes in which perpetrators are distinguishable from the general public by some kind of extreme deviation in behavior, personality and lifestyle. Our experience suggests that offenses suitable for profiling involve serial, indiscriminate (the offenders and victims are strangers) and relatively rare crimes, in which offenders show no apparent motives, or sexually motivated drives (Tamura 1996). Currently, we are conducting research on serial arson (Tamura and Suzuki 1997), serial "Torima" (non-specific-motive attacks) (Tamura et al. 1998), serial sexual murder and paedophilia. This chapter focuses on the profiling of serial arsonists.

Arson is a more serious threat to Japanese communities than to western ones, as the majority of houses are made from wood and vulnerable to fires. When serial arson occurs in a community, the level of public fear becomes extremely high and the police face strong pressures to arrest the perpetrator.

Purpose

The purpose of this study is to determine the characteristics of serial arsonists and to examine whether the circle hypothesis can be adapted to determine the offender's residential area, and hence serve as a tool in criminal profiling research, and, in turn, as the basis for supporting criminal investigations.

Method

We used MO (*modus operandi*) data of arrested arsonists as recorded by the National Police Agency. The data consist of characteristics of offenders, offenses, and points of arson and residential address. We drew a sample of 107 serial arsonists (those who had committed more than five offenses) who were arrested from 1989 to 1995 in Tokyo and its surrounding suburban area and in Osaka (urban arsonists). Our study analyzed this sample to identify common characteristics of offenders and the geographical relationship between offenders' residences and crime scenes.

Characteristics of Offenders

Female offenders were rather rare, comprising only 12% of the sample. The age of offenders was not young: 22% were in their 20s, 31% in their 30s, 22% in their 40s. The average age of offenders was 35.5 years.

By occupation, 29% of offenders were unemployed and 14% were day laborers. They showed limited levels of education: 7% graduated from schools for the mentally

Table 9.1   Characteristics of offenders

Characteristics of offenders	Sex					
	Male/age				Female	Total
	≤ 29	≤ 39	≤ 49	50 ≥		
	N=31	N=31	N=19	N=13	N=13	107
Unemployed	16.1	32.2	36.8	30.8	38.5	29.0
Day laborer	6.5	12.9	26.3	30.8	0.0	14.0
Living with parent	67.7	51.5	26.3	0.0	23.1	42.1
Alone	25.8	38.7	63.2	76.9	23.1	42.1
With spouse	3.2	9.7	10.5	7.7	38.5	11.2
Criminal record	45.2	54.8	68.4	69.2	15.4	48.6
Arson record	9.7	19.4	36.8	53.8	0.0	21.4
Mental disorder	16.1	29.0	26.3	23.1	23.1	23.4
Physical handicap	12.9	19.4	21.1	61.5	15.4	7.7
Chronic disease	0.0	19.4	5.3	15.4	7.7	9.3
Height ≤ 159 cm	19.4	19.4	31.6	46.2	69.2	3130.8
Motive: irritation and dissatisfaction	64.5	48.4	84.2	61.5	46.2	60.7
Alcohol in crime	12.9	38.7	26.3	46.2	0.0	25.2

retarded, 41% graduated from junior high school and 8% were senior high school dropouts. The majority of offenders belonged to the lower socio-economic strata.

As shown in Table 9.1, approximately 40% of the offenders were living with their parents. Another 40% lived alone, while only 10% lived with their spouse. The majority of middle-aged and elderly offenders consisted of socially isolated persons.

Approximately half of the offenders had police records for criminal offenses and 22% had an arson record. Older people had more extensive records than younger people in both total criminal offenses and arson offenses.

Regarding the mental and physical disabilities of the offenders, 23% showed mental disorders including mental retardation (15%), schizophrenia, epilepsy and others. 22% were physically handicapped with conditions including blindness, deafness, being crippled, having amputated fingers, and so on 9% had severe chronic diseases such as diabetes and gastric ulcers. Their height was lower than the national norms, with the average male offender's height at 163.2 cm.

The serial arsonists were physically and socially handicapped persons with feelings of inadequacy, loneliness, persecution or abuse. Therefore, the most common motivation for setting fires was to vent their feeling of dissatisfaction or irritation (61%) produced in daily life. Some offenders had also set fires while under the influence of alcohol.

The serial arsonists' profiles are as follows; they were not young, and were unemployed or had lower class occupations. Many of them had mental disorders or physical inferiority, a history of crimes, and lived a life of isolation. In short, they were socially handicapped persons, with an inferiority complex and a grudge against people in general. Venting their feeling of dissatisfaction and irritation was the primary motive for their indiscriminate setting of fires.

Comparison of Motives between Japanese and US Serial Arsonist

Comparing the Japanese data with US serial arsonist data (A Motive-Based Offender Analysis of Serial Arsonists) compiled by National Center for the Analysis of Violent Crime (NCAVC) at FBI Academy in Quantico, reveals that the US offenders were younger and had more extensive arrest records than their Japanese counterparts. But the US and Japanese offenders had basically similar physical and mental problems. The motives of arsonists ranged from excitement to revenge against others in the US sample, but were concentrated on revenge, especially societal revenge, in the Japanese sample, as shown in Table 9.2.

Table 9.2   Comparison of motives between Japanese and USA serial arsonists

Arson motives	USA N = 83	Japan N = 107
1. Vandalism	7.2%	0%
2. Excitement	30.1	15.0
3. Revenge	41.0	67.3
Personal revenge	6.0	6.6
Societal retaliation	24.1	60.7
Institutional retaliation	8.4	–
Group retaliation	2.4	–
4. Crime concealment	4.8	–
5. Profit	4.8	0.9
6. Extremist	–	–
7. Others	12.0	16.8
Pyromania	6.0	2.8 (delusion)
Mixed motives	6.0	14.0 (unknown)

Table 9.3   Circle hypothesis

Offender's residence	N	[%]
In the circle	N = 54	50.5%
Around the circle	N = 23	21.5%
Far from the circle	N = 30	28.0%
Neighborhood offender	–	70%
Commuter offender	–	30%

The Circle Hypothesis

The circle hypothesis contends that connecting the two offenses which are the furthest apart defines the diameter of a circle in which the offender lives (Canter and Larkin 1993).

We mapped data of arson incidents and offenders' residences to examine the validity of the circle hypothesis.

In our data shown in Table 9.3, approximately 50% of offenders' residences were in the circle, and 22% were around the circle because the arsonist set fire while coming back from a drinking place to his/her home or from a railway station to his/her home, and another 28% were far from the circle. For practical investigation purpose, when the offenders' residence was in the circle or around the circle, we designated it a neighbourhood offender case. When the offender's residence was far from the circle, we designated it a commuter offender case.

Calculating the cumulative percentage of distance of residence from the center of the circle, offenders' residences are not concentrated in the center of the circle, but rather concentrated near the circumference, both inside and outside.

Regarding the circle hypothesis and the average distance between the offender's residence and arson points, commuter offenders had more than 1km average distance between their residence and arson points, while neighbourhood offenders had rather shorter distances. Concerning the circle hypothesis and the longest-distance between arson points, a concentration of points of arson in a small area was not a characteristic of the neighbourhood offenders' cases. The commuter offenders sometimes concentrated their arson points in a small area.

The Differences between Neighbourhood and Commuter Offenders

Our findings reveal that the differences in characteristics between neighbourhood and commuter offenders were not clear. Regarding the relationship between age and type of offender, the neighbourhood offenders were slightly younger than commuter offenders, but other than that, we could not say neighbourhood offenders had certain characteristics and commuters had others. But in terms of offence characteristics, we found some clearer differences.

Regarding the relationship between main offence time and type of offender, the neighbourhood offender's main offence time was concentrated in the 0:00–6:00 time period (59.8% vs. 34.4%), while the commuter offender had a preference for the evening hours (18:00–4:00, 44.8% vs. 27.3%).

Concerning the relationship between the crime scene and the type of offender, commuter offenders had a slightly greater inclination to commit thefts before setting fires (16.7% vs. 5.2%). Neighbourhood offenders were more inclined to set fire to vehicles and vehicle-related objects (garage, cover sheet and others – 51.9% vs. 20.0%).

Regarding other characteristics, the neighbourhood offenders had more total number of cases of setting fire (on average 16 cases vs. 11 cases), a longer period of crime days (283 days vs. 139 days including intervals) and longer "shortest days of interval" (4.3 days vs. 1.6 days) than commuter offenders.

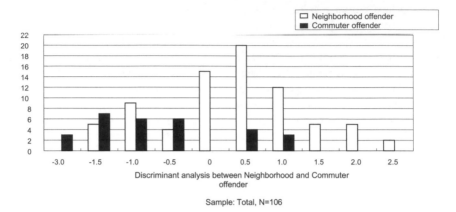

Sample: Total, N=106

Figure 9.1   Discriminant analysis between neighbourhood and commuter offenders

Discriminant Analysis between Neighbourhood and Commuter Offender

Using variables such as:

1. main offence time,
2. committing theft,
3. committing vehicle arson,
4. total number of arson cases,
5. total period of crime days,
6. shortest days of interval,

we conducted discriminant analysis between neighbourhood and commuter offenders.

Figure 9.1 shows the result of discriminant analysis, in which higher discriminant points are neighbourhood offenders and lower points are commuter offenders. In conducting a practical profiling case, we can calculate the discriminant score of a serial arson. And if the score is higher than a certain level (point 0 or more, or point 1.5 or more, in this case), then we can advise investigators with a higher probability that the offender is living in the neighbourhood where the arson took place.

Conclusion

The serial arsonists were older and unemployed or had lower class occupations. Many of them had mental disorders or physical inferiority, a history of crimes, and lived a life of isolation. In short, they were socially handicapped persons, with an inferiority complex and grudges against peoples in general. Venting their feeling of dissatisfaction and irritation was the motive of their indiscriminate starting of fires.

Regarding the circle hypothesis, we found that approximately 50% of offenders' residences were in the circle, 22% were around the circle, and 28% were far from the circle.

Discriminant analysis showed that, in a practical profiling case, if the discriminant score is higher than a certain level, we can estimate with a higher probability that the offender is living in the neighbourhood where the arson took place.

The number of samples was limited in this study. Our next task is to compile a larger data set and to conduct offence-based analysis using Geographic Information Systems. Our intention is to offer a more accurate assessment, in order to support criminal investigations.

References

Canter, D. and Larkin, P. (1993). The environment range of serial rapists. *The Journal of Environment Psychology*, 13, 63–69.

Tamura, M., Watanabe, K., Suzuki, M., Sano, K., Watanabe, S. and Ikegami, S. (1998). Criminal profiling of "Torima" non-specific motive attacking. *Reports of the National Research Institute of Police Science, Research on Prevention of Cringe and Delinquency*, 39(1), 1–20.

Tamura, M. and Suzuki, M. (1997). Criminal profiling research on serial arson. 1. examination of Circle Hypothesis estimating offender's residential area. *Reports of the National Research Institute of Police Science, Research-on Prevention of Crime and Delinquency*, 38(1), 13–25.

Tamura, M. (1996). Two approaches in criminal profiling research. *Reports of the National Research Institute of Police Science, Research on Prevention of Crime and Delinquency*, 37(2), 114–122.

PART 3
Investigative Directions

Chapter 10

Predicting Serial Killers' Home Base Using a Decision Support System

David Canter, Toby Coffey, Malcolm Huntley,
and Christopher Missen

1. Introduction

Studies demonstrate that serial offenders tend to live, or have some form of recognizable base, within an area circumscribed by their offenses (reviewed by Brantingham and Brantingham 1981). One testable formulation of this proposal is the "Circle Hypothesis" described by Canter and Larkin (1993). They showed that 87% of the 45 serial rapists they studied from the South of England each lived within a circle defined by a diameter drawn between that offender's two farthest offenses. Subsequently Kocsis and Irwin (1997) reported that 82% of serial arsonists, 70% of serial rapists, and 49% of burglars in Australia lived within the defined offending circle. In the United States 56% of serial rapists were found in the circle by Warren et al. (1995, 1998) and 86% of the 126 U.S. serial killers studied by Hodge et al. (1998). Tamura and Suzuki (1997) found support for the Circle Hypothesis in Japan for 72% of the serial arsonists they studied.

Canter and Gregory (1994) developed the implications of the circle hypothesis. They showed that a simple computer-based geometric model, incorporating circular regions around the first offense, indicated with considerable success for serial rapists the general area in which an offender was living. The search areas predicted by this system were on average 19 km². This is of some value in assigning priorities to suspects but is not precise enough for general operational utility. It nonetheless supports the utility of developing such approaches further to model serial offenders' geographical behavior and to help identify their base location. The present paper evaluates the effectiveness of one such development.

Whatever the theoretical interest of such geographical models, their practical utility requires that a series of crimes has been linked to a common offender. Such linking can be provided most strongly by forensic evidence such as DNA or fibers. But it can also be indicated by "signature" (Keppel 1997) or distinguishing modus operandi information or multivariate statistics (Green et al. 1976; Canter 1995). Linking is not addressed in any further detail in the present paper. For practical applications it is assumed that linking will be achieved by an appropriate means.

1.1. Investigative Geography

Warren et al. (1998) show that studies of geographical processes for identifying the base location of serial offenders are part of the emerging research that is providing an empirical, scientific basis for "offender profiling" (Ault and Reese 1990; Canter 1995). Rossmo (1993) drew particular attention to the assistance that geographical targeting can provide an investigation. This can include the assignment of priorities to suspects who have come to police attention by other means, giving guidance to police patrols, assistance in determining the areas for house to house inquiries or in the focus for appeals for help from the public.

The "base" in question that provides the anchor for the criminal activity may take many forms. For some forms of base, delimiting the area where this base may be will be of more assistance to an investigation than for others. It will be of particular value when the base is in fact the home or some other location with which the offender will be known to have some affinity, such as a workplace or frequently visited recreation facility. It will be of less value when the base is an anonymous stopover point on a lengthy route that the offender is following, or any other location from which it is difficult to identify the offenders.

If the offender is targeting particular types of victims or particular opportunities for victims, for example, street prostitutes who are available in a particular area of a city, then the association between the base location and the target location may be an accident of the local land use. These "commuters," as Canter and Larkin (1993) call such offenders, may not be so open to decision support modeling as those "marauders" who move out from a fixed base to commit their crimes. It is the marauders whose base is located within the hypothesized circle.

The empirical question therefore arises as to how feasible it is to model the base location of a serial offender, when that base is a location that has a clear link to the offender, notably his place of residence. Furthermore, what mathematical functions best represent the possible relationships between the home and the locations of the offenses in a series? For the present study the focus is on the place of residence, which is referred to as the home.

2. Models of Offender Target Location Selection

Kind (1987) was one of the first forensic scientists to show the direct application of geographical models, such as those studied here, to an ongoing criminal investigation in his pioneering exploration of the location of the offenses of the "Yorkshire Ripper." He showed that a "center of gravity" to the Ripper's crime locations, or as might be termed from geography a "centroid," accurately indicated where the offender was eventually found to live. Being the center of gravity, that point is the only point that simultaneously has the minimum possible distance to each of the offense locations. Kind proposed that the farther a location from this point, the lower the likelihood that that point is the base of the offender.

By using what has become known as "distance decay" functions, Rossmo (1995) indicated that the centroid could be generalized to a probability surface to produce a more detailed model of the likely home of the serial offender, although this would usually be effective only for "marauding" offenders, whose residential base is broadly within an area circumscribed by their offenses. These decay functions are the relationship between the probability of offending and the distance from home. Researchers have demonstrated that as the distance from an offender's home increases, the probability of his committing an offense decreases, i.e., the probability "decays" (Rhodes and Conly 1981; Rengert 1999). Turner (1969) pointed out that there is potentially a large family of functions which could characterize distance decay. Eldridge and Jones (1991) considered this in detail, pointing out the behavioral implications of different functions. For example, the home could have a very strong influence on the activity of the offender, in which case the function would be expected to be very steep, decaying quickly. Or there could be a much wider area in which the offender based himself, leading to much shallower functions in which the distances decay very slowly. Turner (1969) also argued that, within this decay, there is likely to be a "buffer zone" directly around the offender's home in which there is a reduced likelihood of offending, possibly due to the higher risk of recognition (Turner 1969).

By using the appropriate decay function, each location around a crime site can be assigned a weighting indicating the likelihood of residence by the offender. For a serial offender the information derived from the weightings around the locations of each of his crimes can then be combined, using, for example, gravitational summation models (Rossmo 1993), to indicate his likely location of residence. Such models will have practical application if the cases in a series have been linked and relevant information is available on the actual crime locations.

Subsequent work by Rossmo (1995) demonstrated that a computer mapping system based on these principles could indicate the area in which a serial offender is likely to be living. Rossmo states that the crucial constants and exponents in the decay functions on which his software is built are "empirically determined" (p. 233). He does not provide full information on what the empirical basis of this determination is, nor does he make it clear if the same exponent is used in all calculations. The question therefore remains as to what the most effective mathematical function would be across a wide range of crimes. Additionally, without an empirical examination of a sample of solved offense series, it is not possible to identify what the actual success rate of any system is. Furthermore, it is not possible to recognize the situations in which the system would and would not be successful or the degree of success for a particular case. To develop these systems further it is thus necessary to explore the various feasible mathematical functions that describe the distance decay to determine which functions are most effective for which offenders under which conditions.

2.1. A Measure of Effectiveness

If a variety of functions is to be compared it is necessary to determine some measure of their effectiveness. One objective is to reduce the demands on police resources. It is therefore proposed that some index of the "costs" of carrying out any search is determined. Different decay functions can then be examined to determine which is the most cost-effective. Such a measure will reflect the ability of a system to prioritize a search area and identify the location of an offender's home.

The proposed measure is based on the definition of a potential search area for each map of offense locations. Within the present study, a slightly broader definition of search area than the Circle Hypothesis is used. Earlier studies have shown that not every offense will be encompassed by a circle defined by a diameter drawn between the two offenses farthest from each other and therefore locations relevant to the analysis may be excluded. Therefore, in the present study a rectangle was used to define the potential search area, drawn to include all the offense locations. Drawing on the hypothesis that the great majority of offenders will have a base somewhere in the region of their offenses, but allowing for those cases in which the offender may not be living inside the rectangle defined, by his offenses, in the present study the potential search area is magnified by 20%.

In the current study the system being used is based around visualization on a computer screen. Therefore the search area rectangle is made up of a finite matrix containing 13,300 square regions, selected to be the minimum size that was just visible on the standard computer monitor screen. This means that any circular structure that emerges from the calculations is an approximation made up of square, "jagged" edges.

The size of the regions as viewed on the screen does not vary, whereas the area represented by the region varies between cases. The software facilitates this by allowing the user to set the scale that the screen size is to represent. This therefore provides a relative search area in which the search for an offender's location can be prioritized. This approach was taken to enable the decision support software to be of value in a range of field conditions.

The effectiveness of any search of this rectangle is then calculated by assigning to each point on the map a weighting indicating the *likelihood* of residence. The weightings are used as an index by which to rank-order locations, referred to as the Base index, which has associated B values. These B-values are derived from the calibrated decay functions as described below. An array of locations ordered by decreasing B-value is then generated. Each point within the array is then searched for the offender's home base, starting at the location with the highest B-value. If B-values are tied, then they count with equal weight to the overall calculations. When the offender's home is reached, the search is terminated and a cost value generated. This value reflects the proportion of all possible locations searched before the location of the offender's home base is identified. A cost value of 0 would indicate that the first location searched (i.e., the location with the highest B-value) contained the offender's home; a cost value of 1 would indicate that the home was in the last location within the array. If the home were not within the search area, the system would give a null value, which would be treated as a failure. The search cost can therefore be seen to reflect the percentage of the rectangle searched. For example, a search cost of 0.5 would mean that 50% of the defined search area rectangle had to be searched before the offender's home was identified.

2.2. Analytical Models

There are a large number of possible mathematical models to describe the decay functions that can be used to determine the likelihood of a location being where an offender is based. Furthermore, no research has been published comparing different functions on any measure of effectiveness, or any set of crime data.

Rhodes and Conly (1981), in their examination of serial burglars, robbers, and rapists, observed that the distance decay displayed by their samples of offenders was negatively exponential in nature. This observation differed from the relatively normal distribution (with the exception of the buffer zone) around the offender's home suggested by Brantingham and Brantingham (1981). This is also true for other forms of serial spatial and behavioral phenomena (Golledge 1987). The present study therefore explored a family of negatively exponential decay functions and function types generated from the equation

$$Y = e^{-\beta x}, \ \beta = 1/10, \ 1/9, \ldots, \ 1, 2, \ldots, 10 \qquad (N = 19) \qquad (1)$$

where Y is the Base index value, x is the distance of that location from the offense site, β is the exponential coefficient, and N is the number of β values tested.

Each of the range of functions that is produced is applied to each offense location within a series. The functions are calibrated so that the maximum B-value is equal to 1 and the minimum is 0.[3] Figure 10.1 shows the range of functions that are tested in the current study. As the function number increases from 1 ($\beta = 10$) to 19 $\beta = 1/10$) the characteristics of the function change from having a short existence and steep gradient, to having a long existence and shallow gradient. The number of functions tested was limited to 19, as such a range represented a broad selection of the forms of distance decay that may be observed within the sample.

Each function is applied over a distance moderated by a normalization parameter linked to the range of each offender's offense distribution as described in the following section. Twenty equally spaced model representation points define all models. These points encompass the 19 model representation units, each point being a value by which to define the function.

---

3   When used operationally in investigations this scale is recalibrated to a range of 0 to 0.5, to reduce the likelihood of unskilled users mistaking the values expressed by the system as direct probabilities.

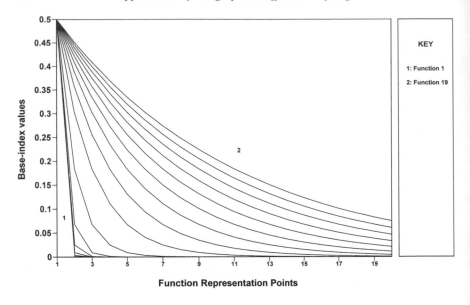

Figure 10.1   Family of analytical functions. (1) Function 1; (2) function 19

To model the presence of a buffer zone, steps, areas with a B-value of 0, and plateaus, areas of a constant B-value (1 in the present study), of varying sizes are inserted in front of the exponential function. This combination of a step and a plateau was a simplified representation of a buffer zone for the present study. Future research may test more stochastic models such as that proposed by Rossmo (1995).

The step is representative of an area in which the offender will not offend, the plateau being a constant region close to the home in which there is the highest likelihood that the offender will offend. For the present study a maximum number of 4 units from the original 19 model representation units was used to define the buffer zone. The analysis was then carried out using each permutation of steps and plateaus up to the maximum of 4 units. Each permutation thereby examines a different form of buffer zone.

Figure 10.2 shows an example function with a step size of 2 units and a plateau of 1 unit. Each permutation within the analysis is referred to as a function "type." A function without a step or plateau is referred to as a "bare" function type. A total of 285 function types were analyzed.

2.3. Normalization Procedure

Offenders differ in the size of the area over which they carry out their crimes. Therefore any analysis that is to allow comparison between offenders must compensate for this by incorporating a normalization procedure. To do this a method based on

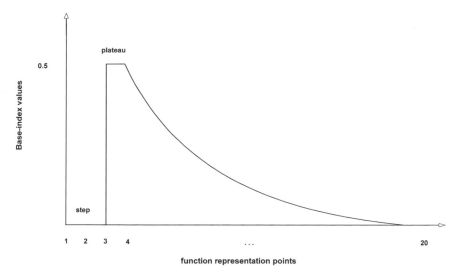

Figure 10.2   Example function type

the average distance between offenses was implemented. However, theoretical considerations and empirical analysis of the actual distribution of offenses indicate that a normalization procedure that takes no account of any possible axis along which the offenses may be distributed may be less effective than one that does. Therefore two normalization parameters were compared. One was the mean interpoint distance between all offenses (MID). The second was a specifically developed index, the QRange.

The QRange is based on the propositions of Brantingham and Brantingham (1981), Fink (1969), and Rengert and Wasilchick (1985) that the arterial pathways of the offender's movements may be of significance to the locations of his offenses. It is therefore feasible that there is some dominant linear structure to the distribution of offenses. The MID gives equal weight to all distances. Therefore an index was developed that provides a numerical indication of the average distribution of offenses around a notional axis. This axis was determined by calculating the linear regression of the crime scene coordinates within an offense distribution. The QRange was then defined as the mean perpendicular distance of all offenses points to the regressional axis inherent within a distribution of offenses. The closer the offenses lie to the regressional axis, the smaller the QRange value. In the present study the MID and the QRange for each offender were used to normalize each offense map.

2.4. Application of the Function

For each run of the analysis, i.e., testing one offense series with one function type and one normalization parameter, the normalization value is calculated. The function

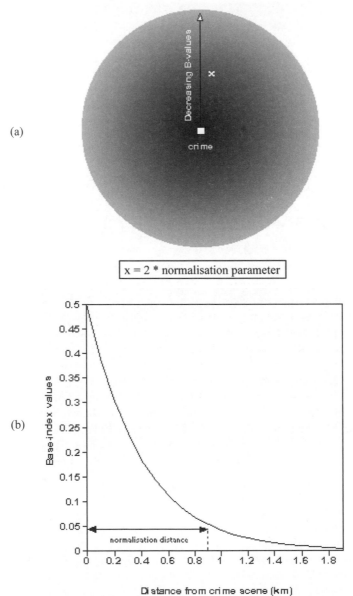

(a)

$$x = 2 * \text{normalisation parameter}$$

(b)

Figure 10.3   Application of function to crime scene: (a) aerial view; (b) profile view

is then applied in a radial fashion around the crime scene to a distance twice the normalization parameter (distance x in Figure 10.3a). The diameter of the resultant circle around the crime scene is therefore four times the normalization parameter. Figure 10.3b gives an example of how one of the bare functions represented in Figure 10.1 is applied to a crime scene and therefore uses physical distances rather than abstract function representation points. This results in the assignment of B-values to the area directly around one crime scene. For this case a normalization value of 0.95 km is used. The radial assignment of the function is repeated for each crime scene location, producing a range of final B-values that can be constructed into a final prioritized map. The distribution of values within the prioritized map can be seen as a field in which each of the crime scenes is an influential body. Thus the B-value for any location is defined as the mean of each of the values assigned to that location by those functions applied to that location. The means are used, as this recognizes the relative reduction in significance of individual crimes by the presence of other crimes as illustrated in Figure 10.4.

To understand further the calculation of the B-values, consider Figure 10.4 as an example. Location x is 0.2 km from the crime scene 1 (cs1). The function (A) applied to the crime assigns a B-value of 0.60 to that location. The radial application of the function (B) around crime scene 2 (cs2) produces an overlap with that around crime scene 1. Location x is 0.2 km from crime scene 1 and 1.6 km from crime scene 2, for which it receives B-values of 0.60 and 0.02, respectively. The relative significance of location x to the location of the offender's home with respect to the first crime

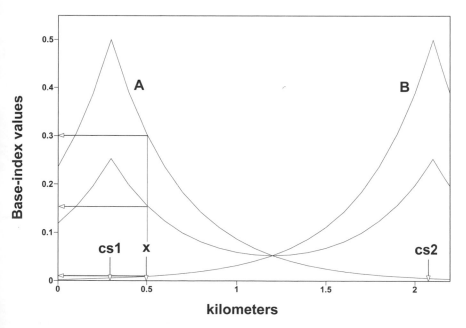

Figure 10.4   Radial assignment of function to two crime scenes

is reduced on the introduction of the new crime scene. Therefore the B-value for that location is calculated as the mean of the two values 0.60 and 0.02 = 0.31. The dashed line in Figure 10.4 indicates the resultant distribution of B-values between the two crime scenes after this process is repeated for each individual location. This process is repeated for each of the functions applied to the crime scene locations, producing a final map that is prioritized by B-values. The B-values for any location is the mean of the values assigned to that location by the calibrated function radially assigned to each crime location within the series. This process is an extension of Kind's (1987) work in that, rather than producing a single point as an indication of the offender's residence, a more comprehensive prioritized map is produced. It is also more detailed than the system studied by Canter and Gregory (1994), in which broad regions were indicated.

The process presented here examines all locations around each of the crime scenes rather than seeking to identify one single point as an indication of the offender's residence. Figure 10.5 provides an example of an actual prioritized search area derived from a recent police investigation. Included within the diagram are the center of gravity (C) for the crime series and the actual location of the offender's home base (H). The range of B-values is displayed from highest to lowest by, respectively, darker to lighter shades of gray (the operational Dragnet system uses a range of different colors). The location of the offender's home within one of the darkest regions illustrates the success of the methodology for this case. The diagram identifies the contrasting amounts of information that are produced from the two forms of analysis and shows how the centrographic method can be misleading as

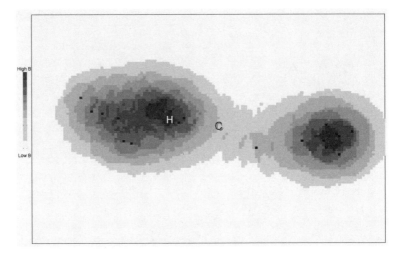

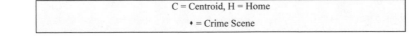

Figure 10.5   Prioritized search map

a result of the geometrical shape of an offense distribution. The center of gravity is actually a unilocational summary or mean of the information represented in the prioritized map.

In this example also, two domains of operation are apparent. After the trial it was found that the area to the right circumscribed the residence of the offenders estranged wife, whom he sometimes visited. The distribution of possible bases in this plot therefore does capture some important aspects of the offender's activity spaces.

Figure 10.5 also serves to illustrate ways in which a mere "eyeballing" of the geographical distribution of offense locations can be unproductive. In this particular case the centroid might be assumed to be the obvious location for a base. The solution provided by the algorithm might be rather unexpected, even though, as it happens, it turns out to be more accurate. Of course, local knowledge about land use, the road network, and sociodemographic and other information that could help indicate where offenders may live can all contribute to formulating a view about an offender's base location beyond the indications of uninformed software. That is why it seems appropriate to regard such software as a decision support tool rather than an "expert system." If it has any validity, it can provide only general guidance to an inquiry, not the precise identification of a residential location.

3. Method

To test the effectiveness of the Dragnet system described, digital offense maps were generated for solved cases in which the home base of the offender was known. The maps contain the location of the offender's home and the location at which a crucial aspect of the crime took place. In the present study, as discussed below, this aspect was the location at which the bodies of the offender's victims were found.

No land use or topographical information is incorporated into the representation. A calibrated decay function of B-values is applied to a normalized map of each of the offense series. As the analysis is working at a level of abstraction that does not take account of land use or topographical characteristics, there are likely to be instances where actual locations such as parks, lakes, or zoos are assigned values indicating the possibility of the offender's living there. In operational use local knowledge would take account of this and limit searches accordingly. The tests applied in this study therefore underestimated the effectiveness of any localization of an offender's residence. The use of the Base index acknowledges this.

Each segment of the map is assigned a specific B-value. The possible B-values decrease from 1 to 0. A rank-ordered search of locations with decreasing B-values is then conducted. A search cost value is then produced, reflecting the proportion of the original rectangular search area that needed to be searched before the offender's home base was identified.

For each offense series this process was repeated using 285 forms of the negative exponential decay function types and 2 normalization parameters. Therefore each of the cases tested in the present study was analyzed 570 times. A mean search cost per function type was produced across all the offense series studied.

3.1. Analysis

3.1.1. Sample

The procedure described is applicable to any series activity that has a geographical location. However, one of the most challenging investigative contexts is in the search for a serial killer. Furthermore, because of the public interest in such offenders, once they are caught, details of their offenses and the locations at which they occurred, as well as where the offender was living at the time, are available from public records for many offense series. The details of these published accounts can also often be checked with investigating officers who, especially in the United States, are prepared to comment on published reports if required.

By consulting published accounts of U.S. serial killers who had been convicted since 1960, a list of offenders was drawn up. The location at which they had been residing at the time of their offenses was then determined from at least two independent sources. If these sources did not corroborate each other, the offender was dropped from the sample. Attempts were then made to contact police officers or local journalists who had worked closely on the cases in question to test further the reliability of the residential location information. At this stage corroboration was also sought for the published information on the locations at which the bodies of the victims were found. By this means information became available on 79 U.S. serial killers. Each of the cases therefore satisfied the aforementioned conditions.

- A series of crimes linked by forensic or other means – murders,
- Specific associated locations – body disposal sites.

Of the geographical information available to the police, the disposal site of the victim's body is the most reliable. Other locations, for example, where the victim was first encountered or abducted or where a body might have been kept before disposal, are of interest but are not often known, or if known published, with the same degree of reliability as the disposal site. It does seem likely, though, that these other forms of location may require types of models different from those studied here. For the current study it was decided to use the location that is consistently the most readily available to a serial murder investigation, the body disposal site.

Using the above conditions of a linked series of crimes and associated locations, it is apparent that not all kinds of serial killers can be analyzed using this methodology. John Wayne Gacy, for example, buried the bodies of 29 victims underneath his house and driveway during his six-year offense series in the 1970s. As a result the identification of the body disposal locations was an integral part of identifying the offender. They were not known until the offender had been identified. Therefore offense series for which the body disposal sites are not known at the time of the investigation are not suitable for this form of analysis and were not included in the present study. In such cases other crime-related sites could be utilized, although as mentioned above, an alternate model to that for the body disposal sites may be more relevant.

The geographical locations of the addresses of the body disposal sites and the offender's residence at the time of the offense were determined through street maps and gazetteers. These were input into a flexible decision support system (Dragnet) as raw coordinates. The decision support system allowed modification of the scale for each "map" so that it would fit a computer screen, and further batch software was applied to this to test the effectiveness of the different functions. Therefore the 79 offenders were an *ad hoc* sample unbiased by any assumptions as to which subsets of offenders may be most open to modeling by the system used.

There are doubtless problems with such data. The information available to the authorities itself may have unreliability within it, they may not have recorded the information correctly, or they may have been misled due to incompetence or malice. Distortions can also arise due to reporting strategies and concern to protect victims' families or avoid sites becoming Meccas for ghoulish tourists. Unreliability is also introduced due to confusion over which victims really were the consequence of the actions of a particular individual and at which location the offender really was residing at the time that any particular victim's body was disposed of. Attempts to counteract all these problems were made during the data collecting process, which took a number of years to complete. However, although the full reliability of the data can probably never be precisely gauged, crosschecks on its internal consistency have been very encouraging. Furthermore, the errors introduced by unreliability are most likely to add noise to the data and thereby reduce the possibility for finding support for the models tested. Any support for the models, through low search costs, may therefore be considered in part as support for the reliability of the source data. But, as in any other area of research, the acid test is through the examination of other data sets by other researchers.

In the sample of 79 serial killers studied, their offense series ranged from 2 to 24 crimes (mean, 8; SD, 4.53) and contained distances from 0 to 845 km (mean, 46.39 km; SD, 85.71 km). The series were drawn from all over the United States across a range of geographical settings. This eliminates the effects of biasing that can be generated from using multiple series from one geographial area of type of land use.

4. Results

4.1. Effectiveness of the Search Area

All of the home bases of the 79 serial killers were located within the search area defined by the decision support system. This 100% result is considerably higher than the results reported for the "marauder circle" in earlier studies. It clearly needs to be tested by replication on other data sets. However, for the present sample at least, this

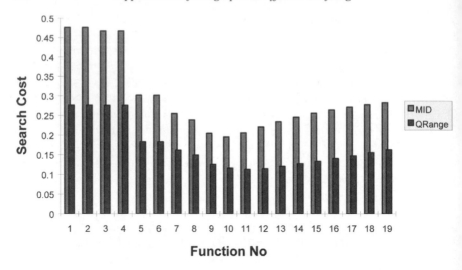

Figure 10.6   Distribution of mean search costs for bare functions

result does support the utility of exploring further the power of different functions in helping to localize the search *within* that overall search area.

4.2. Bare Functions

Figure 10.6 shows the distribution of mean search costs produced from all bare function types with no steps or plateaus. Two major findings are highlighted from this chart.

1. For both the MID and the QRange there are optimal functions which produce minimal search costs. The optimal functions for the MID and QRange are 10 and 11, respectively, producing mean search costs of 0.19 and 0.11. This shows that the original potential search areas were reduced to mean, actual search areas of 19% and 11% of their original size, respectively.
2. For each bare function the QRange is a more economical normalization parameter than the MID.

The difference between the two normalization parameters was found to be significant using a paired-samples t test (t = 14.45, P < 0.05). It is evident that the mean search costs produced using the MID are more sensitive to changes in the function than the search costs produced using the QRange due to the steeper well of lower search costs for the MID distribution. Additionally, the search costs are more sensitive to a reduction in the depth and existence of the function than an increase, for both parameters.

4.3. The MID

The search costs using the MID for bare function 10 are displayed in Figure 10.7. The graph highlights that search costs are distributed in an approximately negatively exponential fashion, with the higher percentage of the sample having a low search cost. If the home of the offender lay outside the potential search area, a search cost of "null" would be produced. As no searches produced this value, the rectangle defining the potential search area encompassed the offender's home in all cases. Fifty-five percent of the sample required searches of less than 15% of the search area; 74%, less than 30%. Figure 10.8 gives a detailed representation of those search costs below 0.3.

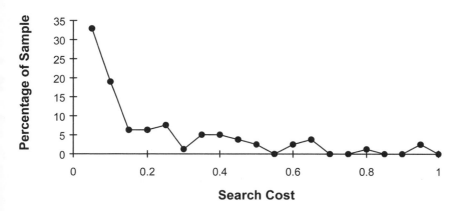

Figure 10.7   Range of search costs for optimal QRange function

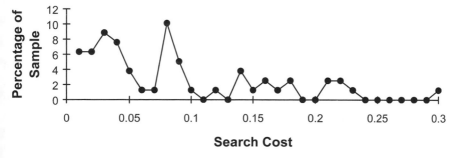

Figure 10.8   Range of search costs below 0.25 for optimal QRange function

4.4. The QRange

The search costs using the QRange for bare function 11 are displayed in Figure 10.9. The graph reveals that there is a high frequency of small search costs accompanied by a small number of larger search costs, generating the average requirement to search 11% of the potential search area. For 51% of the offenders (N=40), less than 5% of the area needs to be searched; or 87% of offenders (N= 69), less than 25%.

A closer examination of the 87% of the sample in which the search cost was less than 0.25, indicated in Figure 10.10, reveals that for 15% of the sample, the search cost was below 0.01.

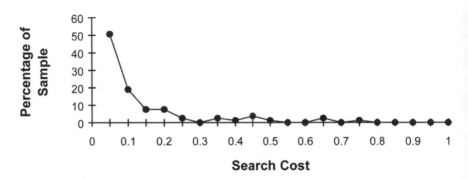

Figure 10.9   Range of search costs for optimal QRange function

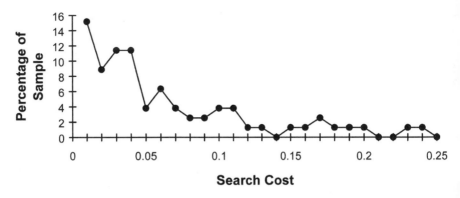

Figure 10.10 Range of search costs below 0.25 for optimal QRange function

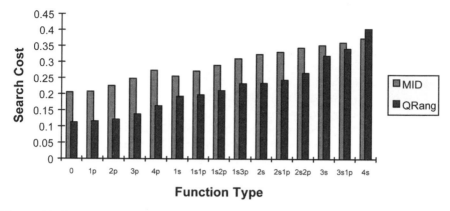

Function Type

Figure 10.11 The effects of steps and plateaus

4.5. Steps and Plateaus

Figure 10.11 shows that the inclusion of steps and plateas for function 11 using the QRange increases the mean search costs. It is evident that including a plateau is more economical than including a step, which is more economical than including a combination of a step and plateau. Furthermore, the inclusion of up to four plateaus is more economical than the inclusion of one step or any combination of steps and plateaus. The same trend is also apparent for the MID normalized functions, with the exception that for this parameter the use of four plateaus is less economical than the use of one step. With the inclusion of three steps and all subsequent combinations of function type, the mean search cost using the QRange becomes increasingly sensitive until it becomes more economical to use the MID than the QRange when the function type with four steps is implemented.

The most economical search value produced from all 285 function types was that of bare function using the QRange normalization parameter, requiring on average a search of only 11% of the total designated search to find the home location.

5. Conclusions

The current methodology has shown that for each of the bare functions, normalization using the QRange provides more cost effective searches than the MID. The identification of an optimal search function has additionally shown that it is possible to generate a mean search cost of 0.11, therefore, on average, reducing the rectangular potential search area to just below 11% of the original size.

Using the optimal function, and QRange normalization parameter, the home base for 15% of the sample was identified within the first 1% of the rank-ordered locations, 51% within the first 5% of locations, and 87% within the first 25%. Such a high proportion of accurate findings indicates that, for the current sample of 79 U.S. serial killers,

(a)   the use of function 11 with the QRange parameter is highly effective in identifying the location of a serial killer's home base, and

(b)   there is a high degree of substantive import within the psychological principles on which the system is built.

Such accurate results are complemented further by the fact that the maps used within the analysis contained no land use or topographical information. Hence within any search the current system will have included areas in which the offender is very unlikely to have lived, such as rivers and lakes. The subsequent inclusion of any such information would therefore improve the results already obtained.

The increased search costs generated with the use of various combinations of steps and plateaus do not support the assumption of a simple buffer zone of the form studied here.

The limitations on the results presented are a function of the data set used. Only offenders who have been caught were included in the sample, so it is an open question whether their parameters of movement are the same as those of offenders who evade detection. Similarly, the models apply to offenders who come to police attention due to the discovery of the locations where the victims' bodies have been disposed of. Those offenders who bury the bodies in their own house or garden would not be drawn into the type of investigation in which the offender's residential location is problematic, and thus the current models would not be relevant.

Perhaps of more general interest at this stage, beyond the practical implications, is the fact that, despite the vagaries of the data used, some strong and consistent patterns have been found. These are consistent with the many claims in the published literature that a criminal's choice of location can be modeled using relatively simple, relatively context-free mathematics. That makes the further test of current and related models a worthwhile enterprise that offers further routes toward the understanding of the geography of criminal behavior.

In principle, any series of offenses in which the offender has direct contact with a geographical location to commit his crime is open to this form of geographical profiling. The models presented here can therefore be used to test the possibility that offenders are operating according to similar mathematical functions. By carrying out analyses similar to the present study with other crimes, such as burglary, it will be possible to determine the same methodology to other serial crimes such as rape and arson as well as the higher-volume crime of burglary. Functions may also be developed in relation to local topographical constraints, land use, target distributions, and transport networks, as Canter and Snook (1999) have reported. However, to evaluate the effectiveness of such explorations, a measure that takes account of the relationship between the proportion of offenders accurately located and the proportion of the area searched needs to be used. The "search cost" described in the present study seems to be one productive way of doing this.

References

Ault, R.L. and Reese, J.T. (1980). A psychological assessment of crime profiling. *FBI Law Enforce. Bull.*, 49(3), 22–25.

Brantingham, P.J. and Brantingham, P.L. (1981). Notes on the geometry of crime. In Brantingham, P.J. and Brantingham, P.L. (eds), *Environmental Criminology*, Sage, London, pp.27–54.

Canter, D. (1995). *Criminal Shadows*. Harper Collins, London.

Canter, D., and Gregory, A. (1994). Identifying the residential location of rapists. *J. Forens. Sci. Soc.*, 34(3), 169–175.

Canter, D. and Larkin, P. (1993). The environmental range of serial rapists. *J. Environ. Psychol.*, 13, 63–69.

Canter, D. and Snook, B. (1999). Modeling the home location of serial offenders. Paper presented to *Expanding the Boundaries: The Third Annual International Crime Mapping Research Conference*, Orlando, FL, Dec.

Eldridge, J.E. and Jones, J.P. (1991). Warped space: A geography of distance decay. *Prof. Geogr.*, 43(4), 500–511.

Fink, G. (1969). Einsbruchstatorte vornehmlich an einfallstrassen? *Kriminalistik*, 23, 358–360.

Golledge, R.G. (1987). *Analytical Behavioural Geography*. Croom Helm, London.

Green, E.J., Bootyh, C.E. and Biderman, M. (1976). Cluster analysis of burglary M/O's. *J. Police Sci. Admin.*, 4, 382–388.

Hodge, S. and Canter, D.V. (1998). *Predatory Patterns of Serial Murderers*. Internal Report, Centre for Investigative Psychology, Liverpool.

Keppel, R. (1997). *Signature Killers*. Pocket Books, New York.

Kind, S.S. (1987). Navigational ideas and the Yorkshire Ripper investigation. *J. Navigat.*, 40(3), 385–393.

Kocsis, R.N. and Irwin, H.J. (1997). An analysis of spatial patterns in serial rape, arson, and burglary: The utility of the Circle Theory of environmental range for psychological profiling. *Psychiatry Psychol. Law*, 4(2), 195–206.

Rengert, G. and Wasilchik, J. (1985). *Suburban Burglary*. Charles C. Thomas, London.

Rengert, G., Piquero, A. and Jones, P.R. (1999). Distance decay re-examined. *Criminology*, 2, 427–445.

Rhodes, W.M. and Conly, C. (1981). Crime and mobility: An empirical study. In Brantingham, P.J. and Brantingham, P.L. (eds), *Environmental Criminology*, Sage, London, pp.167–188.

Rossmo, D.K. (1993). Target patterns of serial murderers: A methodological model. *Am. J. Crim. Just.*, 17, 1–21.

Rossmo, D.K. (1995). Place, space, and police investigations: Hunting serial violent criminals. In Eck, J.E. and Weisburd, D. (eds), *Crime and Place,* Criminal Justice Prcss, New York, pp. 217–235.

Tamura, M. and Suzuki, M. (1997). Criminal profiling research on serial arson: Examination of Circle Hypothesis estimating offender's residential area. *Rep. Natl. Res. Inst. Police Sci. Res. Prev. Crime Delinq.,* 38, 1.

Turner, S. (1969). Delinquency and distance. In Wolfgang, M.E. and Sellin, T. (eds), *Delinquency: Selected Studies*, John Wiley, New York, pp. 11–26.

Warren, J., Reboussin, R. and Hazelwood, R.R. (1995). *The Geographic and Temporal Seqencing* of *Serial Rape*, Final Report submitted to the National Institute of Justice, July 15.

Warren, J., Reboussin, R., Hazelwood, R.R., Cummings, A., Gibbs, N. and Trumbetta, S. (1998). Crime scene and distance correlates of serial rape. *J. Quant. Criminol.*, 14(1), 35–59.

Chapter 11

Linking Commercial Burglaries by *Modus Operandi*: Tests Using Regression and ROC Analysis

C. Bennell and D.V. Canter

This chapter uses statistical models to test directly the police practice of utilising *modus operandi* to link crimes to a common offender. Data from 86 solved commercial burglaries committed by 43 offenders are analysed using logistic regression analysis to identify behavioural features that reliably distinguish between linked and unlinked crime pairs. Receiver operating characteristic analysis is then used to assign each behavioural feature an overall level of predictive accuracy. The results indicate that certain features, in particular the distances between burglary locations, lead to high levels of predictive accuracy. This study therefore reveals some of the important consistencies in commercial burglary behaviour. These have theoretical value in helping to explain criminal activity. They also have practical value by providing the basis for a diagnostic tool that could be used in comparative case analysis.

Introduction

The behavioural linking task, or comparative case analysis (CCA) as it is now commonly called, has the goal of demonstrating that the same offender has committed two or more crimes [1,2]. The task is of particular importance in the absence of a confession, eyewitness testimony or other forensic evidence such as fibres, fingerprints, or DNA. In these cases, behavioural information must be relied upon to link crimes and the task usually involves an examination of what happened at the crime scenes and where the crimes took place. These aspects of the criminal event are popularly regarded as the offender's *modus operandi* (MO) and they have been the subject of limited empirical study.

MO is a rather vague term used in various ways by different police officers and different crime fiction writers. The use of the concept assumes that there will typically be a high degree of similarity between what an offender does in one crime and what he or she does in another. CCA also assumes that police officers are able to recognise these similarities and use them to make effective investigative decisions. Yet research has shown that linking decisions are often based on the limited, subjective impressions of investigating officers [3], that these impressions often differ from officer to officer [4], and that investigators often perform poorly on tasks like CCA[5]. There is, therefore, value in determining precisely which aspects of offenders'crime scene actions are most often repeated across crimes. This will move the consideration of MO onto a firmer objective footing. Identified areas of behavioural repeatability may also have practical value as a basis for decision support tools in CCA.

Defining the possible decision outcomes in CCA

CCA can be fruitfully thought of as a diagnostic task similar, for example, to diagnosing cancer in radiology, assessing risk in psychiatry, predicting storms in meteorology, etc. [6]. The central issue is the validity of linking two or more crimes to a common offender. With two possible decisions (linked or unlinked), and two possible realities (actually linked or actually unlinked), there are four potential decision outcomes for the task (Table 11.1). The goal in studying any system of diagnosis is to increase validity, either by increasing the frequency of correct decisions (hits or correct rejections) or by decreasing the frequency of incorrect decisions (false alarms or misses).

Identifying effective linking features

If the criteria available for making a diagnosis form clear-cut categories, then using these categories directly as diagnostic criteria can lead to effective diagnostic decisions [6]. The accurate diagnosis of cancer, for example, can be made in some cases from readily observable features seen in people with cancer that are not present in people without the disease [7,8]. The use of this approach in linking crimes would require the identification of some linking feature, or set of features, reliably associated with crimes committed by the same offender(s) that are not associated with crimes committed by different offenders.

Table 11.1   Possible decision outcomes in CCA

		Truth:		
		actually linked	actually unlinked	
	linked	a	b	
		hits	false alarms	$a + b$
Decision:				
	unlinked	c	d	
		misses	correct rejections	$c + d$
		$a + c$	$b + d$	$a+b+c+d=N$

However, research suggests that perfect discriminators are unlikely to be found in the criminal context. Although claims have been made for the existence of such criminal 'signatures' [9,10] there are strong grounds for thinking they are likely to be rare and unlikely to be identifiable for very frequent crimes such as burglary [11]. While some studies have found some degree of behavioural similarity across crimes committed by the same offender [1,2], the extensive literature on offender versatility [12] suggests that high levels of behavioural similarity will not be categorically associated with linked offences. Therefore, it is of value to identify the degree to which features of an offence may help link that offence to others committed by the same offender.

The primary objective of the present study is the identification of predictive accuracy levels for various linking features, by themselves, or in combination with each other.

Identifying Appropriate Decision Thresholds

If categorical diagnostic criteria are not available in CCA, such that their presence or absence indicates the correct decision, then an appropriate decision threshold needs to be established. A decision threshold refers to a cut-off point along a continuum of evidence whereby any value obtained above that point results in a positive decision [6]. In our case, this threshold may correspond to a particular across-crime similarity score that defines how similar two crimes must be before we predict they are linked. According to Swets et al. [6], the general goal is to set decision thresholds in order to "...produce the best balance among the four possible decision outcomes for the situation at hand" (p. 3).

For each of the four decision outcomes in Table 11.1, conditional probabilities can be estimated from their frequencies, defined as a, b, c and d. These estimates refer to probabilities of making certain decisions given, or conditional upon, certain truths. For example, the hit probability, pH, indicates the probability of deciding two crimes are linked given that they are in fact linked. This probability is estimated by dividing the number of linked decisions made when the crimes in question are in fact linked, by the total number of crimes that are in fact linked ($a/(a+c)$). The other three conditional probabilities relating to misses (pM), false alarms (pFA) and correct rejections (pCR) are estimated in a similar fashion.

Since the two probabilities of each column in Table 11.1 add up to 1, only one cell in each column is needed to measure accuracy [6]. The probability of hits and false alarms, pH and pFA, are the two values that are most commonly used. However, in deciding where to set the decision threshold it is important to recognise that pH and pFA are related and vary systematically with the exact position of the threshold. As Swets et al. [6] make clear, it is impossible to make the threshold more lenient (e.g., by basing linking decisions on lower across-crime similarity scores) to increase pH without also increasing pFA. Alternatively, it is impossible to make the threshold more strict (e.g., by basing linking decisions on higher across-crime similarity scores) in order to decrease pFA without also decreasing pH.

There are a variety of ways to identify appropriate decision thresholds when carrying out CCA. The most effective procedure is to consider the probabilities that linked crimes and unlinked crimes will actually occur (which can also be estimated using the frequencies in Table 11.1) as well as the costs and benefits associated with incorrect and correct decision outcomes [13]. If

$$p(\text{unlinked}) = \frac{b+d}{N}$$

and

$$p(\text{unlinked}) = \frac{a+c}{N}$$

then multiplying the ratio of probabilities by the ratio of costs (C) and benefits (B) as in

$$\frac{p(\text{unlinked})}{p(\text{linked})} \times \frac{B_{CR} + C_{FA}}{B_H + C_M}$$

will indicate a threshold point that results in optimal decision making performance. The problem with this approach, however, is that assigning specific costs and benefits to decision outcomes in CCA can be extremely difficult. For example, how does one calculate the cost of arresting an innocent suspect or the benefit of arresting a guilty one?

As an alternative, it is also possible to set an appropriate decision threshold without considering individual costs and benefits, by simply taking their ratio [13]. For example, a police force may decide it is ten times more important to make correct decisions when faced with linked crimes compared to unlinked crimes. This ratio (1/10) can then be substituted into the above formula in place of specific costs and benefits. Perhaps even more realistically, the above formula can be abandoned altogether and an appropriate decision threshold can be set based on some predetermined limit relating to the rate of false alarms or hits [13]. For example, a police force may decide they do not have the resources to exceed pFA=0.20, and therefore this rate will determine what the appropriate decision threshold is.

The secondary objective of the present study is to explore the impact that different decision thresholds have on linking crimes.

Accurately Evaluating Linking Performance

To achieve the objectives of the present study, a procedure is required that can evaluate the diagnostic accuracy of various linking features and the impact of setting different decision thresholds. Evaluating hit and false alarm rates without also examining

he effect of setting different thresholds will provide only a partial, and potentially
)iased, picture of linking validity. Receiver operating characteristic (ROC) analysis
assesses these two aspects of linking performance simultaneously, thereby providing
a foundation for overall measures of predictive accuracy independent of decision
hresholds [6]. Throughout the past two decades, this technique has become the
evaluation method of choice for assessing decision-making performance across a
wide range of diagnostic settings [6,13,14].

ROC analysis demonstrates how pH and pFA change for a particular diagnostic
eature, or set of features, as decision thresholds are varied from strict to lenient
6]. Both probabilities are calculated across numerous decision thresholds. These
probabilities are then plotted on a ROC graph resulting in a concave curve starting
from the lower left corner of the graph and ending at the upper right corner, as shown
n Figure 11.1. As Swets and his colleagues [6] explain:

> At the far lower left [of the graph] both probabilities are near 0, as they would be for
> a very strict decision threshold, under which the diagnostician rarely makes a positive
> decision [e.g., that two crimes are linked]. At the far upper right both probabilities are
> near 1.0, as they would be for a very lenient threshold, under which the diagnostician
> almost always makes a positive decision. In between the curve rises smoothly, with a
> smoothly decreasing slope, to represent all of the possible decision thresholds (for a given
> accuracy). (p. 6)

he area under a ROC curve, denoted by the symbol A, is a measure of diagnostic
ccuracy for the particular feature(s) that gave rise to that curve [6]. This measure
an range in value from 0.5 (indicating chance accuracy) to 1.0 (indicating perfect
ccuracy). Thus, the area under the ROC curve will be higher as decision-making
ccuracy increases. Specifically, $A=1.0$ is indicated by a curve that follows the
ft and upper axes, and $A=0.5$ is indicated by a diagonal line on the ROC graph
eferred to as the positive diagonal) going from the lower left corner to the upper
ght corner.

Our study, therefore, sets out to determine initially if readily available information
)out burglaries can be shown to provide a statistically significant basis for linking
em to a common offender. The next stage is to carry out ROC analyses in order to
alibrate the validity of the various criteria used on their own and in combination,
nd to examine the effects of setting different decision thresholds.

Iethod

1e Sample

1e present sample of solved serial commercial burglaries was extracted directly
om a database of offences housed in one division of a large metropolitan UK police
rce. The sample consists of two randomly selected crimes from each of 43 serial
urglars who committed burglaries between January 1999 and January 2000. For the

purpose of the present study, a commercial burglary was defined as any burglary where an offender targeted a commercial property rather than a domestic dwelling. A serial burglar was defined as any offender convicted of two or more commercial burglaries.

There were two primary reasons for selecting just two offences from each burglar's crime series. First, the majority of offenders (55%) included in the entire sample were known to be responsible for just two commercial burglaries. Second, maintaining a constant distribution of offences across offenders ensures that the results will not be biased by undue weighting being given to very prolific offenders who may have displayed particularly high (or low) levels of behavioural similarity across their crimes.

Trained crime analysts coded all of the offence information pertaining to these crimes. However, because the information was entered directly into a database immediately after each crime took place, an assessment of coding reliability was not possible. This potentially weakens the quality of the information utilised, but that weakness is likely to add noise to the data and therefore reduce the chance of any significant patterns emerging. The data has the advantage that it is from genuine police records, collected for statutory and crime management purposes. Any findings from such data, therefore, can claim some important ecological validity and consequent practical relevance.

Potential Sources of Bias

It should also be noted that the validity of any findings emerging from this study would be limited by biases in the data. One source of potential bias is a result of focusing solely on serial burglaries and not including non-serial burglaries. While some research suggests that non-serial burglaries may actually be quite rare [15], their absence from the present sample will likely bias the results.

Another source of bias arises from the fact that all burglaries examined in this study have been solved. It is possible that solved burglaries are characterised by higher levels of behavioural similarity than unsolved burglaries. Indeed, this may be one of the reasons why solved burglaries are linked in the first place. If this were true, it would limit the extent to which the findings could be generalised to unsolved offences occurring in the same police division.

The data could also be potentially biased because only commercial burglaries were examined, with each offence having been committed within only one police division during a relatively restricted time period. However, preliminary analyses carried out by the authors suggest that the levels of predictive accuracy found in the present study generally exist for residential as well as commercial burglary, across a number of police divisions, during different time periods (though appropriate decision thresholds appear to be more context dependent). Having said this, no claims are being made that the results from the present study can be directly applied to these other contexts. To make such a statement, more detailed studies would obviously be required.

Lastly, relying on police records as the only source of data in the present study could create potential biases. While there is no obvious alternative method for collecting such data, besides the equally biased option of conducting interviews with offenders, it must be acknowledged that police data can be, and often is, inaccurate [16,17].

Selecting Linking Features

No comprehensive model exists in the published literature that describes the components of burglars' MO. However, drawing on Green et al.'s [13] cluster analysis study and Maguire and Bennett's [18] extensive interviews with offenders, as well as Merry and Harsent's [19] more recent study of burglary, a number of behavioural domains can be identified. These include: (1) entry behaviours (e.g., whether the offender entered through the front door), (2) target selection choices (e.g., whether the offender targeted a filling station), (3) property stolen (e.g., whether the offender stole jewellery) and (4) internal behaviours (e.g., whether the offender consumed food while in the property).

Within the police database used for this study, information pertaining to entry behaviours, target selection choices and property stolen was coded in dichotomous form across all of the offences, indicating the presence or absence of particular crime scene behaviours. This information was extracted from the database for the present study. However, information pertaining to internal behaviours was not coded by the police force, and therefore this aspect of burglary behaviour could not be examined.

In addition to these three behavioural domains, an important fourth aspect of the crimes, involving offender spatial behaviour, was also examined. This information took the form of the distance in kilometres between every pair of burglary locations. The reason for considering this aspect of burglary behaviour is the growing body of literature indicating that many offenders, including burglars, do not travel far to commit their crimes [20–22]. Within the police database used for this study, information pertaining to this aspect of burglary behaviour was available in geo-coded x-y co-ordinates. This information was also extracted from the database for the present study.

Computational Procedures

The dependent variable in the present study was whether the same offender or different offenders committed a pair of crimes. The independent variables were all continuous and included: (1) the distance in kilometres between every pair of crimes, and across-crime similarity measures pertaining to (2) entry behaviours, (3) target selection choices and (4) property stolen. Each of these independent variables is based on the premise that a higher degree of behavioural similarity will be exhibited across crimes committed by the same offender. Thus, it was expected that crimes committed by the same offender would be characterised by shorter inter-crime distances and higher across-crime similarity scores for entry behaviours, target selection choices, and property stolen.

Due to the large number of crime pairs that result from a sample of 86 offences, two computer programs were developed to automate the process of calculating measures of behavioural and spatial similarity. The first computer program takes as input a series of dichotomously coded variables pertaining to each of the three behavioural domains. These variables indicate the presence or absence of the specific behavioural features making up these domains. For example, variables related to entry behaviour include such things as 'entered through front door' (*yes/ no*), 'entered on ground floor' (*yes/no*), and 'used a screwdriver to gain entry' (*yes/ no*). This program then provides as output a similarity measure between every pair of crimes. These similarity measures provide the basis for the subsequent regression and ROC analyses dealing with each behavioural domain.

Jaccard's coefficient was used as the similarity measure for each of the three behavioural domains. Jaccard's coefficient is a measure of association that does not take account of joint nonoccurrences. In other words, if a particular behaviour is absent across two crimes, the level of similarity between those crimes will not increase. As an example, consider two burglaries that have been dichotomously coded across 17 entry behaviours, where 0 indicates a behaviour that was absent and 1 indicates a behaviour that was present. The pattern of entry behaviours in crime 1 is 00000000000001111 and in crime 2 it is 11000000001111111. If a equals the number of behaviours present in both crimes (1/1), b and c equal the number of behaviours present in one crime but not the other (1/0 and 0/1), and d equals the number of behaviours absent from both crimes (0/0), Jaccard's coefficient can be calculated by

$$\frac{a}{a+b+c}$$

Thus, in the above example, where $a=4$, $b=5$ and $c=0$, Jaccard's coefficient is equal to 0.44 (a value of 1 would indicate total similarity in the behaviours expressed and a value of 0 would indicate no similarity in the behaviours expressed).

Considering the unverifiable nature of burglary data, and the distinct possibility that variables were not recorded as being present when they were in fact present, it may be useful to ignore joint non-occurrences when assessing across-crime similarity. The use of Jaccard's coefficient for this purpose is also in line with previous examinations of CCA [23], as well as numerous other studies that have utilised police data to identify patterns in offending behaviour [24–27]. However, it should be pointed out that Jaccard's coefficient is a relatively coarse-grained coefficient and therefore it may be useful in the future to develop a more refined similarity measure.

The second computer program takes as input the geo-coded x-y co-ordinates from the police database and provides as output the distance in kilometres between every pair of crimes. These intercrime distances provide the basis for the subsequent regression and ROC analyses dealing with distances.

Statistical Procedures

Logistic regression analysis was used in the present study to examine the possibility of utilising various linking features to carry out CCA. In this context, the log odds of a crime pair being linked are expressed as a linear combination of across-crime similarity scores. This combination of scores can be expressed in the form of a logistic regression equation, as in

$$\log\left(\frac{p}{1-p}\right) = \alpha + \beta_1 X_1 + \beta_2 X_2 + ... + \beta_n X_n$$

where p is the probability of a crime pair being linked, α is a constant, and $\beta_1...\beta_n$ are logit coefficients with which to multiply the observed across-crime similarity scores, represented as $X_1...X_n$.

The log odds, calculated using the above formula, can easily be transformed into the odds of a crime pair being linked, which is a ratio of the probability that a crime pair is linked to the probability that the crime pair is unlinked. To calculate the odds, the log odds are simply exponentiated, as in

$$\text{odds(linked)} = e^{\alpha + \beta_1 X_1 + \beta_2 X_2 + ... + \beta_n X_n}$$

If the odds are equal to 1, a crime pair is just as likely to be linked as it is to be unlinked. In contrast, if the odds are less than 1 a crime pair is more likely to be unlinked, and if the odds are greater than 1 a crime pair is more likely to be linked.

The odds can also be converted into a probability that a crime pair is linked. These probabilities are calculated by dividing the odds by 1 plus the odds, as in

$$p\text{(linked)} = \frac{\text{odds}}{1 + \text{odds}} = \frac{e^{\alpha + \beta_1 X_1 + \beta_2 X_2 + ... + \beta_n X_n}}{1 + e^{\alpha + \beta_1 X_1 + \beta_2 X_2 + ... + \beta_n X_n}}$$

The probability of a crime pair being linked can range from 0 to 1, with higher values indicating a greater chance of being linked. Two different logistic regression methods were used in the present study. The first method was direct logistic regression where linking features are entered into the regression model simultaneously [28]. This method was used to examine the linking features separately. The second method was forward stepwise logistic regression where linking features are entered into the regression model in a stepwise fashion [28]. As Getty et al. [7] explain, the variable added at each step is the one that, "...most improves the predictive power of the [model] given the set of variables already included" (p. 473). This process stops once the addition of any more variables fails to result in a significant increase in the models predictive power. Forward stepwise logistic regression was used to identify the optimal combination of features for linking purposes.

Statistical Issues

When working with log odds, odds and probabilities in logistic regression analysis, it is important to remember two general points. The first point is that all three values provide the same information, only in a slightly different form. Therefore, which values are used is simply a matter of preference. The second point is that all three values are effected by how often linked crime pairs occur. For example, since linked crime pairs will usually be rare compared to unlinked crimes pairs it should come as no surprise when linked crime pairs are associated with relatively low probabilities. What is important in this case are not the actual values of these probabilities, but rather how these probabilities compare to the probabilities associated with unlinked crime pairs.

Also in relation to the use of logistic regression analysis in this study, another important point must be addressed. Typically, the dependent variable used when carrying out regression analysis is statistically independent, in the sense that error associated with one observation is not associated with error from any other observation [29]. This is as it should be. In the present study, however, sampling all possible pairs of crimes consists of observations that may not be statistically independent, since different pairs include crimes committed by the same offender. When the dependent variable is not independent, problems can arise. In such cases, the estimates of standard error corresponding to regression coefficients tend to be smaller than they actually are, though the coefficients themselves will not be biased. This is problematic because it means that inferential tests that depend on these estimates of error cannot be relied upon [30]. Thus, while goodness-of-fit tests will not be problematic in the present study, tests used to measure the predictive accuracy of specific independent variables (e.g., Wald's test) might be.

In this study, the problem of independence is avoided to a large extent because measures of predictive accuracy for each linking feature, or combination of features, are generated from their corresponding ROC curves rather than from regression analysis (see below). The measures of accuracy used in ROC analysis do not rely on estimates of standard error in the same way that formal inferential tests in logistic regression do. As a result, the derived measures of predictive accuracy should not be biased in the way just described even if the dependent variable examined in the present study is not statistically independent.

Evaluating Linking Performance

In order to reduce the potential bias that exists if regression models are developed and tested on the same sample of commercial burglaries, the present sample was randomly split in half to form an *experimental sample* and a *test sample* [31,32]. Logistic regression models were developed using only the data in the experimental sample and ROC analyses were carried out using only the data in the test sample. The data in the test sample consists of estimated probabilities for each crime pair, calculated using the logistic regression models constructed from the experimental sample. All ROC analyses were carried out using ROCKIT©, a computer package designed by the Department of Radiology at the University of Chicago [33].

　　This procedure of developing and testing the regression models on two separate samples provides some indication of model validity. The degree of validity, however, will depend on how closely the test sample approximates reality and the potential biases previously discussed must again be considered. The solved serial burglaries examined in the present study are probably similar to a portion of commercial burglaries that will occur within this police force in the future. Consequently, it is appropriate for these offences to form part of the test sample. In spite of this, a more realistic test sample would also have included non-serial burglaries as well as unsolved burglaries if this were in fact possible. Since non-serial burglaries are not included in the test sample, the results in the present study should be interpreted with an appropriate level of caution.

Results

Single Feature Regression Models

Direct logistic regression analysis was first run on each of the linking features separately to determine the extent to which single feature regression models can successfully predict whether crime pairs are linked or unlinked. The first four columns in Table 11.2 contain a summary of these models, including their logit coefficients, standard errors, model X^2 values and R^2 values.

　　The results in Table 11.2 suggest that the single feature regression models are able to reliably distinguish between linked and unlinked crimes. This is reflected in the fact that all regression models have X^2 values that are significant at the 10% level (at least) indicating a good degree of fit with the data. However, these X^2 values also suggest that the models differ with respect to their level of fit. Specifically, the model including inter-crime distances appears to be the most accurate, followed respectively by the models including entry behaviours, target selection choices and property stolen. This ordering of the models is also consistent with the R^2 values presented in Table 11.2, which indicate the proportion of variance explained in the dependent variable by each regression model. Excluding the model containing intercrime distances, all of the R^2 values are extremely low.

　　As expected, the signs of the logit coefficients included in the first four columns of Table 11.2 suggest that crimes pairs committed by the same offender tend to be shorter distances from one another (logit $= -0.97$) but have higher levels of across-crime similarity for entry behaviours (logit $= +2.68$), target selection choices (logit $=$

Table 11.2   Summary of logistic regression analyses

Variables	Statistics	Model 1	Model 2	Model 3	Model 4	Model 5 (optimal)
Constant	Logit coeff.	−2.17	−5.08	−5.16	−4.72	−2.82
	Standard error	0.34	0.33	0.43	0.30	0.44
Distance	Logit coeff.	−0.97				−0.88
	Standard error	0.19				0.19
Entry	Logit coeff.		2.68			2.05
	Standard error		0.70			0.73
Target	Logit coeff.			1.98		
	Standard error			0.87		
Property	Logit coeff.				1.33	
	Standard error				0.71	
	Model X^2	43.80	11.80	4.25	3.08	50.88
	Sig. of X^2	$p<0.001$	$p<0.001$	$p<0.05$	$p<0.10$	$p<0.001$
	R^2	0.19	0.05	0.02	0.02	0.023

Models 1–4: method of analysis was direct logistic regression
Model 5: method of analysis was forward stepwise logistic regression (inclusion criteria: $p<0.05$)
Dependent variable: linked crime pair (1), unlinked crime pair (0)

+1.98), and property stolen (logit = +1.33). To determine what these logit coefficients mean in more practical terms, they can be exponentiated. This procedure indicates how a change of 'c' units in any of the independent variables affects the odds that two crimes are linked [34].

As an example, the effect of increasing the distance between two crimes by 1.00 km is

$$\text{odds} = e^{(c \times \text{logit})} = e^{(1.0 \times -0.97)} = 0.38$$

which suggests that for every increase of 1.00 km between any two crimes, the odds that the crimes are linked are multiplied by 0.38 (which would reduce them).

Alternatively, the impact of changes in the independent variables can be examined in terms of changes in probability. For example, given the model for distance in Table 11.2, and a pair of crimes that are 1.00 km apart, the probability that those crimes are linked can be estimated

$$\text{log odds (linked)} = -2.17 - 0.97(1.00) = -3.14$$
$$\text{odds(linked)} = 0.04$$
$$p(\text{linked}) = 0.04$$

Thus, the probability of two crimes being linked when they are 1.00 km apart is 0.04, which is relatively high considering the extremely low percentage of linked crime pairs in the sample.

In contrast, given a pair of crimes that are 2.00 km apart, the estimated probability of the crimes being linked can be seen to decrease by 0.02

$$\text{log odds (linked)} = -2.17 - 0.97(2.00) = -4.11$$
$$\text{odds(linked)} = 0.02$$
$$p(\text{linked}) = 0.02$$

confirming that linked crime pairs do tend to be characterised by shorter inter-crime distances.

Similarly, each of the other logit coefficients in Table 11.2 can be exponentiated to determine how changes in their values affect the odds that two crimes are linked. In these cases, however, a change of 1 unit will not be particularly meaningful considering that each similarity measure has a potential range from 0 to 1. Instead, it makes more sense to examine the effect of increasing the measures by 0.10, which can be calculated by multiplying the logit coefficients by 0.10 before exponentiating them. Given the three models for entry behaviours, target selection choices and property stolen in Table 11.2, the effect of increasing the across-crime similarity measures between any two crimes by 0.10 is 1.31, 1.22 and 1.14 respectively. In other words, for every increase of 0.10 units, the odds that the crimes are linked would be multiplied by 1.31 for entry behaviours, 1.22 for target selection choices, and 1.14 for property stolen.

Multiple Feature Regression Models

To determine the extent to which combinations of linking features can successfully predict whether crime pairs are linked or unlinked, forward stepwise logistic regression analysis was used. The last column in Table 11.2 contains a summary of the optimal regression model. As would be expected, the optimal model contains the two most effective predictors from the previous analysis, which were inter-crime distances and entry behaviours. Also unsurprisingly, the optimal model is able to distinguish between linked and unlinked crimes more accurately than any single feature regression model, as indicated by the significantly higher X^2 value associated with this model as well as the higher R^2 value.

As indicated in Table 11.3, one reason why target selection choices and property stolen were not included in the optimal model, even though they were relatively accurate as single linking features, is because significant correlations exist between

Table 11.3   Correlations between linking features

	Entry	Target	Property
Distance	−0.03 $p>0.05$	−0.12 $p<0.001$	−0.10 $p<0.001$
Entry		0.16 $p<0.001$	0.18 $p<0.001$
Target			0.14 $p<0.001$

Table 11.4   Correlations and partial correlations between linking features and the dependent variable

	Correlations	Partial correlations
Distance	−0.13 $p>0.05$	−0.12 $p<0.001$
Entry	0.09 $p<0.001$	0.08 $p<0.001$
Target	0.06 $p<0.05$	0.03 $p>0.10$
Property	0.05 $p<0.10$	0.01 $p>0.10$

the linking features. The important exception to this is the correlation between inter-crime distances and entry behaviours. As a result, it is highly likely that each linking feature will not *uniquely* account for a significant portion of the variance in the dependent variable, which would enable them all to be included in the optimal model [36]. The correlations presented in Table 11.4 support this argument. They show that while each linking feature is significantly correlated with the dependent variable, only two features remain highly correlated when the effects of all other features are removed. The remaining two features are inter-crime distances and entry behaviours, which explains why they form the optimal regression model.

As before, the practical significance of the logit coefficients in this optimal regression model can be explored by exponentiating them. When these calculations are carried out, it can be seen that for every increase of 1.00 km between any two

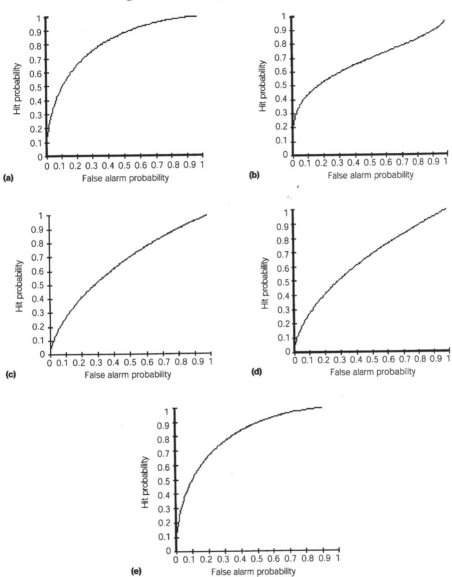

**Figure 11.1 ROC graphs for single and optimal linking features. (a) Distance
A=0.80 (b) Target *A*=0.68 (c) Entry *A*=0.65 (d) Property *A*=0.63
(c) Optimal *A*=0.18**

crimes, the odds that the crimes are linked are multiplied by 0.41. When increasing
similarity measures pertaining to entry behaviours by 0.10, the odds that the crimes
are linked are multiplied by 1.23.

Evaluating Linking Performance

In order to get some general measure of model validity that indicates how well each model might perform on other solved commercial burglaries in the same police division, the regression models presented in Table 11.2 were used to calculate estimated probabilities for every possible crime pair in the test sample. These probabilities were then used to construct five ROC graphs, one for each linking feature separately and one for the optimal combination of features. These ROC graphs are presented in Figure 11.1 along with their overall levels of predictive accuracy as measured by the area under each ROC curve.

Consistent with the analysis of the experimental sample, the ROC curves generated from the single linking features indicate that each feature results in overall levels of accuracy that are significantly greater than chance ($p<0.001$). However, in terms of their predictive accuracy, the ordering of linking features is slightly different than expected from the experimental sample. Clearly, inter-crime distances are still the most accurate linking feature ($A=0.80$), but this is now followed respectively by similarity measures pertaining to target selection choices ($A=0.68$), entry behaviours ($A=0.65$) and property stolen ($A=0.63$). The level of accuracy resulting from the use of intercrime distances is significantly greater than the levels of accuracy obtained when using target selection choices, entry behaviours or property stolen ($p<0.05$). However, no significant differences were found between these three aspects of burglary behaviour ($p>0.10$).

Also consistent with the analysis of the experimental sample, the ROC curve generated from the optimal linking features indicates that this combination of features result in an overall level of accuracy slightly higher than any single linking feature ($A=0.81$). However, the level of overall accuracy obtained when using inter-crime distances and entry behaviours is not significantly greater than the level of accuracy obtained when using inter-crime distances alone ($p>0.10$). This result may seem at odds with the finding in the experimental sample, where the optimal regression model fit the data significantly better than the distance-only model. This can be explained by the fact that the similarity measure pertaining to entry behaviours has a lower level of predictive accuracy in the test sample compared to what they had in the experimental sample.

The Impact of Setting Different Decision Thresholds

The impact that different decision thresholds have on linking performance is also made clear in the ROC graphs. Regardless of the model used, as decision thresholds are made more lenient, pH and pFA both increase. This can be illustrated in Figure 11.1 using the ROC curve generated from inter-crime distances. Consider a decision threshold of $p\geq0.05$, which corresponds to an approximate inter-crime distance of 0.70 km. At this particular threshold, 52.4% of linked crime pairs are correctly classified while 93.2% of unlinked crime pairs are correctly classified. However, at the more lenient threshold of p≥0.01, which corresponds to an approximate inter-crime distance of 2.50 km, 61.9% of linked crime pairs are correctly classified while only 67.7% of unlinked crime pairs are.

The practical significance of using different linking features is also made clear in the ROC graphs by considering how many more hits (or how many less false alarms) will be made at a particular decision threshold depending upon the feature selected for analysis. Take the previously mentioned example where a police force decides to set a limit on the rate of false alarms at $pFA=0.20$. For the ROC curve corresponding to property stolen in Figure 11.1, this particular threshold results in ROC co-ordinates of $pH=0.40$ and $pFA=0.20$. The threshold point for the ROC curve corresponding to inter-crime distances at the same pFA has a $pH=0.64$. Thus, if an investigator is primarily concerned with making additional hits, they could identify 24 additional linked crime pairs for every 100 pairs encountered if inter-crime distances were drawn on instead of property stolen. Similar comparisons can be made between any of the other linking features.

Discussion and Conclusion

Logistic regression and ROC analysis have been used to determine if the degree of across-crime similarity in cases of commercial burglary is high enough for selected aspects of burglary behaviour to allow different crimes to be validly linked to the same offender. Both forms of analysis support the possibility of utilising objectively available aspects of a burglar's MO in a systematic way to carry out valid CCA.

Linking Crimes Through Spatial Similarity

It has been demonstrated that the distance between burglary locations is an extremely consistent and stable aspect of commercial burglary behaviour within the particular police division where the present study was carried out. At a theoretical level then, this study adds something to the growing body of literature that has indicated, since the work of White [36] and Shaw [37], that offenders typically do not travel very far to commit their crimes. The results reported here take the understanding of criminal mobility a stage further by indicating that burglars within a given police jurisdiction, who do not live too close to one another, may have relatively distinct areas of criminal activity. This accords well with Grubin et al.'s [2] recent study of rapists where it was shown that linking accuracy could be enhanced by using spatial information. However, Grubin et al.'s study suffered from the possible artefact that the rape series they examined were drawn from all over the UK. Distinguishing such offence series by the locality in which the offences occurred is therefore not as stringent a test as the present study of commercial burglaries where a relatively small area of the country was examined.

In practical terms, this finding suggests that inter-crime distances can provide a powerful, and relatively simple way of linking commercial burglaries. Specifically, this linking feature may prove useful as an effective first filter when carrying out CCA to reduce the number of potential links that initially need to be examined. Considering the current state of technology in the majority of modern police forces, it would be feasible to draw on the results presented in this chapter and combine them with digital maps of police divisions to create likely 'linkage areas'. Crimes committed within certain distances of one another could be given a high priority and then additional analytical techniques could be used to further reduce the number of false alarms. Drawing on different burglary behaviours, obvious signature aspects, temporal information, or police intelligence could prove useful for this purpose.

Linking Crimes Through Behavioural Similarity

The present study also indicates that similarity measures pertaining to other behavioural domains can be used to link commercial burglaries, though not to the same degree as inter-crime distances. Consequently, the validity of CCA, in its initial stages at least, will depend on what features are used to perform the analysis. The lower level of predictive accuracy for target selection choices, entry behaviours and property stolen is generally consistent with existing research. This research suggests that crime scene behaviours often change across crimes due to external situational influences and internal learning processes [38,39]. Nevertheless, the police often use these behaviours for linking purposes, either formally or informally, and in some cases they form the basis for a legal argument of similar fact evidence [40]. Therefore, there is some value in assessing the accuracy of each behavioural domain in order to understand the patterns of activity that burglars exhibit.

While similarity measures pertaining to target selection choices, entry behaviours and property stolen provide a basis for linking crimes committed by the same offender, their level of predictive accuracy (relative to one another) appears to vary across different samples of offences. This finding supports the idea that these behaviours are more context-dependent than inter-crime distances. Indeed, the results presented in this chapter provide preliminary evidence that the differences in predictive accuracy levels across all linking features may relate to how situation dependent the features are. The property an offender steals, for example, is perhaps the most situation-specific set of behaviours in burglary, depending as they do on what is available to be stolen. The recording of this information in official records may also be unreliable both because of what the police choose to record and because of what the property owner chooses to say was stolen [16]. This may explain why property stolen leads to the least accurate predictions in both the experimental sample and the test sample.

In general, as linking validity increases so to does the apparent extent to which linking features consist of behaviours that can be determined by the offender – from the property they steal, to their entry and targeting behaviour, to where they initially go to commit the crime. This finding is consistent with studies of noncriminal consistency, where operant behaviours (i.e., behaviours emitted by the person across a range of situations) are usually exhibited in a more consistent fashion than respondent behaviours (i.e., behaviours that require specific, eliciting stimuli within situations) [41,42]. The practical importance of such a finding is that it may provide investigators with a means of predicting, *a priori*, what aspects of burglary behaviour will be most useful for CCA.

Combining Linking Features to Enhance Linking Performance

Another significant finding in the present study is the possibility of achieving higher levels of accuracy in CCA when combinations of carefully chosen features are used. Compared to the single feature models, an increase in the overall level of predictive accuracy was observed in the experimental sample and the test sample when inter-crime distances and entry behaviours were used simultaneously. However, in the test sample this increase did not reach the point of being statistically significant compared to the distance-only model. One of the reasons for this was that entry behaviours had less predictive power in the test sample. This reinforces the need to identify stable linking features when developing optimal linking models; features that maintain a high level of predictive accuracy across different samples of offences. If such features can be identified in commercial burglary, beyond those related to spatial behaviour, then combining these features with the distances that exist between burglary locations will likely result in models with significantly more predictive power.

Despite the lack of a significant finding in the test sample, examining the accuracy of feature combinations is important for CCA because of the inherent unreliability in any single piece of information collected as part of a police investigation. A careful combination of selected features could counteract problems there might be in recording such material. Discovering a way of achieving maximum predictive power in CCA using the fewest possible number of linking features is also important because it would reduce the need to collect a great deal of information on a crime, with the attendant problems of such large-scale data collection. It implies that collecting appropriate, possibly limited, information carefully may be more effective than collecting a great deal of information in the hope that some of it may turn out to be of value. Thus, instead of developing longer, more comprehensive linking pro formas, the methods of analysis presented in this study open up the possibility of finding ways to provide more manageable guidance that is just as effective, simply by cutting out unneeded redundancies in the behavioural features that are used.

The Importance of Decision Thresholds

Lastly, the present study demonstrates the impact that decision thresholds have on linking performance. When using single linking features or combinations of features, linking accuracy was shown to depend on the exact position of the decision threshold. Specifically, both pH and pFA could be seen to increase in value as decision thresholds became more lenient. This highlights the need to identify appropriate decision thresholds in CCA that produce a desired balance between the four possible decision outcomes.

One possible strategy for accomplishing this goal was examined here, whereby a limit was set on the rate of false alarms that could be made. However, alternative strategies also exist. These alternatives require the costs and benefits associated with the various decision outcomes in CCA to be made explicit. Such decisions may be extremely difficult to make, in particular when human rights and lives are at stake, and the decisions will necessarily involve both economic as well as ethical considerations. However, carrying out such cost-benefit analyses could lead to decision support tools in CCA that are fine-tuned to quite specific investigative situations, in a similar way to what is being done in other diagnostic settings [43].

Acknowledgements

This research was supported by an Overseas Research Scholarship awarded to the first author by the Overseas Research Students Awards Scheme. The authors would like to thank Chris Setzkorn for his assistance with software development. The authors are also grateful to Brent Snook, Laurence Alison and two anonymous reviewers for their helpful comments on an earlier version of this article.

References

1 Green, E.J., Booth, C.E. and Biderman, M.D. (1976). Cluster analysis of burglary MO's. *Journal of Police Science and Administration*, 4, 382–387.
2 Grubin, D., Kelly, P. and Brunsdon, C. (2001). *Linking Serious Sexual Assaults Through Behaviour*. London: Home Office.
3 Canter, D.V. (2000). *Criminal Shadows: The Inner Narratives of Evil*. Texas: Authorlink Press.
4 Maltz, M.D., Gordon, A.C. and Friedman, W. (1990). Understanding and using information about crime. In: Maltz, M.D., Gordon, A.C. and Friedman, F., (eds), *Mapping Crime in its Community: Event Geography Analysis*. New York: Springer-Verlag, 44–58.
5 Wilson, M., Canter, D.V., Jack, K. and Butterworth, D. (1996). *The Psychology of Rape Investigations*. ESRC Report, University of Liverpool, Liverpool.
6 Swets, J.A., Dawes, R.M. and Monahan, J. (2000). Psychological science can improve diagnostic decisions. *Psychological Science in the Public Interest*, 1, 1–26.
7 Getty, D.J., Seltzer, S.E., Tempany, C.M.C., Pickett, R.M., Swets, J.A. and McNeil, B.J. (1997). Prostate cancer: Relative effects of demographic, clinical, histologic, and MR imaging variables on the accuracy of staging. *Radiology*, 204, 471–479.

8 Lo, J.Y., Baker, J.A., Kornguth, P.J., Iglehart, J.D. and Floyd, C.E. (1997). Predicting breast cancer invasion with artificial neural networks on the basis of mammographic features. *Radiology*, 203, 159–163.

9 Keppel, R.D. and Birnes, W.J. (1997). *Signature Killers: Interpreting the Calling Cards of the Serial Murderer*. New York: Pocket Books, 1997.

10 Keppel, R.D. (2000). Signature murders: A report of the 1984 Cranbrook, British Columbia cases. *Journal of Forensic Sciences*, 45, 508–511.

11 Canter, D.V. (2000). Offender profiling and criminal differentiation. *Legal and Criminological Psychology*, 5, 23–46.

12 Klein, M.W. (1984). Offence specialisation and versatility among juveniles. *British Journal of Criminology*, 24, 185–194.

13 Swets, J.A. (1996). *Signal Detection Theory and ROC Analysis in Psychology and Diagnostics*. Mahwah, NJ: Lawrence Erlbaum Associates.

14 Swets, J.A. and Pickett, R.M. (1982). *Evaluation of Diagnostic Systems: Methods from Signal Detection Theory*. New York: Academic Press.

15 Hindelang, M.J., Hirschi, T. and Weis, J.G. (1981). *Measuring Delinquency*. Beverley Hills, CA: Sage Publications.

16 Alison, L.J., Snook, B. and Stein, K. (2001). Unobtrusive measurement: Using police information for forensic research. *Qualitative Research*, 1, 241–254.

17 Farrington, D.P. and Lambert, S. (1992). *The Feasibility of a Statistical Approach to Offender Profiling: Burglary and Violence in Nottinghamshire*. London: Home Office.

18 Maguire, M. and Bennett, T. (1982). *Burglary in a Dwelling: The Offence, the Offender and the Victim*. London: Home Office.

19 Merry, S. and Harsent, L. (2000). Intruders, pilferers, raiders and invaders: The interpersonal dimension of burglary. In Canter, D.V. and Alison, L.J. (eds), *Profiling Property Crimes*. Aldershot: Ashgate Publishing Limited, 33–56.

20 Canter, D.V. and Larkin, P. (1993). The environmental range of serial rapists. *Journal of Environmental Psychology*, 13, 63–69.

21 Rossmo, D.K. (1993). Target patterns of serial murderers: A methodological model. *American Journal of Criminal Justice*, 17, 1–21.

22 Wiles, P. and Costello, A. (2000). *The Road to Nowhere: The Evidence for Travelling Criminals*. London: Home Office.

23 Canter, D.V. and Heritage, R. (1991). *A Facet Approach to Offender Profiling*. London: Home Office.

24 Bennell, C., Alison, L.J., Stein, K., Alison, E. and Canter, D.V. (2001). Sexual offences against children as the abusive exploitation of conventional adult-child relationships. *Journal of Social and Personal Relationships*, 18, 149–165.

25 Canter, D.V. and Fritzon, K. (1998). Differentiating arsonists: A model of fire-setting actions and characteristics. *Legal and Criminological Psychology*, 3, 73–96.

26 Canter, D.V., Hughes, D. and Kirby, S. (1998). Paedophilia: Pathology, criminality or both? The development of a multivariate model of offence behaviour in child sexual abuse. *Journal of Forensic Psychiatry*, 9, 532–555.

27 Salfati, C.G. and Canter, D.V. (1999). Differentiating stranger murders: Profiling offender characteristics from behavioural styles. *Behavioural Sciences and the Law*, 17, 391–406.

28 Tabachnick, B.G. and Fidell, L.S. (1996). *Using Multivariate Statistics*. New York: Harper Collins Publishers.

29 Lewis-Beck, M.S. (1980). *Applied Regression: An Introduction*. London: Sage Publications.

30 Chatterjee, S. and Price, B. (1977). *Regression Analysis by Example*. New York: John Wiley and Sons.

31 Efron, B. (1982). *The Jackknife, the Bootstrap and Other Re-sampling Plans*. Philadelphia, PA: Society for Industrial and Applied Mathematics.

32 Gong, G. (1986). Cross-validation, the jackknife, and the bootstrap: Excess error estimation in forward logistic regression. *Journal of the American Statistical Association*, 81, 108–113.

33 Metz, C.E., Herman, B.A. and Roe, C.A. (1998). Statistical comparison of two ROC curve estimates obtained from partially paired data sets. *Medical Decision Making*, 18, 110–121.

34 Hosmer, D.W. and Lemeshow, S. (1989). *Applied Logistic Regression*. New York: John Wiley and Sons.

35 Cohen, J. and Cohen, P. (1983). *Applied Multiple Regression/Correlation Analysis for the Behavioural Sciences*. London: Lawrence Erlbaum Associates.

36 White, R.C. (1932). The relation of felonies to environmental factors in Indianapolis. *Social Forces*, 10, 459–467.

37 Shaw, C. (1942). *Juvenile Delinquency and Urban Areas*. Chicago: University of Chicago Press.

38 Douglas, J.E. and Munn, C. (1992). Violent crime scene analysis: *Modus operandi*, signature and staging. *FBI Law Enforcement Bulletin*, 61, 1–10.

39 Davies, A. (1992). Rapist's behaviour: A three-aspect model as a basis for analysis and the identification of serial crime. *Forensic Science International*, 55, 173–194.

40 Ormerod, D. (1999). Criminal profiling: Trial by judge and jury, not criminal psychologist. In Canter, D.V. and Alison, L.J. (eds), *Profiling in Policy and Practice*. Aldershot: Ashgate Publishing Limited, 207–261.

41 Funder, D.C. and Colvin, C.R. (1991). Explorations of behavioural consistency: Properties of persons, situations, and behaviours. *Journal of Personality and Social Psychology*, 60, 773–794.

42 McClelland, D. (1984). Is personality consistent? In: McClelland, D. (ed.), *Motives, Personality and Society*. New York: Praeger, 185–211.

43 Schwartz, J.S., Dans, P.E. and Kinosian, B.P. (1988). Human immunodeficiency virus test evaluation, performance, and use: Proposals to make good tests better. *Journal of the American Medical Association*, 259, 2574–2579.

Chapter 12

Predicting the Home Location of Serial Offenders: A Preliminary Comparison of the Accuracy of Human Judges with a Geographic Profiling System

Brent Snook, M.Sc.,* David Canter, Ph.D., and Craig Bennell, M.Sc.

Introduction

In recent years, a variety of algorithms have been used to predict the home location of unknown serial offenders on the basis of crime locations that have been linked to one offender (Canter and Larkin 1993; Rossmo 1993). These have evolved from spatial typologies such as the marauder/commuter distinction (Canter and Gregory 1994) to software packages that can provide direct support to investigations, often known as geographic profiling systems (Canter, Coffey, Huntley, and Missen 2000; Levine & Associates 2000; Rossmo 1993, 2000). Until very recently, however, the predictive accuracy of these geographic profiling systems had not been compared to other predictive methods.

Levine and Associates (2000) compared a variety of predictive methods, such as those used in geographic profiling systems, to identify those methods that were most accurate. In a task that involved using crime site locations to predict the home location of 50 serial offenders they compared the accuracy of spatial distribution methods (e.g., spatial, geometric, and harmonic means) with the accuracy of journey-to-crime methods (e.g., mathematical and kernel density functions). The distance (in miles) between the predicted home base and the actual home location produced similar results for each method. So, although no statistical tests were reported, Levine and his associates concluded that all methods were of equal utility. As a consequence, they suggested that crime analysts should continue to look at the distribution of crime locations and make predictions about where the offender may

*This research was supported by Overseas Research Scholarships awarded to Snook and Bennell by the Overseas Research Students Award Scheme. The authors would like to thank Gareth Norris for assisting in the data collection and Andreas Mokros and Pavel Toropov for their helpful comments on earlier versions of this chapter.

be residing without needing the support of software packages or other computer based geographic profiling systems.

If the various procedures tested by Levine and his associates give similar results this raises the possibility that the essential principles of geographic profiling are relatively straightforward and could therefore be utilized by crime analysts with minimal training without the need for a geographic profiling system. In other words, it is hypothesized that if individuals are informed of some clear principles that may underlie offender spatial behavior they will make predictions that are as accurate as those produced by geographic profiling systems.

This is an important hypothesis to test because, if supported, it would question Rossmo's (2000) suggestion that in order for individuals to be qualified to use a geographic profiling system to make geographic predictions they should have three years experience investigating interpersonal crimes and a superior level of investigative skill. Support of the hypothesis would also question the need for police forces with limited resources and technological capabilities to invest in geographic profiling systems.

Therefore, as a preliminary examination of these issues, the current study tested the extent to which human judges could accurately predict the home location of serial offenders before and after training. This study also compared the accuracy of these predictions to those produced using a geographic profiling system.

Study Design

Defining Predictive Accuracy
At the most basic level, a geographic profile is a prediction of the most likely location at which the search for a serial offender's home should commence. A geographic profile may also include consideration of temporal and behavioral information, and a search strategy beyond the most likely home location. For the current study, however, the consideration of accuracy was limited to the prediction of the most likely home location. This accuracy was measured from the distance between the predicted and actual home location on the spatial displays used (henceforth referred to as error distance, measured in millimeters).

Two Heuristics for Predicting Home Locations
Part one of the study investigated the extent to which participants could improve in their predictive accuracy if provided with two heuristics frequently mentioned in the geographic profiling literature: 'distance decay' and 'the circle hypothesis.'

The first heuristic emanated from the consistent finding that offenders do not travel far from home to offend and that the frequency of offending decreases with increased distance from an offender's home location; a concept known as 'distance decay' (Capone and Nichols 1976; Turner 1969). The second heuristic originated from tests of the 'circle hypothesis' first proposed by Canter and Larkin (1993). They found that the majority of serial rapists did not typically commit crimes outside a circle with its diameter defined by the distance between the offender's two furthermost offences. Subsequent research by Kocsis and Irwin (1997) and Tamura and Suzuki (1997), using different types of crime, has also found support for this hypothesis.

A significant reduction in error distance after being provided with the two heuristics would indicate that participants are able to use the heuristics to improve and structure their geographic predictions.

Predicting Home Locations Using Dragnet
The second part of the study examined the possibility that participants told about these heuristics could make predictions that are as accurate as those produced by a geographic profiling system. The geographic profiling system used in the current study was Dragnet, described in detail by Canter et al. (2000). In essence, it uses a distance-decay function selected by the user from the negative exponential family. The function identified as optimal by Canter and his associates for a sample of U.S. serial murderers was used in the current study. This function is converted into probabilities around each crime location, indicating the likelihood that any location around an offence contains the home/base of the offender. These probabilities are then combined at each point in the total search area. In the current study, the point on each map where the average probability was highest is taken as the predicted home and was used to measure error distance.

If error distances when using Dragnet were found to be significantly smaller than error distances for the trained human judges this would suggest that the participants were unable to make predictions that were as accurate as Dragnet, even when using appropriate heuristics.

Method

Participants

Participants in the control group consisted of 21 students (four undergraduates, 17 postgraduates), without any knowledge of geographic profiling, studying a variety of disciplines at the University of Liverpool. The 21 students included ten males and 11 females from a variety of nationalities. The age of the students ranged from 19 years to 40 years with an average age of 25.90 years (SD = 5.23).

The experimental group consisted of 21 students (eight undergraduate, 13 postgraduate), without any knowledge of geographic profiling, studying a variety of disciplines. The 21 students included 13 males and eight females from a variety of nationalities. The age of the students ranged from 21 years to 61 years with an average age of 27.67 years (SD = 8.75).

Procedure

In phase 1 of the experiment each of the 21 participants in the control and experimental groups were given ten different spatial displays. Each display represented the locations of five offences for an American serial murderer as points on an otherwise blank sheet of paper. These points were drawn from actual maps but were all adjusted to fit comfortably onto a sheet of A4 paper (21 × 29.7 cm). These spatial displays were used because current geographic profiling systems do not take account of land use or other topographical features. The heuristics and algorithms built into these systems are purely geometric. Participants in both groups were asked to indicate, by marking an 'X' somewhere on each display, where they thought the home of each of the serial murderers was likely to be found. Participants were also given the opportunity to indicate the heuristics they used to reach their conclusions.

Control Group

After the spatial displays given out in phase 1 were collected, participants in the control group were again given the same displays as those used in phase 1. They were asked to indicate a second time where they thought the home location of each of the serial murderers was likely to be located and how they came to their conclusions. They were not given any feedback between the two phases, which were just a few minutes apart.

Experimental Group

For the experimental group, phase 1 was identical to the control group, but after phase 1 they were told

1. the majority of offenders commit offences close to home and
2. the majority of offenders' homes can be located within a circle with its diameter defined by the distance between the offenders two furthermost crimes.

Participants were therefore being provided with the essential information that is utilized by geographic profiling systems. They were then given the same displays again and were asked to indicate where they thought the home of each of the ten serial murderers was likely to be located. They were also asked to indicate the heuristics used to make their predictions.

Dragnet Calculations

Dragnet produces a series of probabilities for each location on the display. By searching through these probabilities the highest value was identified and this was taken as the computer prediction of the home location. A display was then produced the same size as that given to participants and the distance on this display between the computer predicted home location and the actual home location was calculated in millimeters. This distance was taken as Dragnet's error distance for comparison with participants' predictions across the two phases.

Results

Control Group

The mean error distance across all ten displays for the control group in phase 1 was 35.30mm (SD = 22.66) and that in phase 2 was 34.22mm (SD = 21.65; two spatial displays in phase 2 were not filled out). Figure 12.1 illustrates the minimal change in the mean error distance across the two phases for the control group. A related-samples *t*-test confirmed that no significant difference existed between the two phases (t_{207} = 1.63, n.s.).

Experimental Group

The mean error distances before and after the participants were given the heuristics are also shown in Figure 12.1. The mean error distance in phase 1 was 33.94mm (SD = 23.45), and it was 25.65mm (SD = 15.17) after the participants were informed about the heuristics. A related-samples t-test established that these error distances were significantly different (t_{209} = 5.45, $p<0.05$). That is, participants made more accurate predictions when they were provided with the two heuristics.

Control Group, Experimental Group, and Dragnet

The mean error distances for the control group, experimental group, and the average Dragnet value are also shown in Figure 12.1. The figure illustrates the existence of similar baseline results in phase 1 for both the control and experimental groups. An independent t-test did not reveal any significant difference in the mean error distance between the control group and the experimental group in phase 1 of the experiment (t_{418} = 0.61, n.s.). The difference in the mean error distance between the control group and the experimental group in phase 2 of the experiment was significant (t_{416} = 4.70, $p<0.05$). This difference can be explained by the fact that participants in phase 2 of the experimental group were provided with and used the two heuristics.

The average distance from the point of highest probability, as indicated by Dragnet, to the actual home was 25.30 mm (SD = 14.83). A one-sample *t*-test revealed that the error distances for the participants in phase 1 of the control group were significantly larger than those produced by Dragnet (t_{20} = 3.14, $p<0.01$), as were the error distances for participants in phase 2 of the control group (t_{20} = 2.94, $p<0.01$). That is, Dragnet was more accurate than the participants in both phases of the control group.

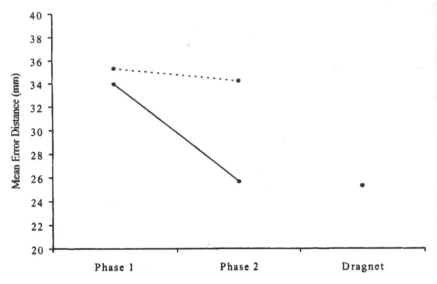

Figure 12.1 Mean error distances for the control group (Dotted Line) and experimental group (Solid Line) across the two phases and Dragnet

A one-sample t-test revealed that the error distances for the participants in phase 1 of the experimental group were also significantly larger than those produced by Dragnet (t_{20} = 2.31, $p<0.05$). However, a one-sample t-test revealed that the error distances for the participants in phase 2 of the experimental group were not significantly different from those produced by Dragnet (t_{20} = 0.40, n.s.). Thus, participants who received a small amount of training on some basic geographic profiling principles were, on average, as accurate as Dragnet.

Offender Spatial Behavior and the Predictions

While there was a general trend for some of the participants provided with heuristics to improve in their predictions, and to make predictions as accurate as Dragnet, there were a number of spatial displays where reductions in error distance were not found, even after participants were provided with the heuristics. Table 12.1 contains the mean error distances for the control group and experimental group in relation to the ten serial murderers across the two phases of the experiment. Results in the table reveal that there are no significant reductions in error distance between phase 1 and phase 2 for the control group. In the experimental group, however, significant reductions in error distance are found between phase 1 and phase 2 for half of the serial offenders.

Table 12.1   Mean error distances and standard deviations for each spatial display for the control group and experimental group across the two phases and Dragnet

Spatial display	Control group		Experimental group		Dragnet
	Phase 1 ($n = 21$)	Phase 2 ($n = 21$)	Phase 1 ($n = 21$)	Phase 2 ($n = 21$)	
1	23.86 (20.17)*	26.10 (25.86)	21.30 (20.88)	15.76 (8.87)	19.00
2	37.33 (21.72)	35.07 (21.07)	35.76 (20.75)	26.00 (7.27)**	21.00
3	43.24 (17.99)	41.38 (17.55)	39.38 (17.89)	39.67 (13.52)	51.00
4	23.62 (17.00)	22.81 (16.19)	25.38 (20.38)	13.85 (7.07)**	20.00
5	37.57 (28.50)	35.05 (26.54)	33.48 (27.67)	19.24 (11.60)**	14.00
6	27.52 (22.12)	25.67 (15.70)	28.29 (19.75)	20.43 (6.11)	23.00
7	29.67 (25.88)	27.57 (25.89)	30.43 (32.64)	13.24 (14.88)**	2.000
8	32.05 (25.56)	33.00 (24.23)	33.43 (25.30)	19.95 (8.39)**	17.00
9	46.05 (12.75)	42.67 (9.23)	41.05 (17.15)	42.67 (8.77)	49.00
10	52.10 (14.31)	52.10 (12.32)	50.86 (17.61)	45.62 (7.31)	37.00
Mean	35.30	34.22	33.94	25.65	25.30

*Numbers in brackets are standard deviations.
**Denotes a significant difference ($p<0.05$) between the error distance in phase 1 and phase 2 for that group in relation to that spatial display.

Inspection of the spatial displays indicated that in each case where there was no error reduction in the experimental group this was because the offenders were commuters (i.e., these offenders lived some distance away from their crime sites). In the case of these offenders it is difficult to accurately identify the likely location of their homes (Canter et al. 2000; Rossmo 2000).

To examine this issue further, Spearman's rank-order correlations were calculated between the mean error distances for every condition in Table 12.1. The only correlation that reached significance was between the phase 2 experimental group error distances and the error distances resulting from Dragnet ($r_s = 0.83, p<0.01$). This indicates that when the heuristics provided to participants were less appropriate (i.e., less accurate) for a particular offender the Dragnet results were also less accurate.

Enhancing Agreement Amongst Participants

An examination of the standard deviations for the predictions made in each phase indicates the extent to which participants agreed upon the most likely home location of each serial murderer. Table 12.2 contains the mean standard deviations for the control and experimental groups in the two phases. A paired samples *t*-test revealed

Table 12.2   **Mean standard deviations for the control group and experimental group across the two phases**

Group	Condition	
	Phase 1	Phase 2
Control	20.60	19.46
Experimental	22.00	9.38

that there was no significant difference in the standard deviations between phase 1 and phase 2 for the control group ($t_9 = 1.18$, n.s.). This suggests that the participants, across the two phases, generally disagreed about the area likely to contain the home of each offender. For the experimental group, however, a statistically significant decrease in the standard deviations existed between phase 1 and phase 2 ($t_9 = 9.75$, $p<0.001$), suggesting that the level of agreement amongst the participants in phase 2 was modified by providing them with the heuristics, such that they tended to carry out the decision task in a more similar way.

What Heuristics Were Used?

The use of inappropriate heuristics by some of the participants in phase 1 of the control and experimental groups was likely to have contributed to the larger error distances. For example, some participants in phase 1 said that 'I guess the perpetrator lives away from the average position of the victims'. In phase 2, participants in the control group reported similar inappropriate heuristics, which explains their consistent performance across the phases. Conversely, participants in the experimental group reported that they were able to adopt the appropriate heuristics provided to them in phase 2 in order to make more structured and accurate predictions.

Discussion

This study indicates that some of the most frequently cited results in the research literature on offender spatial behavior can be summarized as simple heuristics that can be quickly understood and utilized by people without any special training in criminal behavior or experience of criminal investigations. They can understand these well enough to improve their accuracy in predicting the likely home location of serial murderers and can utilize them so effectively that, at least for the sample of serial killers used here, their judgments are, on average, as accurate as a geographic profiling system. These results therefore provide support both for the power of the two heuristics identified – distance decay and circle hypothesis and for the possibility of summarizing those heuristics in ways that make sense to people otherwise uninformed about criminal behavior. It therefore raises the possibility of identifying other aspects of criminal behavior that could be similarly distilled for general application.

The power of the heuristics appears to be that they focus the decision processes of participants, demonstrated by the fact that agreement amongst the participants increased once provided with the heuristics. For these participants, error distance variability was reduced and the strategies they reported became less idiosyncratic and variable. This illustrates a potential problem of those aspects of investigative decision-making often referred to as 'gut feeling', 'intuition', or even 'experience.' The variability in the strategies used for these personal judgments may be so great that no two people will use the same decision rules. This reduces the possibility of general improvement and increases the risk that some individuals will use completely inappropriate procedures.

The second major finding, that participants on average were able to make as accurate predictions as a geographic profiling system, also raises questions about the specific benefits of using specialized geographic profilers and computer based geographic profiling systems. The results of this study indicate that if the basic processes underlying offender spatial behavior are understood, prerequisite qualifications may not be required to make accurate geographic predictions. Moreover, the results from the present study suggest that, on average, individuals with some knowledge of criminals' spatial behavior can make these accurate predictions relatively quickly. Indeed, the experimental respondents here may be less prone to seek novel interpretations or draw on their 'experience' than police officers. They may therefore be able to use the provided heuristics in a more objective manner than experienced investigators. Future research needs to be conducted to test this possibility. Of course, experienced criminal investigators bring other knowledge to their work when preparing geographic profiles. They will have an understanding of the legal context in which an investigation is being carried out as well as the operational possibilities available to those they are advising.

These findings have potential positive implications for police organizations. For example, they indicate that police organizations may be able to correct any use of inappropriate heuristics by providing officers with more appropriate ones, thereby increasing the ability of these officers to make more effective decisions about offenders' residential locations. The significance of these results increases for police agencies that have limited resources and technological capabilities, making low-cost, easy-to-implement alternatives to geographic profiling systems desirable.

The consistent rank ordering of the error distances between the experimental group participants in phase 2 and Dragnet indicates that at the present time when heuristics were ineffective for the participants, Dragnet was also ineffective. This does support the central assumption of the present study that the two heuristics used are the cornerstone of the Dragnet algorithm. It also demonstrates that there is a need for other heuristics that will aid effective spatial decision making in those cases for which the current algorithms are not very effective. For example, there may be some heuristics that are useful for commuting offenders, who are particularly difficult to locate with existing geographic profiling systems. Once appropriate heuristics have been discovered for commuting offenders they may be employed to increase the overall accuracy of both human and computer procedures.

It is also worth noting that geographic profiling systems provide more than a single location as tested in this study. They provide graded areas of differing priorities for investigative searches. These priorities do not fan out evenly from the highest probability but are influenced by the distribution of the crimes. The basis on which these various priorities are calculated can be summarized as a heuristic. Such heuristics could therefore be used as the basis for future studies that are rather more subtle in the comparisons that can be made between human judges and geographic profiling systems. For example, search cost functions (Canter et al. 2000) generated by individuals could be compared with those generated by geographic profiling systems.

Lastly, it is important to point out that the present results are very dependent on the particular spatial distributions selected. The current sample was drawn at random from a larger database, but without full knowledge of the spatial distribution of the population of American serial murderers it is impossible to know how representative this sample is. The results could certainly have been biased against the heuristics used in the current study if a sample had been drawn for which those heuristics were inappropriate, such as a sample of offenders 'commuting' some distance into an area to commit their crimes. It might also be the case that samples could be biased in favor of Dragnet by choosing complex geometries that the computer algorithm could manage but which would be very puzzling for a person, such as uneven distributions and varied sizes of clusters of crime locations. Future research could explore these issues by developing more refined classifications of the geometries of crime locations and determining the roles and effectiveness of different heuristics in relation to those different geometries. Only after such research will it become clear whether the decision rules needed to deal with the complexities of these matters can be readily understood and used by people with little training or whether they require computer support.

References

Canter, D.V., Coffey, T., Huntley, M. and Missen, C. (2000). Predicting serial killers' home base using a decision support system. *Journal of Quantitative Criminology*, 16, 457–478.

Canter, D.V. and Gregory, A. (1994). Identifying the residential location of rapists. *Journal of the Forensic Science Society*, 34, 164–175.

Canter, D.V. and Larkin, P. (1993). The environmental range of serial rapists. *Journal of Environmental Psychology*, 13, 63–69.

Capone, D.L. and Nichols, W.W., Jr. (1976). An analysis of offender behavior. *Proceedings of the American Geographer*, 7, 45–49.

Kocsis, R.N. and Irwin, H.J. (1997). An analysis of spatial patterns in serial rape, arson, and burglary: the utility of the Circle Theory of environmental range for psychological profiling. *Psychiatry, Psychology and Law*, 4, 195–206.

Levine, N. and Associates (2000). *Crimestat: A Spatial Statistics Program for the Analysis of Crime Incident Locations* (version 1.1). National Institute of Justice: Washington, DC.

Rossmo, K.D. (1993). Multivariate spatial profiles as a tool in crime investigation. In *Crime Analysis through Computer Mapping* (pp. 65–97), Block, C.R., Dabdoub, M. and Fregley, S. (eds). Police Executive Research Forum: Washington, DC.

Rossmo, K.D. (2000). *Geographic Profiling*. Chemical Rubber Company: Boca Raton, FL.

Tamura, M. and Suzuki, M. (1997). Criminal profiling research on serial arson: examinations of circle hypothesis estimating offender's residential area. *Research on Prevention of Crime and Delinquency*, 38, 1.

Turner, S. (1969). Delinquency and distance. In *Delinquency: Selected Studies* (pp. 11–26), Sellin, T. and Wolfgang, M.E. (eds). Wiley: New York.

Chapter 13

Commentary –
Confusing Operational Predicaments and Cognitive Explorations: Comments on Rossmo and Snook et al.

David Canter

Snook et al.'s Experimental Paradigm

The discussion by Snook, Taylor, and Bennell (2004) of geographical[1] profiling and the counter-claims from an ex-police officer in Rossmo's (2005) comments obscure the elegant simplicity of the task that Snook et al. set their subjects. In essence, they gave their subjects a straightforward set of geometric rules and asked them to apply those rules to a set of points drawn on a sheet of paper. Broadly these rules amount to asking respondents to mark the spot where they estimate the centre of gravity to be for all the points. In so far as that the dots on the paper reflect actual locations of offences on a geographical map and the offender's home really is near to the centre of gravity of those locations this task can be seen as an analogy for predicting the residential location of an offender from knowledge of where his crimes are committed.

Snook et al.'s (2004) study raises some important, but is has to be admitted not especially profound, questions about the judgements people are able to make when faced with a simplified summary of the spatial distribution of crime locations. If the task did simulate an important component of an investigative decision making process it would raise the possibility that the skills the subjects exhibit could replace intensive training sold at considerable expense and requiring a dedicated computer system. The possibility that geographical profiling may be relatively straightforward is supported by the free availability of one computer system Dragnet, developed as a research tool (Canter, Coffey, Huntley, and Missen 2000) that does not require intensive training but has been effectively used by law enforcement agencies around the world (Canter 2004). The question is thus raised of what the limitations are to

---

1   The term 'geographic profiling' is used in North America and 'geographical profiling' in the UK. In this chapter an attempt is made to distinguish different systems by the use of these different terms.

current models of criminal spatial activity. Should they be considered as operational constraints on the application of geometrical models, and computerized support for those models? Or is it more appropriate to think of these limitations as sources for error in current algorithms that need further research? Furthermore, there is the question of exactly how police investigators do make use of decision support systems.

A Teaching Exercise

The task Snook et al. (2004) and earlier Snook, Canter, and Bennell (2002) used was based in a training exercise employed by Canter (1994) when Snook and his colleagues were students of Canter. In those sessions students were given full details of the crimes committed by serial killers as well as the locations on a map of body disposal sights. The students were asked to guess where the offender lived. Their decisions were then compared with the results obtained from Dragnet (Canter et al. 2000).

This teaching exercise revealed both the distractions and complexities of working with the full details of cases as well as the limitations of computer models of offender spatial behaviour. In some cases students would do better than Dragnet, for example when they took account of useful sequential or land-use information that the computer ignored. In other cases they would do worse, when for instance they made inappropriate inferences about the offender's familiarity with an area or the significance of the body disposal site location. However, what apparently led Snook and his associates to select this as a model for experimental study was that, in general, when students were provided with the broad principles on which computerized geographical profiling systems operate they could often make a reasonable guess of what the computer would produce. This therefore showed that students could, on average, estimate the offenders' residential location with more or less the same accuracy as the computer.

That students can often be quite accurate in estimating an offender's location should not be a surprise because the advocacy of the computer systems is derived from empirical studies going back over a decade (Canter and Gregory 1994; Canter and Larkin 1993). These studies show that in as many as 80% of cases (and usually in at least half) offenders live within an area circumscribed by their known offences and quite often reasonably close to the centre of gravity of those offence locations. There are many ways of calculating the area in which the offender may be based but as Levine and Associates (2000) have pointed out they all tend to give similar results. Subtle differences in the algorithms used tend to be masked by the lack of precision in the original police data.

As mentioned, students, and possibly more so police officers, may be misled by irrelevant crime details that the computer algorithms ignore. They may also be inconsistent in the criteria that they use in a way that a computer will not. But the effectiveness of people or computers will mainly depend on the generality of the patterns in criminal spatial behaviour not on the whether it is a person or a computer making use of those patterns. It is essential to note, though, that no detailed studies of representative samples of cases show that geographical profiling models are very accurate in more than a small percentage of cases. This small percentage is operationally useful and produces enough impressive case studies to encourage the mass media and police officers to regard geographical profiling as a useful tool. However, the limits to the effectiveness of the systems in use show that there is considerable noise in the data used and many sources of error in the models that further research needs to address.

The errors in the results from current computer algorithms are thus partly a function of how oversimplified are the models of criminal spatial behaviour on which they are built. In essence these models are little more than a set of straightforward geometrical principles. This raises the question of whether criminals draw, at least implicitly, on such uncomplicated cognitive rules when deciding where to commit their crimes. Initial explorations by Canter and Hodge (2000), in which criminals are asked to draw 'mental maps' of where they commit their crimes, are beginning to show how impoverished are current geometrical models. Therefore the limitations in the effectiveness of geographical profiling systems, whether carried out with or without the aid of computers, is like to be due to the simple-mindedness of our models of criminal cognition.

Operational Limitations

In practice police officers select the series of offences for which they consider geo-behavioural analysis to be appropriate. This, or course, biases the sample on which geographical profiling has been operationally tested. This is quite different from the studies of geographical profiling (e.g. Canter et al. 2000), in which a full set of cases unselected in any way, is subject to study. It is that unbiased sample which reveals the broad findings of offender's geo-behavioural consistencies.

The basis for selecting operational cases to work on is sometimes made to seem sophisticated and experience based by the use of an evocatively rich vocabulary such as 'hunting area', 'predatory criminals', 'poachers', etc. This can imply that the geographic profiler is not just a behavioural scientist seeking to develop objective models of criminal actions but a hunter with special skills seeking out a prey. These rhetorical devices can obscure the need to provide detailed definition of concepts and explanations. They suggest that the police officer's decisions can only be a product of intuition and hunch.

There is no definitive account of the objective processes that can be used to select crimes in order to increase the probability of a geographic profiling analysis being effective when applied to those crimes. Various police officers, however, have offered up suggestions derived from cases in which they have been involved that do offer interesting hypotheses for further study. Some of the issues they raise are revealed through published case studies (Canter 2004). These indicate areas in which further understanding of criminal processes would be productive.

One such issue is the question of the minimum number of cases necessary before a geographic profiling analysis can be conducted. A random numbers trial described as a 'Monte Carlo' analysis is sometimes quoted as a way of answering this question, leading to the claim that a minimum of five crimes is necessary before geographic profiling can be of value (Rossmo 2000). This process uses 'a computer program to generate random crime site coordinates based on a fixed-buffer distance decay function' (Rossmo 2000, p. 206). Clearly, such a trial is artificial in the extreme. It is thus not unexpected that detailed published accounts of studies using Dragnet on a non-artificially selected sample of actual crimes (e.g. Canter et al. 2000) have shown that there is no empirical necessity for using five or more crime locations. Indeed there is considerable case study evidence (Canter 2004) to show that serial offenders often indicate their base location in the first two or three crimes they commit. But even in one-off crimes the likelihood of an offender being local to the offence can be of great value to investigators (cf. Jill Dando murder – Canter 2004) and just how local can be estimated by using the decay functions at the heart of geographic profiling software.

Another issue is the claim that in order to use geographic profiling the crimes must be 'linked together and the series relatively complete'. On a statistical basis there is no need for the crime series to be complete, as long as it is a representative, unbiased sample of the crimes the offender has committed. Any subset of the offender's crime locations should give the same result if the model is appropriate.

The need for the crimes to be linked is also a consequence of noise in the information available. In a series with a large number of crimes a small number of inappropriately included crimes that do not distort the overall geometry of the crime locations will have little effect on the outcome of geo-behavioural analysis. In a smaller series and with crimes that would greatly modify the spatial configuration the problem of errant data is more marked. The issue is thus not a matter of police *nous* but one of estimating the consequences of various types of error for the various conclusions that might be reached. The impact of including or omitting various crime locations is one way of determining the sensitivity to possible biases in the data of any inferences drawn.

The question of including crimes inappropriately into the series is thus one of error estimation and its consequences. The same is true for the need to determine if the offender is travelling into an area to commit his crimes, or if the offender has moved home during a crime series. As yet there is no published evidence that police officers are able to determine with any accuracy if the offender is based in the area of his crimes or not. Nor are there any objective guidelines that have been empirically supported. Here again it is a matter of determining the size and nature of any errors introduced by the complexities of criminal mobility and how they may be reduced. The different patterns of offender mobility introduce errors into current geo-behavioural models. That is part of the reasons why the results of published studies of geographical profiling do not reveal complete accuracy for the process. What is needed is more careful determination of how to reduce errors by specifying the measurable influences on criminal actions.

The most problematic issue is the process of linking crimes to a common offender in the absence of clear forensic or other identifying information. Bennel and Canter 2002) have shown that geo-behavioural information can be remarkably productive in doing this. Such findings rather turn on their head any proposal that crimes should first be linked then geographically profiled. It may be of more operational value to deal with crime locations first and use that as part of the process of linking.

Region Not Location

Geographic profiling systems provide probabilities across a region rather than a point location. The idea being that the regional probabilities would be used for setting up police searches for possible suspects. However, in the very detailed accounts Canter (2004) gives of a number of police investigations that used geographical searches it transpires that the police do not often set up searches that closely reflect the probabilities generated on the geographically profiled map. The search strategies of investigators typically seem to draw on the locations of known offenders and distance from key points on the map, only partly determined by the highest probability indicated by geographical profiling. It may therefore be the case that the model that Snook et al. (2004) use is closer to police decision making than may seem apparent at first sight. This raises some intriguing questions about the cognitive processes underlying police geographical search patterns and how they may be best integrated into geo-behaviourally based decision support systems. Such explorations will improve our currently limited understanding of the mental models on which police draw to make their decisions as well as opening the way for a psychologically richer, new generation of geographical profiling systems.

Conclusions

The model of geographic profiling that Snook et al. (2004) utilized is remarkably limited and thus their claims that they are studying processes that are close to operational decision making are over-stated. Nonetheless, the results they draw upon do reveal some interesting simplicities in some aspects of some criminals' geographical behaviour. Therefore to the extent that Snook et al. (2004) used a sample of cases that were typical of the offences they were looking at and to the extent that the simple model they used does actually describe criminals' spatial geometry it is not surprising that relatively untrained respondents can carry out the elementary calculations with a similar success rate to the computer.

There are many limits to the effectiveness of geographic profiling computer models. Rather than regarding these limits as merely practical restriction on selecting the offences that can be subjected to computer analysis it is more productive to regard them as areas in which hypotheses nccd to be developed of the reasons for the limitations of current systems. In so doing we will understand more about criminals' cognitive processes. We will also open the way to exploring the forms of heuristic that police investigators can actually use when drawing on geometrica representations of criminal spatial activity.

Inappropriate use of geographical profiling can have serious consequences. That is all the more reason why we must develop our understanding of wha introduces biases and errors into geo-behavioural decision support systems and into the cognitive processes of those who use those systems. Treating these errors as operational problems that have to remain in the hands of police officers will keep criminal investigation in the dark ages of intuition and hunch.

References

Bennell, C. and Canter, D. (2002). Linking commercial burglaries by *Modu. Operandi*: tests using regression and ROC analysis. *Journal of Science and Justice*, 42(3), 1–12.

Canter, D. (1994). *Criminal Shadows*. London: HarperCollins.

Canter, D. (2004). *Mapping Murder*. London: Virgin Books.

Canter, D. and Gregory, A. (1994). Identifying the residential location of rapists *Journal of the Forensic Science Society*, 34, 169–175.

Canter, D.V. and Hodge, S. (2000). Mental mapping. Criminal's mental maps. In L.S. Turnbull, E.H. Hendrix and B.D. Dent (eds), *Atlas of Crime: Mapping the Criminal Landscape* (pp. 186–191). Phoenix, Arizona: Onyx Press.

Canter, D.V. and Larkin, P. (1993). The environmental range of serial rapists. *Journal of Environmental Psychology*, 13, 63–69.

Canter, D.V., Coffey, T., Huntley, M. and Missen, C. (2000). Predicting serial killers home base using a decision support system. *Journal of Quantitative Criminology* 16, 457–478.

Levine, N. and Associates (2000). *Crimestat: A Spatial Statistics Program for the Analysis of Crime Incident Locations*. Washington, DC: National Institute of Justice.

Rossmo, D.K. (2000). *Geographic Profiling*. Boca Raton, FL: CRC Press.

Rossmo, D.K. (2005). Geographic Heuristics or Shortcuts to Failure?: Response to Snook et al. *Applied Cognitive Psychology*, 19, 651–654.

Snook, B., Canter, D.V. and Bennell, C. (2002). Predicting the home location of serial offenders: a preliminary comparison of the accuracy of human judges with a geographic profiling system. *Behavioral Sciences and the Law*, 20, 109–118.

Snook, B., Taylor, P.J. and Bennell, C. (2004). Geographic profiling: The fast, frugal and accurate way. *Applied Cognitive Psychology*, 18, 105–121.

Chapter 14

A Comparison of the Efficacy of Different Decay Functions in Geographical Profiling for a Sample of US Serial Killers

David Canter and Laura Hammond

Introduction

Research into the spatial behaviour of offending populations has shown that the distribution of distances travelled by offenders in the commission of their crimes is typically characterised by a 'distance decay' function (Canter, Coffey, Huntley and Missen 2000; Phillips 1980; Rengert, Piquero and Jones 1999; Rhodes and Conly 1981; Turner 1969). Essentially, as the distance from an offender's home or base increases, the likelihood and frequency of their offending decreases (Turner 1969). This decline is non-linear in form, with a negative exponential or power function typically used to reflect the relationship between location and distance (ESRI 1996).

As early as 1969, Turner hypothesised that a number of different forms of function could characterise distance decay in criminal spatial behaviour. Indeed, Brantingham and Brantingham (1991), Canter et al. (2000), Hunter and Shannon (1985), Kent (2003), Levene (2002), Phillips (1980), Rhodes and Conly (1981) and Turner (1969) all propose different decay functions as providing the closest approximations for describing the distances travelled to offend for various criminal populations.

Eldridge and Jones (1991) observe that different functions will have different behavioural implications. For example, a steep function that decayed quickly would suggest that the home might have a very strong influence on the behaviour of those offenders, in that they would appear to be reluctant to travel far from it. Conversely, if the decay function were much shallower, with the distances travelled to offend decaying very slowly, then the implication would be that the offender's home had less of an influence on their activity, and that they instead operated over a much broader area (Canter et al. 2000). Therefore, different functions can each be treated as a set of hypotheses about the factors governing the distances that offenders travel in the commission of their crimes.

To date there have been few empirical comparisons of the various decay functions which may characterise offender travel distances. Further, there has been little consideration of what different functions might reveal about the underlying factors and psychological processes governing the journey to crime.

There are, however, published studies of the efficacy of various functions in terms of their accuracy at reflecting the distributions of other distance-based data. For example, De Vries, Nijkamp and Rietveld (2004) considered home-to-work journeys between municipalities in Denmark in a study on commuting flows, and found exponential and power functions to be ineffective at characterizing the decay in distances travelled, providing poor fits to data on such phenomena despite being those functions most frequently used for such purposes. Conversely, a logarithmic function was found to work better, and they conclude by suggesting that a pragmatic direction for future work would be to utilise functions of this form in representing distance decay (De Vries, Nijkamp and Rietveld 2004). The value of De Vries et al.'s (2004) comparisons indicate a similar likely utility in studying home-to-crime journeys.

Decay functions play an important role in systems that help investigators to infer the location of an offender's base from the location of linked crimes, known as geographical profiling systems (Canter et al. 2000). The significance of the hypotheses presupposed by different decay functions can therefore be tested by comparing how geographical profiling systems perform when different functions are incorporated into the calculations that they use to model the spatial behaviour of offenders.

Geographical profiling systems are becoming increasingly commonplace within the investigative domain, but they also provide a useful research tool for modelling and characterising the journey to crime. However, with the exception of Canter et al. (2000), there has been little consideration of how different functions affect the operation of any system and what might be the most appropriate mathematical algorithm to employ when describing the frequencies of journeys to crime.

A means of assessing the effectiveness of one such geographical profiling system, Dragnet (Canter et al. 2000), used in the present study, is to use a specifically defined measure termed the 'Search Cost Function' (Canter and Snook 1999; Canter et al. 2000). In cases where the location of the offender's home or base is known, the search cost allows the effectiveness of Dragnet in predicting this location to be examined.

The Search Cost is defined as 'the proportion of the total search area that has to be searched in order to find the location of the offender' (Canter and Snook 1999). The Search Cost Function represents the relationship between the proportion of the total area searched and the proportion of offenders located for each search cost.

Canter and Snook (1999) propose that search cost values can be used to determine whether an offender's spatial behaviour followed a particular function, and that low search costs would suggest that such a function accurately represented the relationship between the offender's home and the location of their offences. It should therefore be that the opposite is also true – that if a function accurately represented

1e relationship between home and crime location then the search costs produced sing that function should be low. Essentially, when utilising the decay function 1at provides the best fit to any given distribution, a geographical profiling system vould be expected to perform more effectively for the offenders whose crime trips enerated that distribution than when any other functions are used.

A two-stage analysis process is suggested for determining how effective a decay unction is for use in geographical profiling. First, the efficacy of the function, in erms of the extent to which the function fits data on the distances travelled to offend eeds to be determined. Second, the efficiency of the function when it is utilised vithin a geographical profiling system needs to be established, using the 'Search 'ost Function' to evaluate how accurately and reliably the system operates when sing that function as the basis for its calculations.

Three decay functions were compared: exponential, logarithmic and quadratic. ι fourth function was introduced as a 'control'. This was a straight negative linear unction, which does not display incremental 'decay' characteristics. The fit of the unctions to the raw data was first established in order to determine which best epresented the spatial relationship between an offender's home location and their ffence sites, using R^2 values as a measure of the strength of this relationship. ubsequently, the effect of the type of function on the operation of a geographical rofiling system, Dragnet, was examined. It was predicted that the better the fit of a unction to the raw data, the lower the search costs produced by Dragnet.

tudy 1

he Logarithmic, Exponential and Quadratic Functions

'hree different functions were examined, in terms of the extent to which they fitted distribution of the distances travelled between home and crime location(s) for 1e offenders in the sample. Each of them illustrates the non-linear decay in the requency of offending as the distance from an offender's home or base increases, ut each presupposes somewhat different explanations and hypotheses as to how and vhy this decay occurs.

he Logarithmic Function

'he logarithmic function providing a close approximation to a distribution of ourney to crime lengths would suggest that the frequency of offending decreases ramatically initially, and then in a more gradual fashion, as the distance from the ome or base increases. A best-fit curved line is mathematically calculated that escribes the rate of change as the data decreases quickly and subsequently levels ut (Kent 2003).

An explanation for the form of decay which this function proposes can be drawn om the work of Stevens (1961) and his 'Power Law' of magnitude estimations, in relation to how distances from home to potential crime locations are likely to b estimated by the criminal.

There is a considerable literature, most clearly summarised by Stevens' semina 1961 paper, which indicates that people do not estimate any magnitudes in a linea way. In other words, as magnitudes get larger, a greater increase in magnitude i needed for the same increase in estimation. The relationship between estimate magnitude and actual size has been shown by Stevens to be characterised as specific logarithmic function for each modality being estimated. Therefore, if it i assumed that offenders are considering how far to travel to commit a crime then the must be making some estimate of the length of the journey. This estimate would b distorted by the logarithmic function proposed by Stevens and it may therefore b hypothesised that the frequency of their journeys to different distances would als obey this logarithmic relationship.

The Exponential Function

In their examination of burglars, robbers and rapists, Rhodes and Conly (1981 found that the distance decay displayed by the offenders in their sample wa typically negatively exponential in nature, and that this was the function that bes characterised the journey to crime. Capone and Nichols (1976) also find that a exponential function is that which would be expected to fit most closely th distribution of crime trip distances, both those that are meaningful and purposefu and those that are accidental. Further testimony to the power of the exponentia function in characterising distance distributions can be found in research int many other aspects of spatial and behavioural phenomena as cited, for example, b Golledge (1987).

A close approximation of the exponential function for journey to crime dat would indicate that the likelihood of offending is highest in the region around th offender's home, and then drops off with distance. This decrease is at a constant rat of decline (Kent 2003), thus dropping relatively quickly near the place of residenc and then levelling out until it approaches a zero likelihood.

Phillips (1980) argues that the distance decay in offending behaviour results fron 'the friction of distance; the cost in money, time or energy of overcoming distanc (p. 136). The exponential function is that which most closely reflects this, with th shape and form of the function illustrating the impact of this friction of distanc on the likelihood and frequency of offending. This is analogous to impedance, th impediment (opposition) to electrical flow, a combination of resistance and reactanc (dictionary definition).

This impedance, or 'friction effect', has been found to relate to a wide variet of phenomena, including property values (Richardson, Gordon, Jun, Heikkila an Dale-Johnson 1990), migration (Kothari 2002) and even fishing (Beverton and Ho 1957). The terms refers to resistance to movement over space (Canter 2004), i relation to cost in terms of time, money and effort, as proposed by Phillips (1980 The increased costs incurred are what generate this resistance to longer journeys and the resultant pattern in the distance travelled to offend can be estimated and represented by the form of the exponential function, illustrating this influence of 'friction of distance'.

The Quadratic Function
The form of the quadratic function is somewhat different to any of the others being examined. It merits consideration as, because of its unique shape, it mirrors two different perspectives on the influences on the distances travelled to offend.

A quadratic function providing a close fit to a distribution of journey to crime distances would suggest that the frequency of offending declines rapidly with distance from the home initially, and then levels out so that the frequency of offending is represented as being substantially less for distances further away from the home. However, after a point the frequency of offending begins to increase again, so that more offences would be expected to occur at locations a notable distance from the home compared with those of medium distance (although the frequency of offending at these distances is much less than those for regions immediately proximate to the home).

The quadratic function therefore incorporates both the process captured by the logarithmic and exponential functions of decrease in crime frequency further from the home location and also the process which has been reported whereby criminals sometimes favour locations further away from home, where the risk of recognition and consequently detection may be reduced (Brantingham and Brantingham 1991). There is also the possibility that the opportunities for crime closer to home will become exhausted, forcing an offender to travel further afield to find suitable targets for their crimes (Lundrigan and Canter 2001).

The Control, Negative Linear Function
A simple negative decreasing linear function was also tested for fit to the distance distribution. If it were to provide a close approximation, then this would suggest that the probability of offending at a particular location decreased by a constant amount with increasing distance from an individual's home or base location (Levene 2002).

The linear function has been presented as a valid representation of the relationship between distance from home and frequency of offending (Turner 1969). However, given that most research proposes that the rate of decrease is likely to change, the linear function can be regarded as a form of experimental 'control' that makes fewer assumptions than the other more complex functions.

Data

The data utilised in the present study was derived from the HITS and Missen Corpus databases, detailed by Canter et al. (2000). These incorporate data drawn from published accounts of serial killers operating within the US since 1960. In total, 96 series of offences were used, each representing a single offender, and each consisting of five of the offences committed by that individual.

For each offender, the location at which they had been residing at the time of their offences were determined from at least two independent sources, as were the body disposal locations, which were taken as the crime sites (for a detailed account of the preparation and features of this data set, see Canter et al. 2000).

The home and offence locations were converted into geocoded co-ordinates and subsequently transformed into a format that would enable them to be fed into the Dragnet system (see www.i-psy.com for details of the files used by Dragnet, as well as for a comprehensive introduction to the system and how it operates).

Fitting the Functions to the Data

In order to determine which of the four functions provided the 'best fit' to the raw data a number of steps had to be taken. Initially, the distances travelled between each home and each offence location were calculated and entered into a Microsoft® Excel® database.

Once a full set of all of the journey to crime distances had be compiled, the values could then be grouped into distance intervals, using a method detailed by Kent (2003). First, the home to crime distances were sorted into ascending order. Next, a frequency distribution was applied for each of these distances, and grouped into 1 km intervals (Kent 2003; p. 63). These frequency intervals were then converted into relative frequencies for each distance value. This was done by dividing the frequency values for each interval by the total number of incidences in that interval, and multiplying this figure by 100 in order to obtain the frequency percentage for each distance value.

The distance intervals and the frequencies of offending for each of these intervals are given in Figure 14.1. The shape of the chart shows clear distance decay in the journeys made to commit offences by the present sample.

Using SPSS® 11.0 and Microsoft® Excel®, a scatterplot was constructed with points marking the frequencies of occurrence for each of the distance intervals. Each of the four functions – linear, exponential, logarithmic and quadratic – was calculated for this scatterplot in order to obtain the 'best fit' for the distribution (Figure 14.2).

The equations for each of the functions were determined, and the best-fit formulas for each of the lines were found to be as follows:

Logarithmic
$$y = 5.6735 + (-1.3307) \cdot \ln x \qquad\qquad R^2 = 0.81$$
Negative exponential
$$y = 2.13403 \; e^{-(-0.04574)x} \qquad\qquad R^2 = 0.45$$
Quadratic
$$y = 0.0009811x^2 + (-0.13129)x + 4.14137 \qquad\qquad R^2 = 0.75$$

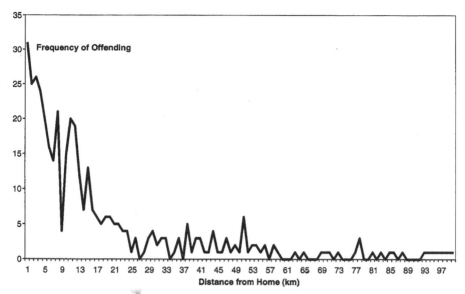

Figure 14.1   The distribution of the distances travelled to offend by all serial murderers in the sample (N = 96)

Linear

$$y = -0.03213x + 2.45555 \qquad\qquad R^2 = 0.46$$

One advantage of Dragnet is that it allows any function to be called up as a specified .fun file as the basis for its calculations of the probabilities of home locations. It was therefore possible to input each of the four best-fit functions in turn and to calculate the search cost for that function. Dragnet also calculates the search cost for each offender and the version used, DragnetK, enables all of the costs to be processed as a batch file, thus reducing inputting and calculation errors.

The best-fit formulas derived for each of the functions were used to create files for each of the functions that could be entered into Dragnet. The same 20 *x* values were put into each of the formulas, and the y values produced were those that were used to characterise each function in its respective Dragnet .fun file.

Findings on the Fit of the Functions

The co-efficient of determination, R^2, measures the strength of the regression relationship to the frequency data. Consequently, it may be used as a measure of how well a mathematical model fits a given distribution (Kent 2003), as it evaluates the extent to which the independent variable, x (in this case the distance between the offender's home and their offence location) can account for the variation in the dependant variable, y (in this instance the frequencies of occurrence of each of the distance intervals).

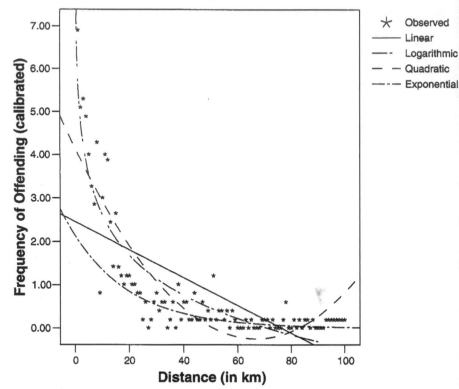

Figure 14.2   **Scatterplot of the frequencies of occurrence for each of the distance intervals, with the calibrated functions 'fitted' to the distribution**

'As a descriptive measure between 0 and 1, R^2 is interpreted as the percentage of variation in the dependant variable that is explained by the independent variable. Analysis of Variance (the F statistic) is used to evaluate the statistical significance of R^2' (Kent 2003; p. 68).

The R^2 values for each of the four functions under consideration in the present work are shown in Table 14.1. For each model the R^2 values were found to be highly significant ($p < 0.01$).

The logarithmic function was found to have the highest R^2 value and thus provided the best fit to the raw data ($R^2 = 0.81$). Consequently, it may be assumed that it was the function that best represented the distribution of the distances travelled from home to crime for offenders in the present sample. The quadratic function was also found to have a relatively high R^2 value ($R^2 = 0.75$), and so proved to fit the data reasonably well, whereas the negative exponential and linear functions both had much smaller R^2 values (0.45 and 0.46 respectively), and so provided the poorest fits of all of the functions. They may therefore be viewed as the weakest representations of the relationship between the distance from home to

Table 14.1 **R and R² values for each of the four functions**

Function	R value	R^2 value
Logarithmic	0.90100	0.81179
Exponential	0.67211	0.45174
Quadratic	0.86612	0.75016
Linear	0.67997	0.46237

time and the frequency of occurrence. The differences between the three functions nd the control linear function, in terms of their fit to the data, were found to be gnificant ($p < 0.05$).

On the basis of these findings, it was hypothesised that, when used in Dragnet, ie logarithmic function would prove to be the most effective, producing the lowest earch costs. Conversely, the linear and negative exponential functions were expected be the least effective functions, and thus to produce the largest search costs.

tudy 2

he Use of Decay Functions Within a Geographical Profiling System

here are a number of systems that draw upon the principle of distance decay in der to predict where an offender's home or base might be located. One such system Dragnet, developed at the Centre for Investigative Psychology at the University f Liverpool by Professor David Canter, Malcom Huntley and colleagues (Canter et . 2000).

Dragnet is a 'geographical offender location system', a decision support package esigned to identify the area in which a serial offender is most likely to reside. The stem operates by adding the estimated probabilities of the location of the home om each crime location (Canter et al. 2000). In common with other systems (e.g. ossmo 2000), for operational support it produces a prioritised probability map of e area in which the crimes occurred. The probability distribution for each crime derived from the particular decay function that is called up by the system. For search purposes the system also provides the actual probability value for each oint on the map. If the location of the home is known then the system calculates the obability value of that location and uses that value in calculating the 'search cost' f reaching that location, i.e. the proportion of the map area that has to be 'searched' efore that probability value is reached. It is these search costs that form the basis of ssessing the effectiveness of any particular decay function.

Research on the efficacy of Dragnet is currently scarce and relatively limited. owever, Canter et al. (2000) found that the system accurately predicted 51% of all

offender residences within the top 5% of the search area, and 87% of the offend
residences within the top 25% of the search area. Overall the model was able
reduce the size of the original rectangular search area to just 11% of the total si
(Canter et al. 2000).

Canter et al. (2000) propose that to enable the development of geographic
profiling systems, like Dragnet, it is necessary to 'explore the various feasib
mathematical functions that describe the distance decay displayed by offenders
order to determine which functions are most effective' (Canter et al. 2000; p. 46C
Further, they note that little empirical research has been published that has compar
different functions on any measure of effectiveness, or any set of crime data, ar
that there is therefore a great need for further consideration of such factors (Cant
et al. 2000).

Canter and Snook (1999) address the significance of the application of differe
functions in geographical profiling, emphasising the importance of establishing tl
impact such functions have when they are built into geographical profiling system
They propose that a key research task would be to delineate what functions may I
used and the impacts that they might have on the Search Cost Function (Canter ai
Snook 1999).

Results of Search Cost Functions

Regardless which of the three decay functions were used, the search costs produc
by Dragnet for this sample were generally very low. Overall, more than 50%
the sample had a search cost of less than 0.1 (i.e. were located within the first 10
of search area as prioritised by the system), and over 80% of the sample produc
search costs of 0.5 or less.

The median search costs produced by Dragnet when each of the functions w
used, as well as means and standard deviations of these values, a
given in Table 14.2.

**Table 14.2   Median search costs produced by
each of the four functions (means and
standard deviations in brackets)**

Function	Median
Logarithmic	0.08342 (M = 0.2109, SD = 0.2448)
Exponential	0.08376 (M = 0.2132, SD = 0.2427)
Quadratic	0.08360 (M = 0.2130, SD = 0.2423)
Linear	0.08996 (M = 0.2391, SD = 0.2791)

The logarithmic function, the model which provided the best fit to the raw data ($R^2 = 0.81$), was found to produce the lowest average search cost (median = 0.083). However, the quadratic and exponential functions both produced median search costs of 0.084 which was only marginally different from the logarithmic search costs. The linear function produced the highest search costs overall, with a median of 0.090.

However, whilst the logarithmic function produced the best results and the straight linear the worst, as predicted, the differences between the various functions, in terms of the search costs that they generated when used within the Dragnet system, were not significant.

The median search cost value is only a gross indicator of the effectiveness of any geographical profiling system. It is very likely that the distribution of the search costs is not symmetrical and from an operational point of view the proportion of low cost searches is possibly a more important indicator. It is therefore of value to look at the 'Search Cost Function', which relates the proportion of the sample to the search cost, as illustrated in Figure 14.3. This shows that the search cost function is positively monotonic for all decay functions with a distinct change in gradients around 58% of the sample regardless of the function employed. The curves of each of the search cost functions displays a distinct 'elbow' at the 0.1 value (10% of the total search area needed to be searched in order to locate the offender), with the curves then tapering off at a much slower rate across the higher search cost values.

The point at which this elbow, the distinct change in the gradient of the search cost function, occurs can be viewed as an indication of a point at which some qualitative change occurs in the operation of the system. The point at which the

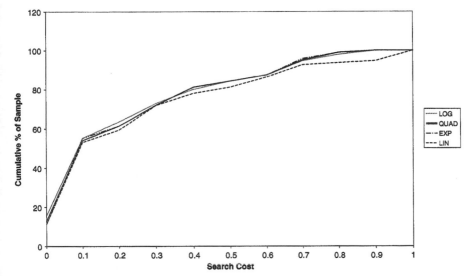

Figure 14.3 Cumulative search cost percentages produced by each of the functions

curve starts to level out and flatten may be indicative of a decreased likelihood of offenders committing crimes around their home/base as 'marauders', and instead becoming increasingly likely to display a 'commuting' style of offending (Canter and Larkin 1993). In this instance, the fact that this is at the 0.1 search cost value, for 58% of the sample, is testament to the power and effectiveness of the Dragnet system in reducing the search for an offender. The elbow, at such a low search cost value, indicates that the system is highly productive in this respect.

Discussion

Two different issues have been explored in the present paper. One is an attempt to explicate the theoretical basis for the often found decay function in offender journey to crime distances. It was proposed that different explanations of why such a decay function occurs would lead to the function itself taking different forms. Explanations based on the cognitive processes of offenders, relating to their estimation of the distances that they are traveling from home, were postulated as being supported by a strong logarithmic function. The finding that, for the present sample of serial killers, this was the function which provided the closest approximation to the distribution of the distances travelled to offend therefore lends support to the role of magnitude estimation in offenders' crime location choice.

However, the fact that each of the other functions, including the straight linear function, produced significant R^2 values with the distribution of distances travelled would suggest that a complex set of other processes are also involved, notably some form of 'impedance' generated by the increasing costs of lengthier journeys and even the increased attractiveness of distant locations as supported by the quadratic function. These results support the view that friction of distance, cost in terms of time, money and effort, familiarity with an area, the influence of the home and the risk of detection associated with regions closer to the residential location all play a part in the decision of how far an individual will travel to commit a crime. A three function model that takes account of a) the cognitive processes of the offender, b) the effort involved in the journey to crime, and c) the opportunities and attractiveness of the target may therefore be necessary to fully model offenders' journeys to crime.

However, the dominance of the logarithmic function with the present sample is worth emphasising because it reflects results found for distance decay for other aspects of human behaviour, for example commuting, or shopping trips. De Vries, Nijkamp and Rietveld (2004) found that the logarithmic function was far more effective at characterising distance decay than other functions, such as the exponential. Therefore the parallels between the extreme and bizarre activities of serial killers may be usefully compared with the more mundane actions of commuting to work or shopping, lending support to the view expressed by Lundrigan and Canter (2001) that, although the actions of serial killers are difficult to explain, their choice of site for disposal of the body may have quite direct and everyday causations.

A second aspect of the present paper was to explore the impact of different decay functions on the effectiveness of the geographical profiling system Dragnet. The results show that with the current data set Dragnet is not especially sensitive to the particular decay function employed. This is likely to be the case for all other geographical profiling systems that incorporate decay functions. The reasons for this may, in part, be due to limits in the precision of the original data, and to the averaging processes that take place within the software. In the present case only five offences were considered for each offender and this may have curtailed the range of values generated. The normalisation process which adjusts the calculations against the average inter-point distance (Canter et al. 2000) may also have reduced the impact of more extreme values which is where the decay functions have their largest differences.

Other factors may also be reducing the impact of the more extreme distances where fewer offences are likely to be occurring. It may therefore be that, were a different sample utilised in which there were bigger variations between the distances travelled by any given offender, the influence of different decay functions might be more marked.

It is plausible that different decay functions would provide the best for different offending subsets (Canter et al. 2000; Hunter and Shannon 1985; Turner 1969). For example, a large body of research has shown that those committing crimes against property tend to, on average, travel further to commit their offences than those committing crimes against the person (Phillips 1980; Pyle 1974; Rhodes and Conly 1981; White 1932). The implications this may have on the decay functions for these different crimes have not yet been fully explored. Yet, as Capone and Nichols (1976) pointed out over a quarter of a century ago, it seems logical to assume that different functions might provide the best fits to distance distributions for different crime types, and future research would need to determine whether this is in fact the case.

The operational implications of the present findings are that, at least for a sample such as the present one, the particular function employed will not make a very great difference to the efficacy of the system. This is likely to be true for any geographical profiling system incorporating decay functions. Broadly speaking, such systems when applied to the present type of data can be expected to give impressive results in approximately half of the offence series. Whether that can be improved by more accurate and precise data and with more complex models remains to be established. It may turn out that the value of studies of different ways of modelling the journey to crime may be of more use in enriching our understanding of criminal behaviour than in improving police investigations.

References

Brantingham, P.J. and Brantingham, P. (1981). *Environmental Criminology*. Prospect Heights, Illinois: Waveland Press Inc.

Beverton, R.J.H. and Holt, S.J. (1957). *On the Dynamics of Exploited Fish Populations*. Fisheries Investment Series 2, Vol. 19, U.K. Ministry of Agriculture and Fisheries, London.

Canter, D. (2004). *Mapping Murder*. London: Virgin Books.

Canter, D., Coffey, T., Huntley, M. and Missen, C. (2000). 'Predicting serial killers' home base using a decision support system. *Journal of Quantitative Criminology*, 16, 457–478.

Canter, D. and Larkin, P. (1993). The environmental range of serial rapists. *Journal of Environmental Psychology*, 13, 63–69.

Canter, D. and Snook, B. (1999). *Modelling the Home Location of Serial Offenders*. Paper for Expanding the Boundaries: The Third Annual International Crime Mapping Research Conference – Orlando, December, 1999.

Capone, D.L. and Nichols, W.W. (1976). An analysis of offender behaviour. *Proceedings of the American Geographer*, 7, 45–49.

de Vries, J.J., Nijkamp, P. and Rietveld, P. (2004). *Exponential or Power Distance-decay for Commuting? An Alternative Specification*. Tinbergen Institute discussion paper; TI: 2004-097/3.

Eldridge, J.E. and Jones, J.P. (1991). Warped space: a geography of distance decay. *Professional Geographer*, 43, 500–511.

ESRI (1996). *The GIS. Glossary*. U.S.: Environmental Systems Research Institute, Inc. www.esri.com.

Golledge, R.G. (1987). *Analytical Behavioural Geography*. London: Croom Helm.

Hunter, J.M. and Shannon, G.W. (1985). Jarvis revisited: distance decay and service areas of mid-19th century asylums. *Professional Geographer*, 37, 296–302.

Kent, J. (2003). *Using Functional Distance Measures when Calibrating Journey to Crime Distance Decay Algorithms*. MSc thesis: Louisiana State University.

Kothari U. (2002). *Migration and Chronic Poverty*. Institute for Development, Policy and Management: University of Manchester. Working Paper No. 16.

Levene, N. (2002). *Crimestat II: spatial modeling*. Report for the US Department of Justice, 13 August , 2002.

Lundrigan, S. and Canter, D. (2001). A multivariate analysis of serial murderer's disposal site location choice. *Journal of Environmental Psychology*, 21, 423–432.

Phillips, P.D. (1980). Characteristics and typology of the journey to crime. In D.E. Georges-Abeyie and K.D. Harries (eds), *Crime: A Spatial Perspective*. New York: Colombia University Press.

Pyle, G F. (1974). *The Spatial Dynamics of Crime*. Research Paper No.159. Chicago: Department of Geography, University of Chicago.

Rengert, G., Piquero, A.R. and Jones, P.R. (1999). Distance decay re-examined. *Criminology*, 37, 427–445.

Richardson, H.W., Gordon, P., Jun, M.J., Heikkila, E., Peiser, R. and Dale-Johnson, D. (1990). Residential property values, the CBD, and multiple nodes: further analysis. *Environment and Planning*, 22(A), 829–833.

Rhodes, W.M. and Conly, C. (1981). Crime and mobility: an empirical study. In P.J. Brantingham and P. Brantingham (eds), *Environmental Criminology*. Prospect Heights, Illinois: Waveland Press Inc.

Rossmo, D.K. (2000). *Geographic Profiling*. Boca Raton, FL: CRC Press, LLC.

Stevens, S.S. (1961). To honor Fechner and repeal his law. *Science*, 133, 80–86.

Turner, S. (1969). Delinquency and distance. In T. Sellen and M.E. Wolfgang (eds), *Delinquency: Selected Studies*. New York: Colombia University Press.

Van Koppen, P.J. and De Keiser, J.W. (1997). Desisting distance decay: on the aggregation of individual crime trips. *Criminology*, 35, 505–513.

White, C.R. (1932). The relation of felonies to environmental factors in Indianapolis. *Social Forces*, 10, 498–509.

Bibliography of Geographical Profiling

Alston, J. D. (1994). *The Serial Rapist's Spatial Pattern of Target Selection.* Unpublished master's thesis, Simon Fraser University, Burnaby, BC.

Amir, M. (1971). *Patterns in Forcible Rape.* Chicago: University of Chicago Press.

Anselin, L., Cohen, J., Cook, D., Gorr, W. and Tita, G. (2000). Spatial analysis of crime. *Criminal Justice*, 4, 213–262.

Bair, S. (2005). *Movement-Based Forecasting of Serial Crime Events.* Paper presented at the 3rd National Crime Mapping Conference: Jill Dando Institute of Crime Science. Stream 3a: Where will the Offender Strike Next? 13th April 2005: London.

Baldwin, J. (1974). Social area analysis and studies of delinquency. *Social Science Research*, 3, 151–168.

Baldwin, J. and Bottoms, A.E. (1976). *The Urban Criminal. A Study in Sheffield.* London: Tavistock Publications.

Barker, M. (2000). The criminal range of small-town burglars. In D. Canter and L. Alison. (eds), *Profiling Property Crimes* (pp. 57–73). Aldershot, UK: Dartmouth.

Bennell, C. and Canter, D.V. (2002). Linking commercial burglaries by *modus operandi*: tests using regression and ROC analysis. *Science & Justice*, 42(3), 1–12.

Bennell, C. and Jones, N.J. (2005). Between a ROC and a hard place: A method for linking serial burglaries using an offender's *modus operandi*. *Journal of Investigative Psychology*, 2, 23–41.

Bennell, C., Snook, B., Taylor, P.J., Corey, S. and Keyton, J. (2007). It's no riddle, choose the middle: The effect of number of crimes and topographical detail on police officer predictions of serial burglars' home locations. *Criminal Justice and Behavior*, 34(1), 119–132.

Bennell, C., Taylor, P.J. and Snook, B. (2007). Clinical versus actuarial geographic profiling approaches: A review of the research. In press.

Bernasco, W. (2005). *The Use of Opportunity Structures in Geographic Offender Profiling: A Theoretical Analysis.* Paper presented at the 3rd National Crime Mapping Conference: Jill Dando Institute of Crime Science. Stream 3a: Where Will the Offender Strike Next? 13th April 2005: London.

Bernasco, W. (2006). Co-offending and the choice of target areas in burglary. *Journal of Investigative Psychology and Offender Profiling*, 3, 139–155.

Bernasco, W. (2007). The usefulness of measuring spatial opportunity structures for tracking down offenders: A theoretical analysis of geographic offenders profiling using simulation studies. *Psychology, Crime & Law, 13(2),* 155–171.

242   *Applications of Geographical Offender Profiling*

Bernasco, W. and Luyxk, F. (2003). Effects of attractiveness, opportunity and accessibility to burglars on residential burglary rates of urban neighborhoods. *Criminology*, 41, 981–1001.

Beverton, R.J.H. and Holt, S.J. (1957). On the dynamics of exploited fish populations. *Fish.Invest.Lond.* Ser II, Vol. XIX.

Bernasco, W. and Nieuwbeerta, P. (2005). How do residential burglars select target areas? A new approach to the analysis of criminal location choice. *British Journal of Criminology*, 45, 296–315.

Block, R.L. and Block, C.R. (1995). Space, place and crime: Hot spot areas and hot places of liquor-related crime. In J.E. Eck and D. Weisburd (eds), *Crime and Place*. Monsey, NY: Criminal Justice Press.

Boggs, S. (1965). Urban crime patterns. *American Sociological Review*, 30(6), 899–908.

Bowers, K. and Hirschfield, A. (1999). Exploring links between crime and disadvantage in north west England: An analysis using geographical information systems. *International Journal of Geographical Information Science*, 13, 159–184.

Bowers, K.J. and Johnson, S.D. (2004). Who commits near repeats? A Test of the boost explanation. *Western Criminology Review*, 5(3), 12–24.

Bowers, K., Johnson, S.D. and Pease, K. (2004). Prospective hot-spotting: The future of crime mapping? *The British Journal of Criminology*, 44(5), 641–658.

Brantingham, P.L. and Brantingham, P.J. (1975). Spatial patterning of burglary. *Howard Journal of Penology and Crime Prevention*, 14, 11–24.

Brantingham, P.L. and Brantingham P.J. (1981). Notes on the geometry of crime. In P.J. Brantingham and P.L Brantingham (eds), *Environmental Criminology* (pp. 27–54). Beverly Hills: Sage Publications.

Brantingham, P.J. and Brantingham, P.L. (1984). *Patterns in Crime*. New York: Macmillan.

Brantingham, P. and Brantingham, P. (1994). Burglar mobility and crime prevention. In R. Clarke and T. Hope (eds), *Coping with Burglary.* Boston; MA: Kluwer Nijhoff.

Bromley, R.J. (1980). Trader mobility in systems of periodic and daily markets. In D.T. Herbert and R.J. Johnston (eds), *Geography and the Urban Environment* (pp. 133–174). New York: John Wiley & Sons Ltd.

Brown, M.A. (1982). Modelling the spatial distribution of suburban crime. *Economic Geography*, 58(3), 247–261.

Canter, D. (1977). *The Psychology of Place*. London: The Architectural Press.

Canter, D. (2004). Geographical profiling of criminals. *Medico-legal Journal*, 72, 53–66.

Canter, D. (2005). Confusing operational predicaments and cognitive explorations: Comments on Rossmo and Snook et al. *Applied Cognitive Psychology*, 19(5), 663–668.

Canter, D. and Alison, L.J. (2003). Converting evidence into data: The use of law enforcement archives as unobtrusive measurement. *The Qualitative Report*, June, 8(2).

Canter, D., Coffey, T., Huntley, M. and Missen, C. (2000). Predicting serial killers' home base using a decision support system. *Journal of Quantitative Criminology*, 16, 457–478.

Canter, D.V. and Gregory, A. (1994). Identifying the residential location of rapists. *Journal of the Forensic Science Society*, 34, 169–175.

Canter, D. and Hammond, L. (2006). A comparison of the efficacy of different decay functions in geographical profiling for a sample of US serial killers. *Journal of Investigative Psychology and Offender Profiling*, 3, 91–103.

Canter, D. and Hammond, L. (2007). Prioritizing burglars: Comparing the effectiveness of geographic profiling methods. In press.

Canter, D. and Hodge, S. (2000). Criminals' Mental Maps. In L.S. Turnbull, E.H. Hendrix and B.D. Dent (eds), *Atlas of Crime, Mapping the Criminal Landscape* (pp. 187–191). Phoenix, Arizona: Oryx Press.

Canter, D. and Larkin, P. (1993). The environmental range of serial rapists. *Journal of Environmental Psychology*, 13, 63–69.

Canter, D. and Shalev, K. (2000). *Putting Crime in its Place: Psychological Process in Crime Site Location.* Paper for Wheredunit? Investigating the Role of Place in Crime and Criminality. Crime Mapping Research Center of the NIJ, San Diego.

Canter, D. and Snook, B. (1999). *Modelling the Home Location of Serial Offenders.* Paper presented at the Third Annual International Crime Mapping Research Conference, Orlando, December.

Canter, D. and Youngs, D. (2003). Beyond offender profiling: The need for an investigative psychology. In R. Bull and D. Carson (eds), *Handbook of Psychology and Legal Contexts* (pp. 171–205). John Wiley and Sons Ltd.

Capone, D. and Nichols, W.W., Jr. (1976). Urban structure and criminal mobility. *American Behavioral Scientist*, 20, 199–213.

Carter, R.L. and Hill, K.Q. (1975). *The Criminal's Image of the City.* New York: Pergamon.

Catalano, P. (2000). *Applying Geographical Analysis to Serial Crime Investigations to Predict the Location of Future Targets and Determine Offender Residence.* Unpublished master's thesis, University of Western Australia, Australia.

Ceccato, V. (2005). Homicide in Sao Paulo, Brazil: Assessing spatial-temporal and weather variations. *Journal of Environmental Psychology*, 25(3), 307–321.

Chainey, S. (2005). *The Police Role in Community Cohesion: Using Geographic Information to Identify Vulnerable Localities.* Paper presented at the 3rd National Crime Mapping Conference: Jill Dando Institute of Crime Science. Stream 2a: Crime, Communities and Offenders. 12th April 2005: London.

Clarke, R. and Felson, M. (1993). *Routine Activity and Rational Choice.* New Brunswick: Transaction Publishers.

Cohen, J. and Tita, G. (1999). Diffusion in homicide: Exploring a general method for detecting spatial diffusion processes. *Journal of Quantitative Criminology*, 15(4), 451–493.

Cohen, L.E. and Cantor, D.C. (1981). Residential burglary in the United States: Lifestyle and demographic factors associated with the probability of victimization. *Journal of Research in Crime and Delinquency*, 18(1), 113–127.

Cohen, L.E. and Felson, M. (1979). Social change and crime rate trends: A routine activity approach. *American Sociological Review*, 44, 588–608.

Collins, P.I., Johnson, G.F., Choy, A., Davidson, K.T. and Mackay, R.E. (1998). Advances in violent crime analysis: The Canadian violent crime linkage analysis system. *Journal of Government Information*, 25, 277–284.

Conklin, J.E. and Bittner, E. (1973). Burglary in a suburb. *Criminology*, 11(2), 206–232.

Cook, D., Symanzik, J., Majure, J. and Cressie, N. (1996). Dynamic graphics in a GIS: Exploring and analysing multivariate and spatial data using linked software. *Computational Statistics*, 11, 467–480.

Cornish, D.B. and Clarke, R.V. (1986). *The Reasoning Criminal: Rational Choice Perspectives on Offending*. New York: Springer-Verlag.

Costello, A. and Wiles, P. (2001). GIS and the journey to crime: An analysis of patterns in South Yorkshire. In A. Hirschfield and K. Bowers (eds), *Mapping and Analysing Crime Data: Lessons from Research and Practice* (pp. 27–60). London: Taylor and Francis.

Craglia, M., Haining, R. and Wiles, P. (2000). A comparative evaluation of approaches to urban crime pattern analysis. *Urban Studies*, 37(4), 711–729.

Cromwell, P.F., Olson, J.N. and Avery, D.W. (1991). *Breaking and Entering. An Ethnographic Analysis of Burglary*. Newbury Park, NJ: Sage.

Curtis, L.A. (1974). *Criminal Violence*. Lexington, MA: Lexington Books.

Davidson, R.N. (1981). *Crime and Environment*. London: Croom Helm.

Davies, A. and Dale, A. (1995). Locating the stranger rapist. *London Home Office Police Department*, Special Interest Series Paper 3.

Douglas, J.E. and Munn, C. (1992). Violent crime scene analysis: *Modus operandi*, signature, and staging. *FBI Law Enforcement Bulletin*, 6, 1–10.

Downs, R.M. and Stea, D. (1973). Cognitive maps and spatial behaviour: Process and products. In R. Downs and D. Stea (eds), *Image and Environment* (pp. 8–26). Chicago: Aldine.

Downs, R.M. and Stea, D. (1977). *Maps in Minds*. London: Harper and Row.

Edwards, M.J. and Grace, R.C. (2006). Analysing the offence locations and residential base of serial arsonists in New Zealand. *Australian Psychologist*, 41(3), 219–226.

Eldridge, J.E. and Jones, J.P. (1991). Warped space: A geography of distance decay. *The Professional Geographer*, 43(4), 500–511.

Engstad, P.A. (1975). Environmental opportunities and the ecology of crime. In R.A. Silverman and J.J. Teevan (eds), *Crime in Canadian Society*. (pp. 193–211). Toronto: Butterworths.

Erlanson, O. (1946). The scene of a sex offence as related to the residence of the offender. *American Journal of Police Science*, 31, 338–342.

Evans, D.J. (1989). Geographical analyses of residential burglary. In D.J. Evans and D.T. Herbert (eds), *The Geography of Crime* (pp. 86–107). London: Routledge.

Everson, S. and Pease, K. (2001). Crime against the same person and place: Detection, opportunity and offender targeting. In G. Farrell and K. Pease (eds), *Crime Prevention Studies Volume 12: Repeat Victimisation*. New York: Criminal Justice Press.

Ewart, B.W., Oatley, G.C. and Burn, K. (2005). Matching crimes using burglars' *modus operandi*: A test of three models. *International Journal of Police Science and Management, 7*, 160–174.

Farrington, D.P (1989). Self-reported and official offending in adolescence and adulthood. In M.W. Kelin (ed.) *Cross-National Research in Self-Reported Crime and Delinquency*, (pp. 399 –423). Dordrecht: Kluwer.

Fritzon, K. (2001). An examination of the relationship between distance travelled and motivational aspects of arson. *Journal of Environmental Psychology*, 21, 45–60.

Gabor, T. and Gottheil, E. (1984). Offender characteristics and spatial mobility: An empirical study and some policy implications. *Journal of Criminology*, 26, 267–281.

Getis, A. (1995). Spatial filtering in a regression framework: Examples using data on urban crime, regional inequality, and government expenditures. In L. Anselin and R. Florax (eds), *New Directions in Spatial Econometrics*. Berlin: Springer- Verlag.

Godwin, M. (1999). *Hunting Serial Predators: A Multivariate Classification Approach to Profiling Violent Behaviour*. New York: CRC Press.

Godwin, M. and Canter, D. (1997). Encounter and death: The spatial behaviour of U.S. serial killers. *Journal of Police Strategy and Management*, 1, 24–38.

Golledge, R.G. (1987). *Analytical Behavioural Geography*. London: Croom Helm.

Goodwill, A.M. and Alison, L.J. (in press). The development of a filter model for prioritising suspects in burglary offences. *Psychology, Crime and Law*.

Gorr, W. and Olligschlaeger, A. (1994). Weighted spatial adaptive filtering: Monte Carlo studies and application to illicit drug market modelling. *Geographic Analysis*, 26, 67–87.

Gould, L. (1969). The changing structure of property crime in an affluent society. *Social Forces*, 48, 50–59.

Green E.J., Booth, C.E. and Biderman, M.D. (1976). Cluster analysis of burglary M/Os. *Journal of Police Science and Administration*, 4, 382–287.

Groth, A.N., Longo, R.E. and McFadin, J.B. (1982). Undetected recidivism among rapists and child molesters. *Crime & Delinquency*, 28, 450–458.

Grubin, D., Kelly, P. and Brunsdon, C. (2001). *Linking serious sexual assaults through behaviour*. Home Office Research Study 215.

Guerry, A.M. (1833). *Essai sur la Statistique Morale de la France*. Paris: Crochard.

Hakim, S., Rengert, G.F. and Shachmurove, Y. (2001). Target Search of Burglars: A Revised Economic Model. *Papers in Regional Science*, 80, 121–137.

Harbort, S. and Mokros, A. (2001). Serial murderers in Germany from 1945 to 1995: A descriptive study. *Homicide Studies*, 5(4), 311–334.

Harries, K.D. (1980). *Crime and the Environment*. Springfield: Charles C. Thomas Press.

Harries, K. (1999). *Mapping Crime: Principle and Practice*. National Institute of Justice. NJC 178919.

Harries, K. and LeBeau, J. (2007). Issues in the geographic profiling of crime: Review and commentary. In press.

Hartley, L. and Morrissey, P. (2005). *The Thames Gateway Crime and Design Project*. Paper presented at the 3rd National Crime Mapping Conference: Jill Dando Institute of Crime Science. Stream 1b: Profiling Neighbourhoods. 12th April 2005: London.

Hayden, C., Williamson, T. and Webber, R. (2007). Schools, pupil behaviour and young offenders: Using postcode classification to target behaviour support and crime prevention programmes. *British Journal of Criminology*, 47, 293–310.

Hesseling, R.B.P. (1992). Using Data on Offender Mobility in Ecological Research. *Journal of Quantitative Criminology*, 34, 95–112.

Holmes, R.M. and Holmes S.T. (1996). *Murder in America*. Beverley Hills: Sage.

Hull, C.L. (1952). *Principles of Behavior*. New York: Appleton Century Croft.

Hunter, J.M. and Shannon, G.W. (1985). Jarvis revisited: Distance decay and service areas of mid-19th century asylums. *Professional Geographer*, 37(3), 296–302.

Johnson, S. and Bowers, K. (2004). The stability of space-time clusters of burglary. *British Journal of Criminology*, 44, 55–65.

Johnson, S.D., Bowers, K. and Hirschfield, A. (1997). New insights in the spatial and temporal distribution of repeat victimisation. *British Journal of Criminology*, 37, 224–241.

Johnson, S.D., Bowers, K.J., Young, C.A. and Hirschfield, A. (2001). Uncovering the true picture: Evaluating crime reduction initiatives using disaggregate crime data. *Crime Prevention and Community Safety: An International Journal,* 3(4), 7–24.

Johnson, S.D., Bowers, K.J. and Pease, K. (2004). Predicting the future or summarising the past? Crime mapping as anticipation. In M. Smith and N. Tilley (eds), *Launching Crime* Science. London: Willan.

Keppel, R.D. and Weiss, J.G. (1992). *Improving the Investigation of Violent Crime: The Homicide Investigation and Tracking System (HITS)*. Washington, DC: U.S. Department of Justice, National Institute of Justice.

Keppel, R. and Weis, J. (1994). Time and distance as solvability factors in murder cases. *Journal of Forensic Science, JFSCA*, 39(2), 386–401.

Kind, S. (1987). Navigational ideas and the Yorkshire Ripper investigation. *Journal of Navigation*, 40, 385–393.

Kind, S. (1999). *The Sceptical Witness: Concerning the Scientific Investigation of Crime against a Human Background*. Harrogate: The Forensic Science Society.

Kitchen, R.M. (1994). Cognitive maps: What Are they and why study them? *Journal of Environmental Psychology*, 14, 1–19.

Kocsis, R.N. and Irwin, H.J. (1997). An analysis of spatial patterns in serial rape, arson and burglary: The utility of the Circle Theory of environmental range for psychological profiling. *Psychiatry, Psychology & Law*, 4(2), 195–206.

Kothari, U. (2002). *Migration and Chronic Poverty*. Institute for Development, Policy and Management, University of Manchester. Working Paper No. 16.

Land, K., McCall, P. and Cohen, L. (1990). Structural covariates of homicide rates: Are there invariances across time and social space? *American Journal of Sociology*, 95, 922–963.

Ladd, F.C. (1970). Black youths view their environment: Neighbourhood maps. *Environment and Behaviour*, 2(1), 74–99.

Laukkanen, M. and Santtila, P. (2005). Predicting the residential location of a serial commercial robber. *Forensic Science International*, 157, 71–82.

LeBeau, J.L. (1978). The spatial dynamics of rape: The San Diego example. Unpublished Ph.D dissertation. Department of Geography, Michigan State University.

LeBeau, J.L. (1985). Some problems with measuring and describing rape presented by the serial offender. *Justice Quarterly*, 2, 385–398.

LeBeau, J.L. (1987a). The journey to rape: Geographic distance and the rapist's method of approaching the victim. *Journal of Police Science and Administration*, 15, 129–136.

LeBeau, J.L. (1987b). The methods and measures of centrography and the spatial dynamics of rape. *Journal of Quantitative Criminology*, 3, 125–141.

LeBeau, J.L. (1987c). Patterns of stranger and serial rape offending: Factors distinguishing apprehended and at large offenders. *The Journal of Criminal Law & Criminology*, 78(2), 309–326.

Leitner, M., Kent, J., Oldfield, I. and Swoope, E. (2007). Geoforensic analysis revisited: The application of Newton's geographic profiling method to serial burglaries in London, UK. In Press.

Levine, N. (1999). *CrimeStat: A Spatial Statistics Program for the Analysis of Crime Incident Locations*. Washington, D.C.: U.S. Department of Justice, National Institute of Justice.

Levine, N. (2006). Crime mapping and the *Crimestat* program. *Geographical Analysis*, 38, 41–56.

Listi, G.A., Manhein, M.H. and Leitner, M. (2007). Use of the global positioning system in the field recovery of scattered human remains. *Journal of Forensic Science*, 52(1), 11–15.

Liu, H. and Brown, D.E. (2003). Criminal incident prediction using a point-pattern-based density model. *International Journal of Forecasting*, 19, 603–622.

Lowe, J.C. and Moryodas, S. (1976). *The Geography of Movement*. Boston, MA: Houghton Mifflin Company.

Lundrigan, S. and Canter, D. (2001a). A multivariate analysis of serial murderers' disposal site location choice. *Journal of Environmental Psychology*, 21, 423–432.

Lundrigan, S. and Canter, D. (2001b). Research report: Spatial patterns of serial murder: An analysis of disposal site location choice. *Behavioural Sciences and the Law*, 19, 595–610.

Lynch, K. (1960). *The Image of the City.* Cambridge, Mass: MIT Press.

MacKay, R.E. (1999, December). Geographic profiling: A new tool for law enforcement. *The Police Chief*, 66(12), 51–59.

Maguire, M., Morgan, R. and Reiner, R. (2002). *The Oxford Handbook of Criminology.* Oxford: Oxford University Press.

Mayhew, H. (1861). *London Labour and the London Poor: A Cyclopaedia of the Condition and Earnings of Those That Will Work, Those That Cannot Work, and Those That Will Not Work.* London: Griffin, Bohn.

Meaney, R. (2004). Commuters and marauders: An examination of the spatial behaviour of serial criminals. *Journal of Investigative Psychology and Offender Profiling*, 1(2), 121–137.

Messner, S.F., Anselin, L., Baller, R.D., Hawkins, D.F., Deane, G. and Tolnay, S.E. (1999). The spatial patterning of county homicide rates: An application of exploratory spatial data analysis. *Journal of Quantitative Criminology*, 15(4), 423–450.

Miethe, T.D. and McDowall, D. (1993). Contextual effects in models of criminal victimization. *Social Forces*, 71, 741–759.

Mizutani, F. (1993). Home range of leopards and their impact on livestock on kenyan ranches. *Symposium Zoological Society London*, 65, 425–439.

Mizutani, F. and Jewell, P.A. (1998). Home-range and movements of leopards (Panther pardus) on a livestock ranch in Kenya. *Journal of Zoology, London*, 244, 269–286.

Molumby, T. (1976). Patterns of crime in a university housing project. *American Behavioral Scientist*, 20, 247–259.

Morenoff, J. and Sampson, R.J. (1997). Violent crime and the spatial dynamics of neighbourhood transition: Chicago 1970–1990. *Social Forces*, 76, 31–64.

Nee, C. and Taylor, M. (2000). Examining burglars' target selection: Interview, experiment or ethnomethodology? *Psychology, Crime & Law*, 6, 45–59.

Nelson, S. and Amir, M. (1973). The hitchhike victim of rape: A research report. In I. Drapkin and E. Viano, (eds), *Victimology: A New Focus, Vol. 5* (pp. 47–64). Lexington, MA: D.C. Heath.

Nichols, W.W. Jr. (1980). Mental maps, social characteristics and criminal mobility. In D.E. Georges-Abeyie and K.D. Harries, (eds), *Crime: A Spatial Perspective* (pp. 156–166). Columbia University Press.

Paulsen, D.J. (2006). Connecting the dots: Assessing the accuracy of geographic profiling software. *Policing: An International Journal of Police Strategies and Management*, 29(2), 306–334.

Paulsen, D.J. (2006). Human versus machine: A comparison of the accuracy of geographic profiling methods. *Journal of Investigative Psychology and Offender Profiling*, 3, 77–89.

Paulsen, D.J. (2007). Improving geographic profiling through commuter/ marauder prediction. In Press.

Pettiway, L.E. (1982). Mobility of burglars and robbery offenders. *Urban Affairs Quarterly,* 18(2), 255–270.

Phillips, P.D. (1980). Characteristics and typology of the journey to crime. In D.E. Georges-Abeyie and K.D. Harries, (eds), *Crime: A Spatial Perspective.* Columbia University Press.

Polvi, N., Looman, T., Humphries, C. and Pease, K. (1990). Repeat break and enter victimisation: Time course and crime prevention opportunity. *Journal of Police Science and Administration,* 17(1), 8–11.

Pyle, G.F. et al. (1974). *The Spatial Dynamics of Crime.* Department of Geography Research Paper No. 159. Chicago: The University of Chicago.

Ratcliffe, J.H. (2002). Aoristic signatures and the temporal analysis of high volume crime patterns. *Journal of Quantitative Criminology,* 18(1), 23–43.

Ratcliffe, J.H. (2003). Suburb boundaries and residential burglars. *Trends and Issues in Crime and Criminal Justice,* no.246. Canberra: Australian Institute of Criminology.

Ratcliffe, J.H. (2006). A temporal constraint theory to explain opportunity-based spatial offending patterns. *Journal of Research in Crime and Delinquency,* 43(3), 261–291.

Ratcliffe, J. and McCullagh, M. (2001). Crime repeat victimisation and GIS. In A. Hirschfield and K. Bowers. (eds), *Mapping and Analysing Crime Data: Lessons from Research and Practice.* Taylor and Francis: London.

Rengert, G.F. (1975). Some effects of being female on criminal spatial behavior. *The Pennsylvania Geographer,* 13(2), 10–18.

Rengert, G.F. (1981). Burglary in Philadelphia: A critique of an opportunity structure model. In P.J. Brantingham and P.L. Brantingham (eds), *Environmental Criminology* (pp. 189–201). Beverly Hills: Sage Publications.

Rengert, G.F., Piquero, A.R. and Jones, P.R. (1999). Distance decay re-examined. *Criminology,* 37(2), 427–425.

Rengert, G.F. and Wasilchick, J. (1985). *Suburban Burglary: A Time and a Place for Everything.* Springfield, Illinois: Charles C Thomas.

Repetto, T.A. (1974). *Residential Crime.* Cambridge, MA: Ballinger.

Rey, S.J. and Anselin, L. (2006). Recent advances in software for spatial analysis in the social sciences. *Geographical Analysis, 38,* 1–4.

Rhodes, W.M. and Conly, C. (1981). Crime and mobility: An empirical study. In P.J. Brantingham and P.L. Brantingham (eds), *Environmental Criminology* (pp. 167–188). Beverly Hills: Sage Publications.

Rich, T. and Shively, M. (2004). *A Methodology for Evaluating Geographic Profiling Software: Final Report.* Cambridge, MA: Abt Associates Inc.

Richardson, H.W., Gordon, P., Jun, M.J., Heikkila, E., Peiser, R. and Dale-Johnson, D. (1990). Residential property values, the CBD, and multiple nodes: Further analysis. *Environment and Planning,* 22(A), 829–833.

Roncek, D.W. and Bell, R. (1981). Bars, blocks, and crime. *Journal of Environmental Systems*, 11, 35–47.

Roncek, D. W. and Francik, J. M. A. (1981). Housing projects and crime: Testing the proximity hypothesis. *Social Problems*, 29, 151–166.

Roncek, D. W. and Maier, P. A. (1991). Bars, blocks, and crimes revisited: Linking the theory of routine activities to the empiricism of hotspots. *Criminology*, 29, 725–755.

Roncek, D.W. and Pravatiner, M. A. (1989). Additional evidence that taverns enhance nearby crime. *Sociology and Social Research*, 73, 185–188.

Rose, H. M. and Deskins, D. R. (1980). Felony murder: The case of Detroit. *Urban Geography*, 1, 1–21.

Rossmo, D.K. (1995). Place, space, and police investigations: Hunting serial violent criminals. In J.E. Eck and D.L. Weisburd (eds), *Crime and Place: Crime Prevention Studies, Vol. 4* (pp. 217–235). Monsey, NY: Criminal Justice Press.

Rossmo, K. (1997). Geographic profiling. In J.L. Jackson and D.A. Bekerian (eds), *Offender Profiling: Theory, Research and Practice* (pp. 159–176). New York: John Wiley and Sons.

Rossmo, K. (2002). *Exploring the Geo-demographic Relationship between Stranger Rapists and their Offences*. Interim Report for Police Foundation, Washington, DC.

Rossmo, K. (2005). Geographic heuristics or shortcuts to failure?: Response to Snook et al. *Applied Cognitive Psychology*, 19(5), 531–678.

Santtila, P., Korpela, S. and Hakkanen, H. (2004). Expertise and decision making in the linking of car crime series. *Psychology, Crime & Law*, 10(2), 97–112.

Santtila, P., Zappala, A., Laukkanen, M. and Picozzi, M. (2003). Testing the utility of a geographical profiling approach in three rape series of a single offender: A case study. *Forensic Science International*, 131, 42–52.

Sarangi, S. and Youngs, D. (2006). Spatial patterns of Indian serial burglars with relevance to geographical profiling. *Journal of Investigative Psychology and Offender Profiling*, 3, 105–115.

Scott, D., Lambie, I., Henwood, D. and Lamb, R. (2006). Profiling stranger rapists: Linking offence behaviour to previous criminal histories using a regression model. *Journal of Sexual Aggression*, 12(3), 265–275.

Scott, R. (2005). Targeting resources using Geodemographic profiling. *3rd National Crime Mapping Conference: Jill Dando Institute of Crime Science*. Stream 3b: Reassuring the Public. 13th April 2005: London.

Shaw, C. R. (1929). *Delinquency Areas*. Chicago: University of Chicago Press.

Shaw, K.T. and Gifford, R. (1994). Residents' and burglars' assessment of risk from defensible space cues. *Journal of Environmental Psychology*, 14, 177–194.

Sherman, L.W., Gartin, P.R. and Buerger, M.E. (1989). Hotspots of predatory crime: Routine activities and the criminology of space. *Criminology*, 27, 27–55.

Sherman, L.W. and Weisburd, D. (1995). General deterrent effects of police patrol in crime "hot spots": A randomized controlled trial. *Justice Quarterly*, 12(4), 625–648.

Smith, T.S. (1976). Inverse distance variations for the flow of crime in urban areas. *Social Forces*, 54, 802–815.

Snook, B. (2000, December). *Utility or Futility? A Provisional Examination of the Utility of a Geographical Decision Support System*. Paper presented at the meeting of the Crime Mapping Research Center, San Diego, CA.

Snook, B. (2004). Individual differences in distances travelled by serial burglars. *Journal of Investigative Psychology and Offender Profiling*, 1(1), 53–66.

Snook, B., Canter, D. and Bennell, C. (2002). Predicting the home location of serial offenders: A preliminary comparison of the accuracy of human judges with a geographic profiling system. *Behavioral Sciences and the Law*, 20, 109–118.

Snook, B., Cullen, R.M., Mokros, A. and Harbort, S. (2005). Serial murderers' spatial decisions: Factors that influence crime location choice. *Journal of Investigative Psychology and Offender Profiling*, 2(3), 147–164.

Snook, B., Taylor, P.J. and Bennell, C. (2004). Geographic profiling: The fast, frugal, and accurate way. *Applied Cognitive Psychology*, 18, 105–121.

Snook, B., Wright, M. House, J.C. and Alison, L.J. (2006). Searching for a needle in a needle stack: Combining criminal careers and journey-to-crime research for criminal suspect prioritization. *Police Practice and Research*, 7(3), 217–230.

Snook, B., Zito, M., Bennell, C. and Taylor, P.J. (2005). On the complexity and accuracy of geographic profiling strategies. *Journal of Quantitative Criminology*, 21(1), 1–26.

Snow, J. (1855). *On the Mode of Communication of Cholera*. Explanation of the map showing the situation of the deaths in and around Broad Street, Golden Square. Retrieved February 25, 2006, from http://www.ph.ucla.edu/epi/snow/snowbook2.html.

Stephenson, L.K. (1974). Spatial dispersion of intra-urban juvenile delinquency. *Journal of Geography*, 73, 20–26.

Stephenson, L.K. (1980). Centrographic analysis of crime. In D.E. Georges-Abeyie and K.D. Harries. (eds), *Crime: A Spatial Perspective* (pp. 146–155). Columbia University Press.

Tamura, M. and Suzuki, M. (2000). Characteristics of serial arsonists and crime scene geography in Japan. In A. Czerederecka, T. Jaśkiewicz-Obydzińska and J. Wójcikiewicz (eds) *Forensic Psychology and Law: Traditional Questions and New Ideas* (pp. 259–264). Kraków, Poland: Institute of Forensic Research in Cracow, Poland.

Taylor, P.J. (1977). *Quantitative Methods in Geography*. Prospect Heights, IL: Waveland Press.

Tita, G. and Griffiths, E. (2005). Traveling to violence: The case for a mobility-based spatial typology of homicide. *Journal of Research in Crime and Delinquency*, 42(3), 275–308.

Tolman, E.C. (1948). Cognitive maps in rats and men. *Psychological Review*, 55, 189–208.

Tolnay, S.E., Deane, G. and Beck, E.M. (1996). Vicarious violence: Spatial effects on Southern lynchings, 1890–1919. *American Journal of Sociology*, 102, 788–815.

Townsley, M., Homel, R. and Chaseling, J. (2000). Repeat burglary victimisation: spatial and temporal patterns. *Australian and New Zealand Journal of Criminology*, 33, 37–63.

Townsley, M., Homel, R. and Chaseling, J. (2003). Infectious burglaries: A test of the near repeat hypothesis. *British Journal of Criminology*, 43, 615–633.

Trickett, A., Osborn, D.R., Seymour, J. and Pease, K. (1992). What is different about high crime areas? *British Journal of Criminology*, 32, 81–89.

Turner, S. (1969). Delinquency and distance. In T. Sellin and M.E. Wolfgang (eds). *Delinquency: Selected Studies* (pp. 11–26). New York: John Wiley and Sons.

Van Koppen, P.J. and De Keiser, J.W. (1997). Desisting distance decay: On the aggregation of individual crime trips. *Criminology*, 35(2), 505–513.

Van Koppen, P.J. and Jansen, R.W. (1998). The road to robbery: Travel patterns in commercial robberies. *British Journal of Criminology*, 38(2), 230–246.

Walker, J., Golden, J. and Van Houten, A. (2001). The geographic link between sex offenders and potential victims: A routine activities approach. *Justice Research Policy*, 3(2), 15–33.

Warren, J., Reboussin, R., Hazelwood, R.R., Cummings, A., Gibbs, N. and Trumbetta, S. (1998). Crime scene and distance correlates of serial rape. *Journal of Quantitative Criminology*, 14(1), 35–59.

White, R.C. (1932). The relation of felonies to environmental factors in Indianapolis. *Social Forces*, 10(4), 498–509.

Wiles, P. and Costello, A. (2000). *The 'Road to Nowhere': The Evidence for Travelling Criminals*. Home Office research study 207.

Yokota-Sano, K. and Watanabe, S. (1998). An analysis on the repetition of criminal *modus operandi*. *Reports of the National Research Institute of Police Science, Research on Forensic Science*, 3, 49–55.

Young, G. (2003). Mapping mayhem: The geography of crime. In *ComputerEdge*, August 2003.

Youngs, D., Canter, D. and Cooper, J. (2004). The facets of criminality: A cross-modal and cross-gender validation. *Behaviormetrika*, 31(2), 1–13.

Index

Note: Page numbers in **bold type** following the title of a paper indicate where this paper is printed in full in this volume, with numbers in ordinary type indicating where it is referred to by other authors.
Where a title is followed by page numbers in <u>ordinary type only</u>, the full paper can be found in the companion volume *Principles of Geographical Offender Profiling*.
Page numbers in *italic type* refer to information in figures or tables.

Twentieth-Century Germany